Polish Holiday Cookery

Polish Holiday Cookery

ROBERT STRYBEL

HIPPOCRENE BOOKS, INC.
New York

The cover photographs come from the album Folkore: Polish Folk Culture, published in 2001 by Wydawnictwo BOSZ, and have been reproduced by permission from the publishers.

Paperback edition, 2015

Book design and composition by Susan A. Ahlquist, East Hampton, NY.

For more information, address:
HIPPOCRENE BOOKS, INC.
171 Madison Avenue
New York, NY 10016

ISBN 978-0-7818-1349-5

Contents

Foreword

THERE IS MUCH ABOUT OUR POLISH HERITAGE THAT IS GOOD, VALUABLE AND INTERESTING AND CAN ENRICH PEOPLE'S LIVES. IT SHOULD THEREFORE BE EXPLORED, CULTIVATED AND PASSED ON NOT ONLY TO POLONIA'S YOUNGER GENERATION, BUT ALSO SHARED WITH AMERICA AS A WHOLE. OTHERWISE IT MAY MELT, CRUMBLE AND FADE AWAY UNDER THE PRESSURE OF THE LOUD, AGGRESSIVE, PLASTIC "COMMERPOP" MAINSTREAM "CULTURE" THAT BOMBARDS US AT EVERY TURN OF THE WAY.

When, in the late 1980s, my wife Majka (Maria) and I first began work on a Polish cookery book for New York's Hippocrene Books, little did we imagine that it would evolve into a 900-page colossus. Indeed, *Polish Heritage Cookery*, containing as it does some 2,200 recipes, has been called the definitive English-language work on Polish cuisine. It certainly was the largest Polish cookbook ever published in English. It might have appeared, therefore, that nothing more remained to be said.

But our publishers felt—and the comments of many readers bore this out—that there was still another niche to be filled. True, using *Polish Heritage Cookery*, people could cook 365 dinners a year without ever repeating themselves, but the fact is that fewer and fewer Americans these days are cooking complete dinners at home on a daily basis. A 1999 study showed that 46% of the Americans surveyed said they ate out because they lacked the time for home-cooked meals. Others explained that their families were constantly on the go—busy with commuting, work, school, extracurricular activities—so they just grabbed something to appease their hunger rather than enjoying a sit-down family dinner. Those living alone often claim it doesn't pay to cook meals at home for just one person, and even some retired couples concur.

But you don't see many Americans celebrating Christmas, Easter, First Holy Communions, weddings, anniversaries and other family occasions at the nearest fast-food joint. And no one sends out for tacos, spring rolls or pizza when attending their parish's Polish Harvest Fest *(dożynki)*. The point is that Americans nowadays tend to enjoy the delicacies of their ethnic heritage primarily on special occasions, and Polish Americans are no exception. It was that awareness that gave rise to this book. While it was being prepared, as always the author kept receiving airmail and e-mail queries from readers in America about various aspects of our cultural heritage. Naturally, there were also numerous recipe requests for foods people remembered from their Polonian childhood or had sampled during visits to Poland.

This book is by no means the last word on the subjects dealt with in these pages. Instead, it is intended to pique the interest of readers and encourage them to begin to independently explore various aspects of our ancestral legacy.

How to Use This Book

Any review of Polish calendar-related events begins not with the first of January but with Advent (early December). In keeping with Poland's age-old Catholic tradition, that roughly three-and-a-half-week-long period of preparation for Christmas marks the start of a new liturgical year and with it we began our journey through the world of *Polish Holiday Cookery.*

Since this book is peppered with Polish names, words, phrases and sayings, the reader would do well to have at least a rudimentary knowledge of Polish pronunciation. Hence, let's get acquainted with the Rudiments of Polish Pronunciation:

RUDIMENTS OF POLISH PRONUNCIATION

The Polish alphabet effectively contains 32 letters. The 26 letters of the English alphabet are reduced by the letters Q, V and X, which appear only in a handful of foreign imports, but the Polish alphabet includes nine additional, accented characters: ą, ę, ł, ż, ć, ń, ó, ś, ź. English has only five vowels, but in Polish, there are nine: a, ą, e, ę, i, o, ó, u and y. (In Polish, "y" is never a consonant.) The letters are roughly pronounced as follows:

A, a like the "a" in English "father," e.g., *mak* (mahk) = poppy

Ą, ą nasal "o" as in English "own" without fully pronouncing the "n," e.g., *są* (son) = (they) are

B, b same as English "b," e.g., *barka* (pronounced: BAHR-kah) = barge

C, c like "ts" in English "lets," e.g., *cebula* (tseh-BOO-lah) = onion

Ć, ć very soft "ch," somewhat like "ch" in English "cheese," e.g., *cisza* (CHEE-shah) = silence

D, d same as English "d," e.g., *deska* (DESS-kah) = board, plank

E, e like short "e" in English "set," e.g., *ten* (ten) = this one

Ę, ę nasal "e," close to "in" in French *"fin"* (fen) = end

F, f same as in English "f," e.g., *fala* (FAH-lah) = wave

G, g like English hard "g" (get, go, green), e.g., *góra* (GOO-rah) = mountain

H, h like English "h," e.g., *hałas* (HAH-wahss) = noise

I, I like English "ee" in "feet," e.g., *igła* (EEG-wah) = needle

J, j like English "y" in "yard," e.g., *jajko* (YAHY-kaw) = egg

K, k like English "k," e.g., *kasa* (KAH-sah) = ticket office, cash desk

L, l like soft English "l" in "leek," e.g., *list* (leest) = letter

Ł, ł like English "w" in "wife," e.g., *ławka* (WAHF-kah) = bench

M, m same as English m," e.g., *malina* (mah-LEE-nah) = raspberry

N, n same as English "n," e.g., *nora* (NAW-rah) = (animal's) den

Ń, ń soft "n" as in Spanish *"mañana,"* e.g., *koń* (kawhń) = horse

O, o similar to "aw" sound English "awl," e.g., *rok* (rawk) = year

Ó, ó like English "oo" in "tool," same as Polish "u," e.g., *bór* (boor) = pine forest

P, p like English "p," e.g., *para* (PAH-rah) = steam, couple

R, r like trilled Scottish "r," e.g., *rosa* (RAW-sah) = dew

S, s same as English "s," e.g., *sowa* (SAW-vah) = owl

Ś, ś similar to soft English "sh" in "sheet," e.g., *siwy* (SHEE-vih) = gray

T, t similar to English "t" in "tot," e.g., *tylko* (TILL-kaw) = only

U, u like English "oo" in "tool," same as Polish "ó," e.g., *dusza* (DOO-shah) = soul

W, w like English "v," e.g., *wojna* (VOY-nah) = war

Y, y always a vowel like short English "i" in "bit," e.g., *byt* (bit) = being

Z, z like English "z," e.g., *zamek* (ZAH-mek) = castle

Ź, ź softer than English "z" in "azure," e.g., *źle* (zhleh) = badly

Ż, ż similar to English "z" in "azure," e.g., *żaba* (ZHAH-bah) = frog

COMMON DIAGRAPHS (consonant clusters):

ch like "ch" in Scottish *"loch"* or German *"Nacht,"* e.g., *chór* (hoor) = choir

cz similar to English "ch" in "church," e.g., *czas* (chahss) = time

rz same as Polish "ż," e.g., *burza* (BOO-zhah) = storm

sz similar to English "sh" in "show," e.g., *szopa* (SHAW-pah) = shed

szcz similar to "st" in English "bastion," e.g., *szczotka* (SHCHAWT-kah) = brush

krz similar to English "ksh" in "rickshaw," e.g., *krzak* (kshahk) = bush

prz similar to English "psh" in "dropshot," e.g., *pszenny* (PSHEN-nih = wheat(en)

trz similar to English "tsh" in "hotshot," e.g., *trzy* (tshih) = three

Culinary Prelude

A FEW PRELIMINARY REMARKS

Polish Holiday Cookery contains numerous recipes suited to various special occasions. It should be remembered that most any event, not only Christmas Eve supper, Easter breakfast or an elegant full-course banquet, can be special. With the right atmosphere and company, even *kiełbasa* roasted on sticks over a crackling campfire can be a festive occasion. Before getting into the recipes, some readers may enjoy learning a little more about what in America is still a relatively little-known cuisine. How did it develop in Poland and later in America? What are its general characteristics and typical foods, its strong points and drawbacks? It is hoped that historical background presented in the following pages will shed some light on these and other culinary issues of interest to readers.

This, however, is not obligatory reading and can easily be postponed until time permits. The section entitled "Little Lexicon of Basic Foods and Culinary Concepts" is more important to a better understanding of many of the Poles' daily staples and delicacies. It may refresh the memories of those raised in Polish family settings, who later gradually drifted away from their ancestral foodways. To those largely unfamiliar with Polish cuisine, it may be a rather eye-opening experience. This section also provides the proper pronunciation of foods and dishes that are repeatedly mentioned throughout the book. But it is absolutely essential for readers to acquaint themselves with the following three sections of this Culinary Prelude—"This Book's Incorporated Recipe Ingredients," "Abbreviations" and "Basic Ingredients and Procedures."

Without the information contained therein, using the recipes found in these pages will be confusing and difficult.

POLISH CUISINE IN POLAND AND AMERICA

Polish cuisine reflects the many political, social, economic and cultural cross-currents that have affected the Polish nation over the centuries. When Poland was first emerging as an independent state around the turn of the second millennium, the basic staples for the masses of peasantry were coarse breads, groats, root vegetables and the plentiful wild mushrooms and berries that were there for the taking. Wild honey was the only sweetener available. The upper classes back then ate pretty much the same kind of plain and simple fare with the addition of plenty of fish and meat, especially wild game. The peasant also occasionally feasted on the game he managed to ensnare, except that was called poaching and entailed painful consequences if he got caught.

Foreign monks, merchants and travelers as well as soldiers returning from the Crusades brought with them the foods and eating habits of distant lands, including exotic Middle Eastern spices and fruits. The use or overuse of spices as well as figs, raisins and other ingredients that did not grow in Poland's northerly clime were typical of medieval cookery. A major turning point occurred in the early 16th century when Italian Princess Bona Sforza became the queen of Poland after marrying King Zygmunt the Old. She moved to Poland with her entire court, bringing with her cooks, gardeners and the copious use of hitherto unknown ingredients such as tomatoes, lettuce, leeks, cauliflower, spinach and chives. Even today, Poland's standard soup greens (carrot, parsley root, celeriac, savoy cabbage and leek) are known as *włoszczyzna* (Italian things).

Later, French haute cuisine made its imprint on all of Europe, including Poland. Although the 18th-century partitions deprived Poland of its independent statehood for 123 years, they did enhance Polish foodways through closer contacts with the cuisine of the three occupying powers. Wars, invasions, occupations, annexations, revolutions and counterrevolutions, uprisings and reprisals, destruction and reconstruction also played a part in the overall process. Like everyone else, refugees, exiles and prisoners also had to eat but were often forced to make do with what was available. Perhaps that too has helped to shape Polish culinary ingenuity—the creative ability to whip up a tasty and appetizing repast from next to nothing.

In addition to native preferences and foreign influence, there was also what might be called a trickle-down effect. It was the small but influential aristocracy that first went for imported innovations. Later the more prosperous of the nobility would follow suit and the process would continue trickling down through the petty nobility, to burgher (middle) class and all the way to the peasantry. But as these influences trickled down, they themselves were influenced by native foodways, including Polish culinary preferences and availability. The Polonized end result was often quite different from the original import.

The bottom line of it all is probably the definition that first appeared in my previous book, *Polish Heritage Cookery* (1993): "*Kuchnia polska* (Polish cuisine) is a blend of hearty peasant dishes and more elegant gourmet fare, served with a flair and generous helping of hospitality. . . . It has succeeded in assimilating a broad cross-section of (foreign) cultural influence, but has not lost its distinctly Slavic favor in the process. . . . Polish cookery might be described as a middle-of-the-road European cuisine, meaning that is has wide potential appeal. It is less fiery than the food of Hungary and Mexico, less vinegary than Germany cookery, less starchy than that of Czechoslovakia, and not as sweet as traditional Jewish cuisine. On the whole Polish food is a bit more inclined towards the tart and tangy than mainstream American cooking."

When the first immigrants arrived in America in the mid-1800s, they naturally brought with them their traditional food preferences and eating habits. Accustomed to crusty and flavorful rye bread, almost to a man (or woman), they found American white bread highly unpalatable, so they baked their own bread. They also tried as best they could to replicate the foods they grew up with in the Old Country, but not all the ingredients were readily available. As more and more Polish immigrants flooded into America's cities and towns, ethnic bakeries, groceries, butcher shops and poultry stores sprang up to cater to their needs, and existing farmers' markets expanded their offerings to include the things the Polish newcomers wanted to buy. In such places as Chicago, Wisconsin's Stevens Point, Detroit's Chene Street area, and Buffalo's east side, and in Little Polands across America's northeast and midwest, largely or even exclusively Polish farmers' markets emerged.

But, unlike other ethnic groups, the early Polish pioneers did not set up too many Polish restaurants or other eateries. Perhaps that was because "eating out" had not been the custom among the peasantry, to which most of the immigrants traced their roots. And unlike the ethnically indigenous inns, pubs, chop houses and cafés common to other countries, in Poland, the village inn was usually operated by non-Poles: the legendary Jewish innkeepers or nationals of the partitioning powers. Poles would frequent the *karczma* (public house), *gospoda* (inn) or *zajazd* (roadhouse) while traveling, on market day or to meet their cronies there for a drink and a snack on other occasions. But for serious celebrations (or plotting their next national insurrection!), they would retire to the intimacy of private homes. That practice was largely continued in America. Workers who needed a moment of respite after a backbreaking shift visited the bar or tavern, but it, too, was a largely alien place. The American saloonkeeper of the late 19th and early 20th century served only U.S. mainstream drinks, such as blended whiskey, weak American beer, ginger ale, hot dogs, popcorn, pretzels, salted peanuts and potato chips.

So again the family home was where it was at. That was where the family and close friends gathered at Christmas and Easter, for christenings, First Holy Communion parties, name day get-togethers and festive Sunday dinners. Apart from grandmothers, mothers and daughters who kept their families fed, early Polonia did develop a category of cooks specializing in weddings, funeral banquets and, later (when they came into vogue among Polonia)—wedding and baby showers. An aunt of mine, the late Maria Tanalska of Hamtramck, had been one such cook. Even after she retired and stopped catering weddings, she was no longer able to cook the more modest quantities needed to feed just her and my Uncle Tadek, her retired husband.

Although immigrants retained their preference for the familiar foods to which they had been accustomed, their eating habits did undergo certain changes. Foremost among them was the considerably greater volume of meat consumption than had been the case in the Old Country. The typical Polish villager had his fill of meat only on holidays, at weddings, christenings and a few other occasions, and even then this was stretched by a lot of grain and vegetable fillers. Meat was incomparably more plentiful in America, so newcomers could enjoy their native *kiełbasa, gołąbki, kotlety, golonka, żeberka, flaczki, kiszka* and other meat-based foods on a far more regular basis. They were also exposed to such mainstream American foods as steak, roast beef, flapjacks, fruit pies and corn on the cob.

The breakup of many Polish neighborhoods in the aftermath of World War II sent Polish Americans scattering to ethnically mixed urban areas, suburbs and neighboring towns—a development that also affected their eating habits.

But even Polish Americans who no longer lived in or near their particular Little Poland, often visited it on weekends to stock up on all the great ethnic goodies. Those nice family-run Polish bakeries and sausage shops offered real honest-to-goodness food whose aroma hit you the minute you opened the door. Christmas and Easter were usually held at Busia's (Grandmother's), who often would also have the family over for Sunday dinner as long as her age and health permitted. And there is widespread agreement that the Old Polonian weddings were in a class by themselves.

Polish and other ethnic foods in America underwent various processes including hybridization (melding with the foodways of other ethnic groups), assimilation (tending to increasingly resemble the mainstream culture) and reductionism (the tendency to focus on a handful of dishes and overlook the rest). Like other ethnic cuisines, Polish foods tend to fall into two general categories: in-foods (eaten mainly by those within the ethnic group) and display foods, stereotypical dishes with which the general public associates a given community. For different ethnic groups this would include lasagna (Italian), bratwurst (German), stir-fry dishes (Oriental), onion soup (French), gefilte fish (Jewish), tacos (Mexican) and the like. The best-known Polish display foods are undoubtedly *kiełbasa*, *pierogi* and *gołąbki*. On the other hand, *flaki, kaszanka, czernina, chłodnik, piieróg gryczany* and *oscypek* are likely to be known to and enjoyed by mainly members of the in-group. Since the display foods are viewed as having greater general appeal, they are frequently featured at festivals, community suppers and Polish food concessions at various public events. When Polish Americans themselves start following that general trend, the more esoteric dishes may get pushed into the background and may eventually fade away.

Starting in the 1960s and '70s, Polish food began experiencing a revival, as more and more Polish Americans started traveling to Poland and taking an interest in various aspects of their heritage. That was true of other ethnic cuisines as well. By the late 20th century, awareness of Polish foods and foodways had spread to non-Polish ethnic and mainstream circles alike. Frozen *pierogi* have gone nationwide, and Americans of all ethnic backgrounds now know what *kiełbasa* is—even in parts of the country inhabited by few Polish Americans. One installment of the popular syndicated comic strip "Garfield" showed that ever-irreverent cat burping, thinking it over and finally asking: "When did we last have *kiełbasa*?" Polish sausage is now so widespread that it is even called for in non-Polish ethnic recipes including Fernande Garvin's well-known *The Art of French Cooking*.

For years, American food producers have marketed dill pickles as *polskie ogórki* (Polish pickles) or *polski wyrób,* (Polish-made), often with a white eagle on the label. Their quality may vary, but that marketing gimmick indicates that the term "Polish pickles" is a selling point. Since Poland regained its independence in 1989, more and more imported Polish food brands (Krakus, Hortex, Vavel, Cracovia, Fortuna, Tymbark, Wedel, Winiary, Polonaise, Wyborowa, Luksusowa, Chopin and Belvedere, among others) have been turning up not only at Polonian delis and food shops, but also on the shelves of mainstream American supermarkets. Products imported from Poland, such as brined dill pickles *(ogórki kiszone),* sauerkraut, marinated mushrooms, bottled *żur*, *ćwikła* (beet and horseradish relish), horseradish, mustard, fruit syrups, and confections, as well as North American–made Polish-style foods are becoming increasingly common.

Although Polish-style foods are now more widely available beyond the traditional Polish neighborhoods than ever before, as of this writing the more upscale, gourmet-type Polish dishes are still widely unknown to and largely absent from the Polish-American scene. This becomes especially apparent when Polish Americans go formal at upscale banquets and other such celebrations. Even at events such as Polonaise Balls and Polish Heritage Banquets, there is a visible tendency to resort to the banquet fare of the Anglo-mainstream: scotch, martinis, shrimp cocktails, standing rib roast, lobster, and so forth, as if to say that Polish cuisine has nothing suitably elegant to offer. Sometimes the blame is laid on the management of a major hotel or banquet facility, which claims it has a fixed menu and is unprepared to cook unfamiliar foods. But some Polonians themselves are reluctant to expand their Polish palate, arguing that their *babcia* never made this or that Polish dish.

One of this book's goals is to encourage readers to explore various, previously unknown aspects of their cultural heritage, and that includes Polish cuisine. Not just the stereotypical *kiełbasa, gołąbki* and *pierogi*, not just the dishes of a single social class or region, but a wider spectrum of Polish fare, from the gourmet banquet circuit all the way to the campfire scene. Hopefully, the "Little Lexicon of Basic Foods and Culinary Concepts" that follows will bring the foregoing introductory remarks into sharper focus and give readers a better idea of what Polish cookery is all about.

LITTLE LEXICON OF BASIC FOODS AND CULINARY CONCEPTS

This is but a partial list of some of the better-known foods and culinary concepts meant to give the reader a general idea of Polish culinary traditions, preferences and foodways. Suggestions on how to put them into practice are found in the following section on ingredients. The rough pronunciation of the entries in this section is given in brackets.

Babka (BAHP-kah)—Defining this tall tapered, turban-shaped cake as a "yeast-raised egg bread" is only partially correct, because this name is also applied to a wide variety of different cakes using other types of leavening. Tall iced or sugar-dusted babkas are among the traditional culinary attractions of the Polish Easter table, but they are enjoyed on other festive occasions as well. (NOTE: There are also savory babkas made with potatoes, onions, meat, etc.)

Barszcz (BAHRHCH)—A tart soup of two basic types: red (made with beets) and white (creamed). The *czerwony barszcz* ranges from the hearty *barszcz ukraiński* containing beans, potatoes, other vegetables and meat and/or sausage to the delicate *czysty barszcz czerwony*, a clear burgundy-hued beet-flavored bouillon. The *biały barszcz*, similar to *żurek* (see index), is often served over hard-cooked egg slices. In many families, it is the traditional Easter soup *(biały barszcz wielkanocny)*.

Bigos (BEE-guss)—Often referred to in English as hunter's stew, because of its close connection to the hunts of yesteryear, this ragout or stew is widely regarded as Poland's national dish. Its praises were sung in *Pan Tadeusz*, the epic poem of 19th-century romantic bard Adam Mickiewicz. It contains sauerkraut (with the possible addition of fresh shredded cabbage), bacon, sausage, a variety of cooked meats, including wild game, prunes and mushrooms with a splash of red wine, mead or even beer for good measure. It is best after several days of slow simmering and improves in flavor each time it is reheated. *Bigos* is usually served as a hot starter or supper dish with rye bread and a nip of vodka. In most Polish homes it is a "must" during the long winter season of holiday entertaining and is the favored delicacy of Polish hunters, campers and other outdoor enthusiasts.

Bitki (BEET-kee)—Collops or slices of boneless meat, usually beef, pounded thin, browned and simmered in sauce; short for *bite zrazy* (pounded collops).

Bliny (BLEE-nih)—Yeast-raised pancakes made with buckwheat or wheat flour. Sometimes they team up with caviar to make an interesting starter.

Boczek (BAW-chek)—Bacon is not only fried (as in the U.S.) but is often boiled and baked in a slab. Diced fried bacon nuggets are a smoky version of *skwarki* (see page 17), used to garnish potatoes, *pierogi,* groats, noodles, and other lean foods. Uncooked diced bacon is usually one of the ingredients of *bigos*.

Budyń (BOO-diń)—If you look closely, you'll see that the word comes from the English word *pudding*. It includes both the classic variety cooked in boiling water in special pudding molds as well as the potato-starch–thickened blancmange type of pudding.

Buraczki (boo-RAHCH-kee)—Chopped or grated braised beets, often containing some apples and thickened with a roux or sour cream, are a typical cooked vegetable accompanying beef and game dishes.

Chleb (KHLEP)—According to Polish tradition, the term *chleb* (bread) is mainly reserved for bread containing some proportion of rye flour. *Chleb zwykły* (regular bread) is anywhere from a 30/70, 40/60 to 50/50 combination of rye (the first figure given) and wheat flour. *Razowiec* is a darker bread (sometimes erroneously referred to in the U.S. as pumpernickel) made with whole-rye (also called dark-rye) flour. The best breads are baked using a sourdough starter (*na zakwasie*). Traditional Polish loaves are round or oval.

Some varieties of bread are sprinkled with poppy seeds, caraway or black cumin. Things such as Vienna or French bread are referred to as *biała bułka* (white loaf) or *bułka paryska* (Parisian loaf) and the thin French bread is called a *bagietka* (baguette). American-style white bread is known in Poland as *pieczywo tostowe* (toast loaf). NOTE: Bread is buttered when served with cheese, cold cuts, eggs, cold fish, etc. It is unbuttered when served with soup, since the latter is believed to already contain enough fat.

Chrust, chruściki (KHROOST, khroosh-CHEE-kee)—Also known as *faworki,* these delicate, fried, sugar-dusted pastries are usually associated with Mardi Gras. They are variously referred to in English as angel wings, bowknot pastries, bow ties, crisps, crullers, kindlings, favors, favorites and vanities.

Chrzan (KHSHAHN)—Grated horseradish in vinegar marinade, usually laced with sour cream, is a favorite Polish condiment with meat, fish and hard-cooked eggs. It is also used in a hot creamy horseradish sauce usually served with boiled beef or tongue.

Ciasto (CHAHS-taw)—Depending on its context, this word can mean cake, dough or batter.

Ciastko (CHAHST-kaw)—Pastry, tea cake, biscuit, or cookie.

Czernina (chair-NEE-nah)—A tart and tangy duck (or goose) soup, containing the fowl's blood and dried fruit and usually served over noodles or potatoes; so named because of its dark chocolate-like color (*czerń* means blackness); also spelled *czarnina*. This soup also had a ritual significance as the legendary *czarna polewka* (black pottage) served to a suitor who was being rejected.

Czysty barszcz czerwony (CHIS-tih BAHRHCH chair-VAW-nih)—A clear, ruby-red beet-flavored bouillon with a wine-like tang, often with a hint of garlic and mushroom; usually served with a hot mushroom- or meat-filled pastry on the side; a standard item on Polish restaurant menus often served at banquets and dinner-parties.

Ćwikła (CHFEEK-wah)—This salad or relish made with grated, cooked beet seasoned with horseradish is the most typical Polish accompaniment to roasted and smoked meats and sausages. The first recorded recipe for *ćwikła* was provided by writer Mikołaj Rey (1505–69), known as the "father of Polish literature."

Dziczyzna (jee-CHIZZ-nah)—Game dishes are frequently encountered on restaurant menus of heavily forested Poland. They include wild boar *(dzik),* hare *(zając),* venison (*sarnina*) and wildfowl such as partridge (*kuropatwa*), pheasant (*bażant*) and quail (*przepiórka*). Games dishes are usually served with sauces flavored with mushrooms or juniper and braised beets on the side.

Flaki/flaczki (FLAH-kee, FLAHCH-kee)—Tripe soup, on the spicy side, flavored with black and red pepper, ginger and marjoram; a topping of grated cheese makes it *po warszawsku* (Warsaw-style). Condiments such as additional marjoram, paprika, Turkish pepper and Maggi seasoning are usually provided for those who enjoy a zingier taste. This soup is known as *flaczki* (the diminutive form) to descendants of the old Polonia and *flaki* to more recent Polish immigrants.

Galareta (gah-lah-REH-tah)—Aspic or jelly encasing meat or fish to enhance their flavor and keep them moist and tender; a typically Polish cold starter.

Gałeczki, gałuszki, hałuszki (gah-WECH-kee, gah-WOOSH-kee, hah-WOOSH-kee)—A kind of grated-potato dumpling. Singular: *gałeczka, gałuszka, hałuszka.*

Golonka (gaw-LAWN-kah)—Pork hocks usually boiled and served with sauerkraut or yellow puréed peas. This hearty, stick-to-the-ribs meal is not recommended for the faint-hearted or those requiring easy-to-digest foods. A stein of beer will help wash down this substantial dish.

Gołąbki (gaw-WUMP-kee)—Literally "little pigeons," these are stuffed cabbage rolls, one of the Polish ethnic group's best-known display foods. The ground meat and rice version served in tomato sauce is the most common, but there are numerous other varieties, including vegetarian versions. Singular: *gołąbek.*

Grochówka (graw-HOOF-kah)—This yellow split pea soup is a hearty stick-to-the-ribs pottage containing sausage, bacon, potatoes, carrots and possibly other vegetables (some cooks add a dried mushroom for added depth). It is seasoned with crushed garlic, pepper and marjoram. *Grochówka* is best when allowed to simmer for hours and is often served at fests, street fairs and other outdoor events. Among the best memories Polish men have of their army days is the *żołnierska grochówka* (soldier's pea soup), simmered for hours in huge field kettles.

Grzyby (GZHIH-bih)—In Polish cookery, mushrooms are not only an accompaniment to meat dishes but are often served as the main meal. The most favored are the noble bolete *(cèpes, Steinpilz, porcini)* known in Polish as *borowik* or *prawdziwek.* Fresh boletes are usually stewed in sour cream. Dried boletes, after rehydration and cooking, have a more intense, deep, dusky and delicious flavor. Milky caps *(rydze)* are usually served pan-fried in butter, as are the white domestic champignons *(pieczarki). Kurki* (chanterelles) are good in white sauces and with scrambled eggs. The tall *kania* or umbrella mushroom (portobello) is usually breaded and fried like a pork cutlet. *Podpieńki* (honey mushrooms), *podgrzybki* (bay boletes) and *maślaki* (slippery jack) are but a few of the many varieties picked in Poland's forests. Different varieties of mushrooms are pickled in a seasoned vinegar marinade. Unlike the custom in other countries, oil is generally not added to Polish *grzyby marynowane* (pickled mushrooms).

Indyk (EEN-dick)—Turkey, owing to its size and delicate flavor, has long been associated with festive events in larger company; this native American bird has been misnamed both in English and Polish, for it no more hails from Turkey than from India. (The French have done likewise by calling it the *dinde,* originally: *d'Inde* [from India].) A slightly sweet bread, liver and raisin stuffing is the most popular Polish filling for roast stuffed turkey.

Jajecznica (yah-yech-NEE-tsah)—The Polish have this special word for scrambled eggs, a favorite quick dish that even inexperienced cooks can prepare; *jajecznica* is often fried *na słoninie* (on salt pork) *na boczku* (on bacon), *na szynce* (on ham) or *na kiełbasie* (on Polish sausage).

Jarzynka (yah-ZHIN-kah)—Any cooked vegetable served as a side dish accompanying the main course.

Kaczka (KAHCH-kah)—Duck, usually roasted, stuffed with apples and seasoned with marjoram; also used to prepare *czernina* (duck soup—see page 12).

Kapusta (kah-POOS-tah)—Cabbage and sauerkraut have long been Polish dietary mainstays. *Kapusta kiszona* or *kwaszona* (barrel-cured cabbage or sauerkraut) is the basis for Poland's national dish *bigos*, *kapuśniak* (sauerkraut soup), the Christmas Eve dishes *kapusta z grochem* and *kapusta z grzybami* and a common *pierogi* filling. Sauerkraut is served uncooked as a salad and as a cooked vegetable. Fresh cabbage is also cooked in soups, as a vegetable side dish, in stews and casseroles, and its leaves enwrap the popular *gołąbki.*

Kartofle (kahr-TUFF-leh)—Although of American origin, potatoes have long been a Polish dietary mainstay; they are also known as *ziemniaki* (esp. in the Kraków region), *grule* (in the Tatra Moutnains) and *pyrki* (in Wielkopolska, the Poznań region). Most often Polish cooks serve potatoes boiled or mashed.

Kasza (KAH-shah)—This term can be translated as groats, grits, grain, gruel, cereal, porridge, etc. The favorite is *kasza gryczana (hreczana)*—buckwheat groats. Fine-milled buckwheat is known as *kasza krakowska.* Others include *kasza jęczmienna* (barley), *kasza jaglana* (millet), *kasza manna* (farina, cream of wheat) and *kasza owsiana* (oatmeal).

Kisiel (KEE-shell)—This very old and simple fruit jelly, now usually thickened with potato starch, continues to be a home-style favorite of Polish children. Oat and cranberry *kisiel* are a typical Christmas Eve specialty.

Kluski (KLOOSS-kee)—This term is applied to different kinds of noodles and dumplings.

Knedle (KNEDD-leh)—A kind of potato dumpling, filled with meat, plums or other fillings and boiled.

Kolacja (kaw-LAHTS-yah)—Supper, the last meal of the day, usually a lighter meal than *obiad* (early afternoon dinner).

Kołduny (koh-DOO-nih)—Small, usually meat-filled *pierożki* popular in northeastern Poland along the Lithuanian border.

Kopytka (kaw-PIT-kah)—A kind of unfilled potato dumpling served as a meat accompaniment instead of potatoes or as a meal in itself, garnished with fried salt-pork nuggets or gravy.

Kotlet (KAWT-let)—The connection with the word cutlet is quite obvious. This can be a bone-in chop or a deboned cutlet, which is usually pounded, breaded and fried. It can also be a kind of flattened meatball or thick patty (*kotlet mielony* or *siekany*). Today, one of Poland's favorite meals is *kotlet schabowy* (fried, breaded pork cutlet).

Krupnik (KROOP-neek)—This term is applied to two entirely different products: 1) vegetable-barley soup; 2) hot honey-spice cordial (often served during the Christmas holidays).

Kulebiak (koo-LEBB-yahk)—A kind of loaf-shaped pie encasing various fillings, especially sauerkraut, cabbage, rice, meat and mushrooms. Often served as an accompaniment with soup.

Kurczę po polsku (KOOR-cheh paw PAWL-skoo)—Roast spring chicken polonaise, a classic Polish dish, stuffed with a filling made of milk-soaked white bread, chicken liver (or raw ground meat), seasoned with fresh dill and roasted to golden brown perfection. Typical accompaniments are buttered new potatoes and *mizeria* (sliced cucumbers in sour cream).

Makaron (mah-KAH-rawn)—Derived from the Italian word *macaroni*, these are thin egg noodles usually served in soup.

Makowiec, strucla z makiem (mak-KAWV-yets, STROOTS-lah z MAH-kyem)—A traditional Christmas cake, this yeast-raised roll cake contains a delicious filling of poppy seeds, raisins and nuts, is usually iced and sprinkled with poppy seeds or slivered almonds.

Mazurek (mah-ZOO-rek)—Various kinds of flat cakes cut into serving-sized squares; a typical Easter treat.

Naleśniki (nah-lesh-NEE-kee)—Polish crêpes. The most common fillings for these thin pancakes are white curd cheese *(twaróg),* meat and onion and jam. The *naleśniki* are often folded into a square and browned in butter. Sour cream is a common topping for all except the meat-filled *naleśniki*. Singular: *naleśnik.*

Nalewka (nah-LEFF-kah)—Homemade cordial (alcoholic drink), usually made with grain alcohol or very strong vodka and various flavorings (fruit, honey, herbs, etc.).

Obiad (AWB-yaht)—Dinner, the main meal of the day, generally eaten between 1 and 3 P.M. The traditional Polish dinner consists of soup and a main course (*drugie danie* meaning second course). Dessert is optional.

Okrasa (aw-KRAH-sah)—This can be melted butter, fried fatback or bacon bits, fried onions, pan drippings, etc. used as toppings for potatoes, pasta, dumplings, groats, etc. Also known as *omasta*.

Paszteciki (pahsh-teh-CHEE-kee)—Small handheld pastries or pasties filled with meat, mushrooms, etc. and usually served with clear soups. Singular: *pasztecik.*

Pasztet (PAHSH-tett)—*Pâté*, a meat paste made from finely ground cooked meat. The addition of wild game such as hare or venison gives Polish pâté (mainly containing cooked pork, veal and liver) its characteristic flavor. Horseradish sauce or tartar sauce is a frequently provided condiment.

Pączki (PAUNCH-kee)—Polish doughnuts, usually containing fruit filling, and glazed or sugar-dusted; although available year-round at Polish pastry shops and cafés, they have a ritual significance on *Tłusty Czwartek* (Fat Thursday) and *Ostatki* (Fat Tuesday). In Warsaw, the best *pączki* come from Blikle's Pastry Shops—they are glazed with icing, garnished with candied orange peel and each contains a dollop of rose-petal jam. Singular: *pączek.*

Pieczeń (PYEH-chain)—Meat roast, the most common being *pieczeń wołowa* (roast beef), *pieczeń wieprzowa* (roast pork), *pieczeń cielęca* (roast veal), *pieczeń barania* (roast mutton), *pieczeń z dzika* (roast wild boar).

Pieczyste (pyeh-CHISS-teh)—Roast-meat course at a banquet or other festive repast.

Piernik (PYAIR-neek)—Honey-spice cake (a kind of gingerbread) usually associated with the Christmas season. The northern city of Toruń is Poland's *piernik* capital. Also known as *miodownik* (honey cake).

Pierogi (pyeh-RAW-ghee)—This popular Polish dish has been variously translated by English speakers as dough pockets, filled dumplings and even Polish ravioli. Pierogi can have a variety of fillings, but the most common are minced cooked meat, sauerkraut and mushrooms, cheese and potatoes (these are known as *ruskie* [Ruthenian] *pierogi*), sweet cheese (usually with a touch of vanilla) and blueberries (in summer). Other fillings include buckwheat groats, potatoes and onions, and lentils. Toppings include fried fatback nuggets, sour cream, melted butter, or butter-browned bread crumbs. Singular: *pieróg*.

Pierożki (pyeh-RUSH-kee)—Diminutive of *pierogi*, suggesting smaller, daintier dumplings of the type city-folk would serve. Singular: *pierożek.*

Placek (PLAH-tsek)—Any of a variety of usually yeast-raised cakes baked with fruit, cheese, crumb topping, etc.; plural: *placki* often means pancakes, as in *placki kartoflane* (potato pancakes).

Podwieczorek (pawd-vyeh-CHAW-rek)—Tea, a usually light sweet meal (cakes, preserves, pudding, and tea or coffee) served at about 5 o'clock in the afternoon, roughly midway between *obiad* (dinner) and *kolacja* (supper).

Polędwica (paw-ledn-VEE-tsah)—Tenderloin, the choicest cut of meat; beef tenderloin is usually broiled, while pork tenderloin is most often cured and smoked to create a first-rate cold meat.

Przekąska (psheh-KAWN-skah)—An hors d'oeuvre; finger food; light snack served with drinks; plural: *przekąski*. Often synonymous with *przystawka* (see below).

Przystawka (pshih-STAHF-kah)—Starter course, hot or cold meat, fish, vegetable or egg dish served ahead of the main course; plural: *przystawki*.

Pyzy (PIH-zih)—These dumplings, made from raw and cooked potatoes, are typical of the southern province of Śląsk (Silesia). These potato balls are boiled and served garnished with fried pork fatback nuggets and drippings.

Rachuchy, racuszki (rah-TSOO-khih, rah-TSOOSH-kee)—Golden brown pancakes, often made with sour milk or buttermilk, fried in butter or oil and served dusted with confectioners' sugar or fruit toppings.

Rosół (RAW-soow)—Broth, a clear soup made by cooking meat or meaty bones with soup vegetables. The favorite is *rosół z kury z makaronem* (chicken noodle soup), a typical dish served at Sunday dinner and other family occasions.

Ryba w galarecie (RIH-bah v gah-lah-REH-cheh)—Fish in sparkling clear aspic is a typical Polish cold starter course. Carp is the preferred fish for this dish, but other freshwater species such as trout, pike and walleye (as well as sea fish) are also good. Lemon juice and/or horseradish as well as tartar sauce add tang to this otherwise mild-tasting dish.

Schab pieczony (SKHAP pyeh-CHAW-nih)—Roast pork loin, a favorite Polish cut, may be served hot as a main course or cold as a starter, sometimes encased in aspic. Horseradish sauce is often provided.

Sernik (SARE-neek)—Cheesecake, often studded with raisins and flavored with grated orange peel, has long been a favorite Polish Easter cake, enjoyed by many year-round. It was among the dishes introduced to the Vatican by Polish-born Pontiff John Paul II.

Skwarki (SKFAHR-kee)—Diced pork fatback (*słonina*) fried up into crunchy golden brown nuggets, together with the rendered fat, are a typical Polish topping for potatoes, *pierogi* and other dumplings, groats and vegetables.

Szarlotka (shahr-LAWT-kah)—Apple cake, in terms of popularity the Polish equivalent of America's apple pie. A thick apple filling flavored with a pinch of cinnamon is baked in a flaky crust to produce this delectable treat. Cafés sometimes serve it topped with a dollop of whipped cream.

Śledzie (SHLEDGEH)—After being soaked to remove excess salt, Baltic herring are served up with sliced onions marinated in vinegar or oil or creamed.

Sometimes diced apples are added. A favorite cold snack or starter course that just begs for nips of ice-cold vodka.

Śniadanie (shnyah-DAH-nyeh)—Breakfast, the first meal of the day; may be savory (cheese, cold cuts, eggs) or sweet (jam, raised cakes, sweetened milk soup and hot cereals); *drugie śniadanie* (literally "second breakfast") is often a bagged lunch (sandwich, apple, cake) eaten at work.

Tatar (TAH-tahr)—Beef tartare is a mound of minced beef tenderloin with a raw egg yolk deposited in its volcano-like crater and served in a wreath of chopped onion, pickled cucumbers and pickled mushrooms. A glass of ice-cold vodka is the natural accompaniment to this cold snack or starter.

Zakąska (zah-KAWN-skah)—A bite-down, a small morsel of food (a bite of sausage, herring, pickle, egg, cheese) to follow up a glass of vodka.

Zimne nogi (ZHEEM-neh NAW-ghee)—Literally "cold feet," this is the popular name for jellied pig's and/or calf's feet, a favorite cold dish. Also known as *studzienina* and *galareta z nóżek.*

Zrazy (ZRAH-zih)—Collops or slices or meat, pounded thin, browned and simmered until tender; a favorite of the Old Polish nobility that has remained popular to this day (synonymous with *bitki*—see page 11).

Zrazy zawijane (ZRAH-zih zah-vee-YAH-neh)—Slices of boneless meat are pounded, spread with a filling, rolled up, browned and simmered until tender; an elegant banquet dish, traditionally served with buckwheat groats.

Zupa (ZOO-pah)—Soup, traditionally the first course at daily dinner, followed by the main course. Although hot savory soups predominate, there are also cold soups and sweet ones.

Zupa grzybowa (gzhih-BAW-vah)—Creamed mushroom soup in Poland is made from wild bolete mushrooms that Poles call *prawdziwki* (true mushrooms). Polish menus clearly distinguish them from the rather bland-tasting cultivated champignon type *(pieczarki),* which are considered inferior.

Zupa ogórkowa (aw-goor-KAW-vah)—A tangy, creamy soup containing grated brined cucumbers and diced potatoes.

Zupa pomidorowa (paw-mee-daw-RAW-vah)—Polish tomato soup–lovers are divided over whether it should be served with rice or noodles, but the latter seem to have the edge.

Zupa szczawiowa (shcha-VYAW-vah)—This creamy soup, flecked with tart green sorrel leaves (similar to spinach), is usually served over a hard-cooked egg.

Żurek (ZHOO-rek)—A tart soup made with fermented ryemeal, usually cooked on a sausage-based stock, and seasoned with marjoram. It may be served with a hard-cooked egg in the soup or a serving of potatoes garnished with pork fatback or bacon nuggets on the side. A meatless version of this soup was once a Lenten dietary mainstay.

THIS BOOK'S INCORPORATED RECIPE INGREDIENTS

Most (but not all) cookery books first list ingredients at the start of a recipe and then proceed to tell you what to do with them. When we were writing our voluminous 2,200-recipe *Polish Heritage Cookery* in the late 1980s, we chose to emulate the classic *Gold Cook Book* of the late Master Chef Louis P. De Gouy by foregoing the listing of ingredients and incorporating them into the text. By so doing, we were able to keep our book down to a single volume and thereby provide readers with a maximum number of recipes at a not unreasonable price.

That format has been readily accepted by the thousands of readers who have been buying *Polish Heritage Cookery* since it first appeared in 1993. Since neither reviewers nor individual readers have complained about this departure from the typical practice of prefacing recipes with ingredient lists, we have decided to arrange *Polish Holiday Cookery* the same way.

For the benefit of those unaccustomed to that format, we can only suggest they start by lightly underlining the ingredients in a given recipe in pencil. After preparing two or three recipes in this way, the reader should acquire the knack of glancing at a recipe and picking out the ingredients without having to underline.

ABBREVIATIONS

Another space-saving measure is the following abbreviations commonly used throughout this book:

t = teaspoon(s)	l = liter(s)
T = tablespoon(s)	g = gram(s)
c = cup(s)	kg = kilogram
jg = jigger	lb = pound(s)
pt = pint(s)	oz = ounce(s)
qt = quart(s)	temp = temperature
gal = gallon(s)	min = minute(s)
sm = small	hr = hour(s)
med = medium	lg = large
″ = inch(es)	pkg = package
′ = foot/feet	m/l = more or less
° = degree(s)	esp. = especially

BASIC INGREDIENTS AND PROCEDURES

Beer—Poland's long-standing flagship beers, Żywiec and Okocim, have been joined by such brands as Lech, Krakus, EB, Leżajsk, Tyskie, Piast, Hevelius, Brok, Królewskie and Łomżyńskie. One of the oldest brands is Warka, produced at Kazimierz Pułaski's birthplace. In 2002, the Tychy Brewery of Silesia, Poland, received the prestigious Champion Beer title in the lager category for its Tyskie Gronie at the Brewing Industry International competition held in London. Most Polish breweries produce a basic golden lager usually called *pełne jasne* (meaning full-strength and pale-colored), which usually contains from 5.7% to 6% alcohol by volume. Light beers, which usually contain 5.5% alcohol or less, taste watery to the Polish palate and are not very popular. Strong beers generally have an alcohol content of 7.2% to 7.8%, and porter (a thick, dark beer similar to but stronger and slightly sweeter than Guinness stout) may have an alcohol content of 9% or more. It is next to impossible to differentiate between brands when the beer is used in cooking. Even nonalcoholic beer (which in Poland used to contain 1.2% alcohol, and was lowered to 0.5% in 2002) may be used in cooking, since it imparts the desired hoppy-yeasty taste to foods.

Beet concentrate—This bottled liquid concentrate imported from Poland *(koncentrat z buraków)* enables quick preparation of *barszcz* when there isn't time to cook beets from scratch. The well-known Krakus brand translates this product into English as "red borscht concentrate."

Beets—A Polish staple often used in soups *(barszcz),* as a cooked vegetable *(buraczki),* in salads and in the best-known Polish relish *(ćwikła).* Scrubbed, unpeeled beets may be baked in an oven (1 hr at 375° or until tender) or boiled. Then they are sliced, diced, grated, etc. Plain canned beets may be used instead of fresh beets in all recipes; their liquid should not be discarded. It is a great *barszcz* ingredient and imparts a beautiful color to potato/vegetable salads. Canned pickled beets are good in *ćwikła.*

Beet-sour—This fermented beet liquid *(kwas burakowy)* is used to prepare Poland's traditional, tangy beet *barszcz.* Peel and slice 1 lb beets and place in glass or crockery container. Add 6 c preboiled lukewarm water and on top place a slice of rye or black (whole rye) bread. Cover with gauze and keep in warm place 4–5 days. Check on it daily, skimming away any foam or scum that forms on top. Strain into sterilized bottles, seal and refrigerate until needed. About 1 c beet-sour and 5 c stock are normally needed to make *barszcz,* but individual recipes and tastes may vary.

Bouillon cubes—Also known as stock cubes (and also available in granulated and powdered form) can be used to prepare stocks, soups, gravies and stews in place of traditional meat or vegetable stocks. However, they tend to give foods certain monotonous, store-bought or fast-food taste, so use them sparingly. Use only ⅓–½ the amount suggested by the manufacturer to prepare stocks and other foods. For instance, if the manufacturer tells you to use 2 cubes to make a pint of bouillon, use only one. Bouillon cubes may also be used in small quantities to enhance the flavor of traditional stocks. The traditional chicken, beef and vegetable bouillon has been joined by mushroom bouillon cubes (see page 26), turkey bouillon, chicken and beef broth and even chicken-goose-turkey-flavored bouillon cubes. Winiary and Knorr brands imported from Poland are the best known.

Bread—As a result of today's chemical revolution, unfortunately the bread baked in Poland, North America and elsewhere is getting progressively worse in taste and texture. The big commercial baking companies are interested less in quality and craftsmanship and more in maximizing their profits, hence the copious use of additives known as "bread improvers." What is being passed off as Polish rye bread contains less and less rye flour, or more and more white enriched (wheat) flour. The traditional shiny, crackly crust is also getting rarer. The darker color of some varieties is, more often than not, achieved through coloring additives such as caramel rather than by whole-grain flour. A small private bakery you regularly engage to supply your festivals, weddings, banquets and other large events is more likely to custom-bake genuine Polish-style bread and rolls to your specifications the old-fashioned way, than is a large commercial baker.

Bread crumbs—Use dry, plain, white bread crumbs, not the flavored variety, whenever bread crumbs are called for in this book. If you regularly have stale bread and unused end slices left over, mill them in a processor or roll them with rolling pin and sift. For savory recipes (not cakes or desserts), rye bread crumbs may be added to the white crumbs for sharper flavor.

Bread crumbs, browned in butter—Often referred to as Polonaise topping, this is the classic garnish for various hot foods. Simply brown plain bread crumbs in butter (e.g., 2 T crumbs in 3 T butter), stirring frequently, until nicely browned and spoon over boiled potatoes, other vegetables, various pasta including *pierogi* and other hot dishes. Cauliflower Polonaise is an especially delicious favorite.

Breading—Typically meat, fish or other foods are dredged in flour, dipped in egg wash (1 egg beaten with 1 T water) and rolled in bread crumbs before frying to give the end product a crunchy golden brown crust. The

American way of shaking the egg-dipped food in a plastic bag containing flour and/or bread crumbs is a less messy way of accomplishing this task.

Bread-sour—Proceed as with ryemeal-sour (*żur*—see page 33), but use several slices stale rye bread instead of the flour and/or oatmeal. For best results, use rye bread from a Polish, Slavic or Jewish bakery that still uses traditional bread-making methods. NOTE: If any mold appears on the bread slices floating on top, simply skim it away. Although unsightly, it is not harmful. (Penicillin comes from bread mold!)

Buckwheat groats—The ideal accompaniment to beef dishes, meatballs and wild game, this mildly nut-flavored grain is a nice change of pace from potatoes, rice and pasta. It is also used to make *kaszanka/kiszka* and used in poultry and suckling-pig stuffing. There are three basic varieties: unroasted (white), medium-roasted (pale brown) and dark-roasted (dark brown).

Butter—Use only fresh, unsalted butter in the recipes contained in this book. Salted butter may be old, as the salt simply retards rancidity but does not help butter retain its light, creamery-fresh flavor.

Cake mixes—Many traditional Polish cakes—*babka*, *sernik*, *karpatka*, *piernik*, etc.—are now available in cake-mix versions marketed under such brand names as Delecta, Dr. Oetker and Gellwe. The best that can be said about them is that they are better than nothing. Like American or any other cake mixes, they cannot compete with the real thing.

Cheese, white—Known in Polish as *twaróg* or *biały ser*, in English this is often referred to as farmer cheese, curd cheese, pot cheese or pressed cottage cheese. During a 2002 stateside reconnaissance, I noticed one Chicagoland producer marketing it as white cheese. It is a basic cheese obtained by heating clabbered sour milk to separate the curds from the whey, draining it and pressing it to the desired degree of firmness. This is the cheese used to fill *pierogi*, *naleśniki*, make Polish-style cheesecake and other dishes. It can be mashed with a little sour cream, seasoned and flavored with chives, scallions, radishes, etc. to create a nice cheese spread. It is easy to make at home. Simply heat 2 qt cultured buttermilk on low heat until the curds float to the top. Switch off heat and leave pot intact until it cools to room temp (several hr). Drain in colander or sieve lined with a linen napkin or several thicknesses of cheesecloth. When dripping stops, you will have a nice, soft cheese to season and spread on bread. Twist into a ball through the cloth to extract more moisture, and refrigerate overnight for a firmer, sliceable cheese that can be used in *pierogi* and other dishes.

Cheese, yellow—*Żółty ser* is the Polish term for what is known in English as semihard and semisoft cheeses. Such imported Polish cheeses available in North America include *podlaski, mazowiecki, morski, tylżycki* and *salami* (so-called because of its roll shape and not to be confused with the cold cut). The Wisconsin Cheese Group based in Monroe, Wisconsin, imports from Poland a mild, semihard cheese known as Polish Delight. In Polish recipes calling for yellow cheese, feel free to use Edam, Gouda, brick, Monterey Jack, Muenster and similar domestic varieties. Do not use orange-colored American (or Canadian) cheeses in Polish cooking.

Cheeses, specialty—The famous little, lightly smoked cheese of the Polish Tatra Mountain highlanders is known as *oszczypek* or (in Góral dialect) *oscypek*. Made from sheep's milk, it is spindle-shaped cheese that is brown (from the smoking) and intricately patterned (from the carved wooden cheese mold) on the outside and off-white on the inside. It has a pleasant taste and an unusual, slightly rubbery, "tooth-squeaking" texture makes it an interesting addition to the cheese tray. Another sheep's-milk cheese from the mountain region is *bryndza*—a somewhat grainy, salted, ground cheese that is good in cheese spreads.

Citric acid—Also known as lemon sour or sour salt *(cytrynowy)*, these sour white crystals are widely used by Polish cooks to impart a tart flavor to soups, sauces, gravies, dressings, etc. More stomach-friendly than vinegar, a pinch or two is often all that is needed. A pinch of citric acid dissolved in 1 T water provides "instant vinegar" that can be used wherever real vinegar is called for.

Coffee—For authentic Polish-style *kawa*, a medium-dark roasted, finely ground (espresso or Turkish grind) coffee should be selected. Less water is used to brew Polish-style coffee, resulting in a richer-flavored beverage, and since it is stronger, less is consumed. Polish-style ground coffee is now available at Polish delis and import shops in North America. The most aromatic are Tchibo Excellent and Jacobs Krönung, followed by Elite's Pedro's, Prestige and Sahara Oasis varieties, MK Café Premium, Prima Arabica and Gala Wspaniała. Polish-made Maxwell House is dark and strong but not very aromatic. Personally I like Tchibo's Grand Mocca variety, which combines aroma with an extra caffeine kick for that early-morning or midday pick-me-up. One Chicagoland firm produces a Królewska brand Polish-style coffee that unfortunately I have never had a chance to try. NOTE: When coffee labels are in Polish, *mielona* means espresso (fine) grind and *drobno mielona* means Turkish (extra-fine) grind.

Fatback—Also referred to as salt pork *(słonina)*, fatback is a white slab of pork fat widely used in traditional Polish cooking. It is diced, fried up into crunchy golden nuggets and used as a topping *(skwarki)*, fried with onions and served at room temp as a sandwich spread, used for larding lean meat and is great for frying eggs in. If you have the salted variety, scrape off excess salt before using. If unsalted, sprinkle lightly with salt and rub it in on all sides before dicing and frying.

Flavor enhancers—Popular Polish flavor enhancers used to improve the taste of soups, sauces, stews and meat dishes go by such trade names as Jarzynka, Vegeta, Warzywko and Kucharek. They all contain dried, ground vegetables (carrot, onion, parsnip, celeriac), herbs such as parsley as well as other seasonings and, naturally, the inevitable monosodium glutamate (MSG). A pinch or two will improve the flavor of savory dishes, but it's best not to overdo it. Use less than the amount recommended by the manufacturer who obviously wants you to go through as much of his product as possible. If the manufacturer recommends 1 t per c water, then use ⅓–½ t instead. Using these preparations too generously gives all dishes a monotonous store-bought/fast-food taste, and many people may develop an allergic reaction.

Fork-blending—You can blend different ingredients together using a mixer, blender or processor, but for smaller amounts the cleanup may take more time and effort than it's worth. In many cases, fork-blending (vigorously stirring) the ingredients with a fork in a cup is quicker, more convenient and less messy.

Grating—Various foods can be grated on a handheld grater, which usually has fine-grating and coarse-grating surfaces as well as a slicer blade. Feel free to use a food processor, hand-cranked chopper-grater or other appliance that does the same job. When grating small quantities, the handheld grater may be your best choice since it saves you the time-consuming cleanup of food chopper, blender or processor.

Herbs—Of the fresh herbs, dill is by far the Poles' favorite flavor accent, used on potatoes more often than parsley, in poultry stuffing, in soups, fish dishes, egg dishes, salads, etc. Parsley and chives are next in popularity. Basil and mint are used less frequently, only by some cooks in a limited number of dishes. Marjoram is widely used, and mainly it is dried and rubbed.

Horseradish—Whenever a recipe in this book calls for horseradish, it means prepared, non-creamed horseradish. Check around to find a brand that is not bitter and does not contain cheap fillers such as turnip or rutabaga. It is better to add your own cream to plain prepared horseradish than to buy the cream-style variety out of a jar, which may contain preservatives, stabilizers and other chemicals to prevent the cream from spoiling or separating. Check the ingredients to see whether it contains powdered milk or other dairy additives.

Horseradish root—Some recipes call for fresh grated horseradish. Freshly bought or dug-up horseradish roots should first be soaked in cold water several hr, then peeled or scraped. The white root is grated and added to whatever dish is being prepared. But, in a pinch, prepared horseradish may be used instead of the freshly grated kind. A little more should be used, since it is usually less potent than freshly grated horseradish. (See Fruit and Vegetable Gardening—Polish-style, page 214.) Horseradish root may also be peeled, washed, diced, dried, and processed to a powder. Stored in a sealed jar, this is a convenient way to add horseradish flavor to dishes when you are out of the prepared type. Horseradish powder is often one of the ingredients of Polish seasoned pepper *(pieprz ziołowy).*

Hunter's seasoning—Excellent in game and other meat and poultry dishes, *bigos*, stews, etc. Process 2 heaping T marjoram, 1 T dried juniper berries, 1 T peppercorns, 1 t caraway, 1–2 t garlic powder, 1 t onion powder, 6–8 grains allspice, 3–4 cloves and 1 broken-up bay leaf. Feel free to juggle the ingredients according to preference. You can also add a few T of any of the Vegeta-type flavor enhancers.

Kefir—This kind of liquid yogurt may be used in place of sour milk as a side dish with boiled potatoes or cooked groats and in batters (see sour milk page 30).

Larding—This technique (known in Polish as *szpikowanie)* is used to make lean and dry meat (especially beef and game) juicier. It is easiest to cut fatback into roughly pencil-thick sticks and freeze them until needed. Incisions are made in the meat and the frozen lardoon (fatback stick) is forced into the opening. During roasting it will make the meat around it more succulent. The frozen fatback stick may also be rolled in seasoning (salt and pepper, paprika, hunter's seasoning or your own composition) before inserting into meat, as that helps to season the inside of the roast as well.

Maggi liquid seasoning—Extensively used by Polish cooks since the early 20th century, when the Maggi company first built a factory in Gdańsk, this condiment has sometimes been humorously referred to as "Polish soy sauce." Similar in application but much thinner (less concentrated) than America's familiar Kitchen Bouquet, a few dashes of Maggi will perk up the flavor of most savory dishes. But do not get into the habit of using it in everything because your soups, gravies and meat dishes will end up with a monotonous taste-alike flavor. Also available in cubes. Winiary, Knorr and other companies also produce a similar seasoning.

Marination—Keeping food in a tart liquid (vinegar, oil, wine, sour milk, buttermilk, whey, etc.) to improve its flavor, keep it juicy and/or tenderize it. Even salting and drizzling fresh fish with lemon juice is a form of marination. Often onions and/or vegetables and spices (pepper, allspice, bay leaves, juniper) are added. Wild game and tougher cuts of beef may require steeping in a strong vinegar-wine marinade for several days to tenderize them and (especially in the case of wild game) rid them of their gamey off-flavors.

Mushrooms—The best fresh mushrooms are king boletes (*borowiki, prawdziwki*), but don't expect to find them in the first supermarket you encounter. They may be marketed under other names such as *cèpes, porcini* or *Steinpilze*. They are also nowhere as abundant in the North American wilds as they are in the forestlands of Poland. Polish-American mushroom-pickers are more likely to encounter *pieczarki* (meadow mushrooms—the wild form of the cultivated white mushroom), *opieńki* (honey mushrooms, stumpers), *maślaki* (slippery Jacks), *kurki* (chantrelles) and *smardze* (morels). Store-bought portobello, oyster and shiitake mushrooms may also be used in Polish dishes calling for fresh mushrooms.

Mushroom bouillon cubes—This is one of the most successful convenience items to emerge in the final years of the 20th century. Unlike beef, chicken and vegetable bouillon cubes, which give foods an artificial taste, mushroom bouillon cubes are very close in flavor to genuine rehydrated dried mushrooms. That is probably because they contain dried bolete mushrooms. One 10-g cube (Winiary or Knorr brand) dissolved in 2 c boiling water makes 2 c of clear mushroom bouillon or, with the addition of some milk and flour, delicious mushroom gravy.

Mushrooms, rehydrating dried—When directed to "cook 1 oz rehydrated bolete mushrooms," first scrub the mushrooms with a stiff brush under cold running water. Place them in a small saucepan, drench with 1 c lukewarm water and let stand several hr or overnight. (VARIATION: A shortcut method is to drench the mushrooms with boiling water and let them stand, covered, 30 min.) Cook mushrooms in same water until tender (30–60 min). Leave mushrooms in their stock until cool enough to handle. Slice or dice and return to stock until needed. When instructed to "add cooked, rehydrated mushrooms," that also means the liquid in which they soaked and cooked, unless otherwise indicated. To remove any grit, liquid may be filtered through a cloth napkin, dish towel, several thicknesses of cheesecloth, which should be wrung to squeeze out every drop of mushroom flavor. A coffee filter may also be used.

Mustard—Whenever mustard is called for in this book, it means medium-sharp, brown, prepared Polish-style mustard out of a jar. In the few cases when dry mustard or mustard seed is required, that will be clearly specified. The basic types of Polish imported mustard are *stołowa* (table mustard, a general purpose condiment), *kremska* (a mild, slightly sweet mustard), *sarepska* (a sharper mustard containing black mustard seed), *chrzanowa* (horseradish mustard) and *delikatesowa* (a term suggesting a smooth gourmet-style product). You may also encounter Polish imported mustards labeled *miodowa* (honey-flavored), *czosnkowa* (garlic-flavored) and *grillowa* (barbecue). Polish-style mustard is also produced in America, including brands named after Pułaski and Kościuszko. If Polish-style mustard is not readily available, Düsseldorf-style is a close alternative. Mild Dijon may be used in Polish recipes, but if you have only sharp Dijon, then use half the amount called for in the recipe. Although devoid of any Polish identification on its label, Detroit's Red Pelican sharp brown mustard is very nice in Polish dishes. Avoid those Polish mustards that now contain *kurkuma* (turmeric) or *kurkumina* (synthetic turmeric)—the substance that gives American-style mustard its unappetizingly canary-yellow color and sour taste. Check the label to see if its ingredients include turmeric, and if it does, choose another brand.

Pickles, pickled vegetables and fruits—The most authentically Polish dill pickles are brine-cured (*ogórki kwaszone* or *kiszone*) and do not contain any vinegar. Those pickled in a vinegar-flavored marinade (*ogórki konserwowe*) are more familiar to U.S.-born Polonians, and are produced by both Polish- and American-based companies. Other marinated vegetables include spicy dill pickles, sliced cucumber salad, vegetable salad, *ćwikła*, pickled beets, spiced plums, spiced pears, spiced pumpkin and a variety of pickled mushrooms of various species. (See next entry.)

Polish imports—"If it's imported, it must be expensive" is not necessarily true where Polish food imports are concerned. Before generalizing, compare the prices of Polish food products imported from Poland and their non-Polish counterparts. During an informal price survey I conducted in metro Detroit in May 2002, I found one local Polish supermarket featuring excellent Krakus brand sauerkraut for $1.29 per 1-liter (nearly 34 oz) jar, compared to $1.79 for 1-qt (32 oz) jars of American-made Silver Floss. Many other Polish imports, including condiments (horseradish, *ćwikła*, mustard), marinated mushrooms and veggies, jams, compotes, syrups, juices, etc. are also quite reasonably priced. Be on the lookout for such brands as Krakus, Vavel, Cracovia, Babcia, Fructos, Łowicz, Paola, Runoland, Andros, and Orzeł. Juices in cartons are supplied by Hortex, Fortuna, Tymbark, Garden and Sokpol.

Pork seasoning—Process 1 heaping T marjoram, 2 heaped t peppercorns, 2 t caraway seeds, 1 t garlic powder and (optional) 1 t sage. Use to season all pork dishes, *bigos,* stew, goulash, meatballs, meatloaf and *gołąbki*. For variety, also use on other meats (beef, veal, lamb, game, turkey, chicken, duck, goose).

Potato starch—*Mąka kartoflana* is the most common thickener used in Polish cookery when a glossy, somewhat gelatinous consistency is desired. Feel free to use cornstarch wherever potato starch is called for.

Pounding—The pounding of meat with a special mallet is a widely used Polish technique that helps tenderize it and improve its texture. Worth recommending is the American method of pounding meat through a sheet of plastic wrap, as that prevents bits of meat from splattering your kitchen. When preparing pounded-meat dishes (pork, veal and chicken-breast cutlets, beef collops, roll-ups, etc.), first have the butcher run the meat slices through his tenderizer once. That will break down the meat structure and permit less pounding.

Processing—Anyone handy with their food processor knows that it can perform a variety of once time- and labor-consuming kitchen tasks. If you are among them, be sure to make use of your appliance whenever any of the recipes in this book calls for food to be chopped, crushed, grated, ground, milled, minced, pulverized or puréed. When dealing with small quantities, however, there is always the question whether the cleanup will take more time than manually performing the above tasks.

Roux—A roux *(zasmażka)* is a mixture of flour browned in hot fat used to thicken and improve the flavor and color of soups, gravies and sauces. Heat 3 T flour in dry skillet, stirring constantly until golden. Add 2 T butter (lard, fatback drippings, oil) and simmer briefly, stirring to blend ingredients. Remove from heat. Stir in 1 c room temp stock or water to dissolve, add 1 c hot stock, water or milk, heating and stirring until smooth. Stir into boiling soup.

Ryemeal-sour—See *żur.*

Seasoned pepper—Known in Polish as *pieprz ziołowy* (herb pepper), this may be regarded as a general, all-purpose Polish seasoning. Feel free to use it whenever ordinary black ground pepper is called for. Available at Polish delis, you can also make your own at home. Process together 2 heaped T peppercorns, 1 slightly heaped T caraway and 1 slightly heaped T marjoram. Stir in just enough ground paprika to give the mixture a nice brown color. Feel free to juggle the ingredients to achieve the flavor you like best. One of the commercially available Polish herb peppers contains coriander, mustard seed, caraway, Turkish pepper (cayenne), horseradish root and marjoram.

Sauerkraut, preparing—For most Polish dishes, sauerkraut (straight from the barrel, canned, bottled, in plastic bags, etc.) requires similar preparation. First, the sauerkraut should be drained and the liquid retained. The sauerkraut is then rinsed under cold running water in a colander or sieve or, (to remove more of the acidity) swished around in a pot of cold water and drained. In either case, excess moisture should be pressed out by hand. If shorter strands of sauerkraut are desired, it should be chopped. It is then placed in a pot, covered with cold water and cooked 45–60 min (part of the time uncovered to rid it of its strong odor). Then the sauerkraut is ready to be used in different dishes. (NOTE: The sauerkraut is only rinsed and drained, but not cooked, for sauerkraut salads.) Krakus and other brands of sauerkraut imported from Poland in 1-liter jars are highly recommended when preparing Polish dishes.

Sausage, Polish—The popularity of *kiełbasa* in North America has grown immensely in recent years, spreading to areas devoid of significant Polonian populations. Non-Polish Americans (and Canadians) tend to think of it as a smoked sausage, whereas North American–born Polonians often claim there are two kinds of Polish sausage: fresh and smoked. In reality, there are many different varieties and better Polonian meat markets and delis in areas with a sizable recent influx of Poles usually offer a nice variety to choose from. Polish sausage differs in terms of ingredients and preparation techniques and includes ground or chopped-meat varieties, all-pork, pork and beef or pork and veal. *Kiełbasa* flavored with marjoram is typical of western Poland. Turkey *kiełbasa* is growing in popularity as a leaner, healthier alternative on both sides of the Atlantic. A good all-around smoked kiełbasa is *Podwawelska*, which comes about the closest to being the typical Polish sausage. *Zwyczajna*, an inexpensive utility grade, is good in cooked dishes such as *bigos,* stews, soups, etc. There is smoked *swojska* (down-home) sausage that contains no salt-peter and is therefore not a nice pink in color, and *wiejska* (country-style) that contains saltpeter. There are sausages named after their dominant flavor accent including *jałowcowa* (juniper), *czosnkowa* (garlic), *kminkowa* (caraway), and their place of origin such as *krakowska* (Kraków sausage) and *śląska* (Silesian). *Myśliwska* (hunter's sausage) is a dry sausage that requires no refrigeration and can be taken on hunting and fishing trips. *Kabanosy,* thin dried sausages that need no refrigeration, are an excellent snack any time. Bobak's Sausage Co. of Chicago even produces a Polish-American *kiełbasa,* its Maxwell variety, that is the kind of sausage non–Polish Americans and depolonized Polish Americans think of whenever *kiełbasa* is mentioned. This is typical of *kiełbasa* produced by the big non–Polish American meat packers. It is usually less expensive than the Polonian-butcher-made variety and can be freely used in *bigos* and other cooked multi-ingredient dishes, where the less expensive *kiełbasa* can hardly be detected. Smaller Polish sausages known as grillers (Michigan's Kowalski Sausage Co. calls its version "stadium kiełbasa") are good for serving in buns at Polish-American fests and picnics.

Soup greens, soup vegetables—The standard portion of soup greens or vegetables needed to prepare the 6–8 c stock needed for most soup recipes in this book comprises roughly ½ lb or slightly more of mixed vegetables. Typically such a portion includes 1–2 carrots, 1 parsley root (or small parsnip), 1 leek, 1 slice of celeriac (or 1 stalk of celery) and 1 onion. A few recipes also include a slice of savoy cabbage. Typical seasonings accompanying the soup greens are peppercorns, allspice and bay leaves, which may be thrown into the pot loose or placed in a little cheesecloth bag tied with a string for easy removal.

Soups, instant—Most popular Polish soups are now available as instant powdered mixes, including *żurek, grzybowa, pomidorowa* and *krupnik*, and *flaki* (tripe) and others even come in "hot cup" form—just add boiling water and stir. Their use is recommended only if you already make a steady diet of American-style instants, since these are mainly "chemical" concoctions that have very little in common with the real thing.

Soups, heat and serve—Around the turn of the 21st century, Hortex came up with a very good *barszczyk* (beet and apple juice) in a 1-liter carton that can be simply heated and served as a clear beet broth. Krakus soon followed with its own version as well as other varieties including tomato soup and *żurek*. Cracovia and other companies produce Polish heat and serve soups in jars, including *biały barszcz*, pea soup, sorrel soup, beet soup, sauerkraut soup and tripe. The condensed canned soups (Campbell, Heinz, etc.) so popular in the English-speaking world have so far not gained wide acceptance in Poland. While soups in jars and cartons may be acceptable to many, they cannot compare with the homemade variety and would be rather expensive if served to large crowds.

Sour cream—Commercially available dairy sour cream is referred to whenever sour cream is mentioned in this book.

Sour milk—Homogenized milk (whole or 2%) may be home-soured (see *zsiadłe mleko*), but in recent years it has become commercially available and is sold at Polish delis in America's larger Polish-population centers (see kefir page 25).

Spice-cake seasoning—The main two ingredients of this seasoning used to flavor honey-spice cake *(piernik)* are cinnamon and cloves. Pepper is sometimes added along with other spices. Commercially available as *przyprawa korzenna do pierników*, it may also contain ginger, nutmeg, cardamom, coriander, allspice, anise and fennel. To prepare your own, process together equal parts of cinnamon bark, cloves and peppercorns adding a little of any of the other above-mentioned ingredients you like or happen to have on hand. It may also be prepared from ground spices.

In a pinch (no pun intended!), American pumpkin-pie seasoning or Chinese five-spice seasoning may be used.

Spices and seasonings—The most common spices and seasonings used in Polish cookery, aside from salt and pepper, are caraway (*kminek*), marjoram (*majeranek*), paprika (*papryka*), bay leaves (*listki laurowe/bobkowe*), mustard seed (*gorczyca*), allspice (*ziele angielskie*), herb pepper and other seasoning compositions (see also pork seasoning, hunter's seasoning, spice-cake seasoning). Such spices as cinnamon, nutmeg, ginger, cloves, cardamom, mace and various flavoring extracts (vanilla, rum, lemon, orange) are now used mainly in cakes and other desserts, although in Old Polish cookery they often flavored meats and savory sauces.

Stock cubes—See Bouillon cubes page 21.

Stock, meat—Rinse and (if possible) break into smaller pieces ½ lb or so beef, pork or veal bones or chicken backs or necks. Add 8 c water, bring to boil, skim off scum until no more forms, and cook on med heat 1 hr. Add 1 portion (about ½ lb) soup greens and 2 t–1 T salt and cook, covered, until vegetables are tender and meat comes away from bone. Strain and use as soup base. NOTE: Several peppercorns, a bay leaf and 1–2 grains allspice may be added with the vegetables. OPTIONAL: Intensify your stock's flavor with ½–1 t or so Vegeta-type flavor enhancer, 1 bouillon cube or equivalent amt of bouillon granules.

Stock, smoked-meat—Cook 1 lb smoked-meat bones (hambone, smoked hock or pork-ribs), ¼ lb slab bacon or 1 c mixed ham, bacon, sausage scraps, end slices, etc. in 8 c water 1½ hr. Add 2 onions (or a portion of soup greens, see page 30) and 1 bay leaf and cook at least another hr. The water in which fresh or smoked *kiełbasa* is boiled can also serve as a tasty stock.

Stock, vegetable—This is the basis for vegetarian soups and meatless sauces. With the addition of a little vinegar or white wine, it becomes a poaching stock for fish. Proceed as with meat stock (above), but omit the meat and/or meat bones. To keep it vegetarian, use only vegetable bouillon as a flavor-enhancer, if you insist on using it.

Tea—Known in Polish as *herbata* (from the Latin *herba Thea*), this is Poland's most popular hot beverage and is usually taken with sugar and/or lemon or plain, never the English way with milk. Black tea (known in the U.S. under such trade names as orange pekoe) is the hands-down choice of most Poles. In addition to Poland's Posti and other domestically packed brands, international brands (Tetley, Lipton, Brook Bond, etc.) are also widely used. There is no appreciable difference between most major brands of unflavored black teas, except that the lower-priced ones may contain more tea dust. Teas are often selected on the basis of their place of origin. Posti brand Madras is a good, inexpensive, all-purpose utility blend of Indian teas, while Assam (also from India) is of slightly better quality. Indyjska (Indian) is a mixture of different Indian teas, Cejlońska comes from Sri Lanka and is the favorite of many tea lovers. Yunan is a Chinese tea with slightly smoky undertones. Unfermented green tea is said to be extremely healthy but its taste takes getting used to. Earl Grey (nowadays usually flavored with imitation bergamot) and various herbal and fruit teas (many produced by Poland's Herbapol company) also have their devotees. Traditionally, the River Vistula (Wisła) has divided the tea-drinking eastern half of the country from the coffee-drinking western part. Today, media advertising and greater social mobility are gradually obliterating that difference.

Vanilla sugar—This is often a more convenient way to impart a vanilla aroma than liquid vanilla extract. The commercially available kind usually contains vanillin (imitation vanilla). You can also make your own cutting up 2 or 3 vanilla pods and mixing them into a ½ p jar filled with confectioners' sugar. After about 2 weeks, when the vanilla aroma permeates the sugar, it is ready to use.

Vodka and other spirits—The Poles and Russians have long argued over who was the first to distill this strong, clear spirit, but at the turn of the 21st century Poland's Belvedere and Chopin brands were generally regarded as the world's best vodkas. Other well-known but less expensive brands include Wyborowa, Polonaise, Sobieski and Luksusowa. Even more reasonably priced are Żytnia and Krakus. During the 1990s, a vodka called Siwucha (literally "the old gray one"), in a stylized, old-fashioned-looking bottle, became popular. Flavored vodkas include Starka (a strong vodka aged in oak barrels to produce a brandy-like tipple), Myśliwska (juniper vodka, a kind of Polish gin), Jarzębiak (a brandy-colored spirit flavored with mountain-ash berries), and Żubrówka (bison-grass vodka) with a strand of bison grass in every bottle. Fruit-flavored spirits include Wiśniak (dry cherry cordial), Wiśniówka (sweet cherry cordial) and Nalewka Babuni (Granny's Cordial), a mild, low-alchol-content fruit cordial in a distinctive bottle. Others include Orzechówka (walnut cordial), Malinówka (raspberry cordial), Jerzynówka (blackberry cordial), Tarniówka (sloeberry cordial) and Cassis (blackcurrant cordial marketed under its French name). Winiak, which comes in numerous varieties, is the Polish version of cognac-like brandy aged in oak wine casks.

Wine—At elegant banquets or dinner parties, follow the international practice of serving dry white wine with fish and white meat, and red wine with dark meat. Burgundy, a heavy red wine, is recommended with game dishes. When wine is served as an apéritif, both white and red varieties should be provided for guests to choose from. Sweet wines are generally served after meals. Champagne or other dry sparkling wine can be served at any time but are largely associated with festive occasions and are the preferred choice for toasts at weddings, on New Year's Eve, etc. *Miód pitny* (literally "drinkable honey"), known in English as mead, is an old Polish honey wine still produced today. It can help add an authentically Polish touch to festive gatherings and is sure to win raves because it is simply delicious. The basic varieties of mead are *półtorak* (intensive honey flavor), *dwójniak* (less intense honey flavor) and *trójniak* (faint honey flavor). In addition to *miód pitny*, you can give your event an Old Polish flavor by serving *węgrzyn* (Hungarian-style Tokay), another Sarmatian drink of choice. Poland also produces fruit-flavored wines that are acceptable but not outstanding.

Żur—To prepare your own ryemeal sour *(żur)*, in earthenware crock or glass jar place 1 c rye flour (regular [light rye] or *razowa* [whole-grain, dark rye]), whole-wheat flour or rolled oats or a combination thereof. With wooden spoon gradually stir in 4 c preboiled lukewarm water until smooth and lump-free. Add 1–2 sliced cloves garlic. Cover mouth of container with cheesecloth or a dishtowel and let stand in a warm (75°–80°F) place 3–4 days, or until liquid becomes pleasantly sour. When the desired stage of tartness has been reached, stir up flour sediment at bottom and strain through colander into another container, then pour through funnel into bottles or jars. Seal and refrigerate until needed. (NOTE: A slice of good rye bread will speed up the fermentation process. The bread and any mold that forms on or around it should be discarded before *żur* is strained.) For most kinds of *żur* or *biały barszcz*, the rough proportion is about 1 c ryemeal sour to 5–6 c stock. Shake bottle when adding a portion of *żur* to soup so some of the flour sediment gets included. VARIATION: For a more aromatic ryemeal sour, add 1 bay leaf, 3–4 peppercorns and 1–2 grains allspice to jar. Ready-to-use *żur* is also available, but I strongly favor the bottled liquid type to the paste or gel that comes in jars. NOTE: *Żur* or *żurek* comes close to being a kind of Polish cult soup. Once a common breakfast soup, a meatless version of *żur* was a traditional Lenten staple. The sausage-based variety is a typical Easter soup, and tart-tasting, thirst-quenching *żurek* has also been the traditional eye-opener (and hangover medicine!), served at the crack of dawn "after the ball is over."

Żur powder—This in effect is a way of preparing your own instant ryemeal soup. Crumble up 2 or 3 slices of rye bread and set out to dry. Measure the amount with a measuring cup and add an equal amt of uncooked rolled oats. Mill the dry bread and oats to a powder in food processor or blender. Use about 1 T of żur powder for 1 c stock to make easy ryemeal soup. Simply bring to boil and simmer several min.

Recipes

Since the food of Christmas and Easter (plus the intervening Carnival and Lenten season) loom large in Poland's culinary heritage, the recipes associated with those periods form the basic framework of this section. Other foods, suitable for banquets, home entertaining, festivals, picnics and other special occasions, follow. But the fact that a recipe is presented under the Christmas, Carnival, Lent or Easter heading does not necessarily mean it is restricted to that period. In fact, with only a very few exceptions, all the dishes presented in this section are regularly prepared and enjoyed at different times. Only seasonality influences the choice of menus. Although produce of every kind is now available in Poland year-round, experienced cooks prefer vine-ripened, in-season, locally produced fruits and vegetables, which are of superior taste and nutrition. They are also more economical than the imported green-picked varieties that are artificially ripened, coated, transported and cold-stored for months before they reach the supermarket. NOTE: With the exception of the Polish fest/picnic/community supper foods section, the name of a dish is given first in English in bold upper case, followed by its Polish equivalent, italicized and in brackets.

THE FOOD OF POLISH ADVENT

Unlike Lent, the nearly four-week period preceding Christmas is more preparatory than penitential. Nevertheless, it has traditionally been a time of fasting and doing without. On the Polish-American scene, Advent is not observed as prominently as Lent, so perhaps that is reason enough to look into the potential this season has to offer. Things to consider might include *pierogi* and/or herring and potato suppers, Polish fish fries, Advent specials in restaurants and delis and Advent food and bake sales. The actual foods would include any of the Lenten dishes or *Wigilia* foods. Suggestions for the intervening St. Barbara's Day (December 4) and St. Nicholas's Day (December 6) are provided below.

ST. BARBARA'S DAY SPECIALITIES

St. Barbara's Day festivities are mainly celebrated in Silesia (Śląsk), hence the regional specialities of that area would be most appropriate on that occasion. For Silesian and other dishes suitable for St. Barbara's Day see Family/Country-Style/Regional Favorites, page 131.

ST. NICHOLAS DAY TREATS

HONEY-SPICE HEARTS *(serduszka piernikowe)*: Heat, but do not boil, 1 c honey mixed with 2 T lard and set aside to cool. Mix 1½ c flour with 1 T baking powder and 1 t baking soda. Combine flour and honey mixtures and add 2 t cinnamon, 1 t ginger, ½ t ground cloves, ¼ t pepper, 4 T milk, juice and grated rind of ½ lemon and 2 pinches salt. Work ingredients well into a uniform dough, cover and refrigerate overnight. Next day, roll dough out just under ¼" thick on lightly floured board. Cut with heart-shaped cookie-cutter. Bake on baking sheet in preheated 350°oven 15–20 min. When honey-spice hearts are cool, they may be decorated with lines or swirls of white or chocolate icing or their entire tops and sides may be iced. NOTE: Polish honey-spice hearts of various kinds are now widely available in the U.S. at Polish markets and delis. So are *katarzynki*, chocolate-covered, non-heart-shaped *pierniczki*—just the thing for *Święty Mikołaj* to pass out to well-behaved youngsters on his feastday.

THE DISHES OF POLISH WIGILIA

When Poles think of Christmas Eve supper, they think of fish. That is because fish dishes reign supreme at the Wigilia supper. At the sumptuous feasts of yesteryear, the tables of the *szlachta* (nobility) would traditionally feature twelve different fish dishes, not to mention all the other delicacies. Nowadays, few Polish Americans could afford such extravagance. We are therefore presenting a wide variety of fish and other Christmas Eve dishes both as culinary mementos and to give our readers a good selection to choose from. Many have been simplified and adapted to today's convenience-minded times, but we're starting with the traditional way of preparing herring from scratch.

CHRISTMAS EVE HERRING

PREPARING SALT HERRING *(przygotowanie solonych śledzi)*: Soak 4–6 salt herring in a sinkful or large pan of cold water 24 hr, changing water 2–3 times. If they have heads attached, cut them off and discard them before soaking herring. Carefully remove the skin and backbones from the herring and discard any loose fishbones you see. Slice the herring into 1 or 1½″ pieces. Now you may proceed with any of the traditional recipes below.

PICKLED or MARINATED HERRING *(śledzie marynowane)*: Cut the herring into 1–1½″ pieces and layer with wafer-thin small onion slices in a jar or crockery bowl. In pot combine 1 c 6% distilled vinegar and 1 c water (for zippier herring use 1⅔ c vinegar and ⅔ c water), 1 bay leaf, 6 peppercorns, 2 grains allspice, 1 t mustard seed and 1 heaping t to 1 heaping T sugar. Bring to boil and simmer, covered, on low heat 10 min. Switch off heat and let stand until cooled to room temp, then pour over herring. Seal jar or cover crockery bowl and refrigerate at least 24 hr before serving.

HERRING PICKLED WITH MUSHROOMS *(śledzie z marynowanymi grzybami)*: Cut herring into 1–1½″ pieces, place in jar and cover with pickled mushrooms and their liquid. Seal, turn jar upside down several times to distribute marinade and refrigerate at least 24 hr before serving. To serve, place herring pieces on serving plate, top each piece with a little freshly chopped onion and decorate plate with the pickled mushrooms.

HERRING IN OIL *(śledzie w oleju)*: Into a jar pour a little salad oil, add a layer of herring, then a thin layer of chopped onion, and keep layering until jar is full. Top layer should be chopped onion. Top up with oil, seal and refrigerate. Let stand in fridge at least 24 hr before serving. It will keep in the fridge a week or longer.

CREAMED HERRING *(śledzie w śmietanie)*: Arrange pieces of herring on serving dish. Drizzle with juice of 1 small lemon (through a sieve to catch the pits). Slice 2 small onions wafer thin and place on the herring. Fork-blend ½ to 1 c sour cream, 1 t confectioners' sugar and 1 T mustard. Pour over herring. Cover with plastic wrap and refrigerate overnight. When ready to serve, dust with a little paprika to add a bit of color.

HERRING IN HORSERADISH SAUCE *(śledzie w sosie chrzanowym)*: Arrange herring on serving dish. Fork-blend ⅓ c sour cream, ⅓ c mayonnaise, 1 heaping T prepared noncreamed horseradish (m/l to taste), juice of ½ a lemon and 2 t confectioners' sugar. Pour over herring. Chill at least 1 hr before serving. Cover with plastic wrap if you plan to refrigerate it overnight.

HERRING WITH APPLE AND PICKLE *(śledzie z jabłkiem i ogórkiem)*: In bowl combine 1 finely chopped onion, 2 dill pickles, coarsely grated, and 1–2 small or 1 large apple, peeled and coarsely grated or finely diced. Stir in enough horseradish sauce (above) to bind ingredients together (2–3 heaping T). Top each 1½″ piece of herring with a spoonful of the mixture.

HERRING ROLLS WITH MUSTARD *(ruloniki śledziowe z musztardą)*: Depending on their size, cut 4 soaked and dried herring fillets into 2 or 3 pieces each. Spread each piece with a little prepared brown mustard, roll up tightly and skewer with toothpick. Place in jar or crockery bowl and drench with oil. Seal or cover tightly and refrigerate at least 24 hr before serving.

ROLLMOPS *(rolmopsy)*: Cut 4 herring fillets into 2 or 3 pieces each. At one end of each piece place a slice of dill pickle, a small pickled mushroom and/or a piece of onion and roll up tight. Skewer each roll-up with 2 toothpicks, place in jar or crockery bowl and drench with room-temp marinade (as for pickled herring or marinated fried fish—see pages 37 and 44). Seal or cover and refrigerate at least 24 hr before serving.

HERRING SALAD *(sałatka śledziowa)*: In salad bowl combine 2–3 diced herring, 2 chopped dill pickles, 2 chopped onions or 1 bunch chopped scallions, 2 apples, peeled, cored and diced, 2 c home-cooked or drained canned navy beans or pea-beans, 2 c diced cooked potatoes, 1 green bell pepper plus 1 red bell pepper, chopped. For a gourmet touch add 1 heaping T capers. Toss gently. Lace with sauce made by combining 1 part mayonnaise and 1 part sour cream. Season to taste with salt, pepper, a little lemon juice and a couple of pinches of sugar. Dieters may prepare sauce from low-fat or no-fat yogurt and part light mayonnaise. NOTE: Feel free to alter the amount of individual salad ingredients according to personal preference and availability.

CHRISTMAS EVE SALAD *(sałatka wigilijna)*: Proceed as in preceding recipe but omit bell peppers and add 3–4 chopped hard-cooked eggs, ½–¾ c drained pickled mushrooms, diced, and 3–4 canned pickled beets, diced, and 1 T chopped fresh parsley. Toss gently and stir in enough mayonnaise–sour cream dressing (see preceding recipe)—with a heaping T mustard added—to bind ingredients together. NOTE: If you are serving herring separately, both of the above salads can be made without adding diced herring.

HERRING, EASY *(łatwe śledzie)*: If the prospect of buying, soaking, cleaning and marinating salt herring from scratch seems overwhelming, you can still enjoy this Christmas Eve treat at a fraction of the effort. Simply buy a jar of marinated herring and proceed as follows:

Marinated or Pickled Herring: If you like pickled herring in tangy vinegar marinade just as they are, simply drain a jar of marinated herring, discarding onions and spices, arrange herring on serving dish and top with fresh small onions, sliced wafer-thin. You can also keep the fresh sliced onion in the marinade together with the herring overnight before serving. If you find the herring too vinegary, they can be plunged into cold water briefly before serving.

Herring Garnished in Other Ways: To prepare herring in oil, creamed herring, herring in horseradish sauce, herring salad, etc. the easy way, drain a jar of marinated herring, discarding onion and spices. Cut herring into serving-size pieces, usually 1–1½" in length. Plunge into a large pot of cold water and keep them in it several min. Drain in sieve or colander and allow to drip dry. Proceed as with soaked and trimmed salt herring (above).

SAVORY WIGILIA SOUPS AND ACCOMPANIMENTS

CLEAR BEET SOUP *(czysty barszcz czerwony)*: Rehydrate 2–3 dried bolete mushrooms, cook in same water until tender and set aside. Peel and coarsely grate 1 lb beets and combine with 4 c vegetable stock or fish stock. Add the mushroom liquid (reserve mushrooms for some sauerkraut dish or *uszka*), 1 large, peeled, coarsely grated apple and 1–2 c liquid beet-sour. Bring to boil and simmer 2 min. Add 1 clove crushed garlic and (optional) ¼ c dry red wine. Strain, discarding contents of sieve. Season soup to taste with salt, pepper, lemon juice and a little sugar until you achieve just the right tangy taste you want. Serve in bowls with traditional *uszka* (ear-dumplings, below). You can also serve the clear soup in twin-handled bouillon cups (sometimes known in Polish as *barszczówki*) or, if unavailable, large teacups with a handheld pasty on the side (see page 193).

LITTLE-EAR DUMPLINGS *(uszka)*: Rehydrate and cook 2 oz dried bolete mushrooms. Soak 1 slice French bread in ½ c warm water. Chop and sauté 1 coarsely chopped onion in 2 T butter until tender and lightly browned. Pass mushrooms, onion and squeezed-out pre-soaked bread through food chopper and process briefly. Add ¼ c bread crumbs, stir in 1 egg white, salt and pepper to taste and mix well. Filling should be on the stiff side, so if it's mushy, stir in a little more bread crumbs and set aside. Sift 1 c flour onto breadboard, work in egg yolk and just enough water (roughly ½ c) to bind ingredients into a dough. Knead until smooth, roll out very thin and cut into 1½″ squares. Place a little filling on each square, fold 2 opposite points together to form a triangle and pinch shut. Gently pull 2 ends of the triangle together into a ring and pinch them together. Cook in lightly salted boiling water without crowding until *uszka* float up. Remove with slotted spoon and serve in clear beet soup (see above).

CLEAR BEET SOUP, EASY *(czysty czerwony barszcz najłatwiejszy)*: To 3 c meatless vegetable stock add 3 c beet juice (from canned beets) and ½ mushroom bouillon cube (e.g., Winiary or Knorr brand) dissolved in 1 c boiling water. (VARIATION: Mushroom flavor can also be imparted using mushroom powder or liquid mushroom extract.) Season with pepper, a dash of garlic powder, a pinch of marjoram, 1 T dry red wine and a little sugar and lemon juice to get a balanced tangy, sweet, tart flavor. Serve with freshly baked handheld mushroom pasties on the side (see below).

MUSHROOM/CABBAGE-FILLED PASTIES *(paszteciki z kapustą i grzybami)*: Place 1 c shredded cabbage in small pot, scald with boiling water and cook until tender. Drain in colander. In skillet brown 8 oz diced fresh mushrooms with 2 chopped onions in 3 T oil until fully cooked and nicely browned. Chop mushrooms, onion and cooked cabbage in food processor. Place mixture in sieve and force out excess moisture. If still too mushy, stir in 1 T or so bread crumbs. Salt and pepper to taste. Open pkg of refrigerator crescent-roll dough. Obliterate manufacturer's perforations by pressing down on them with floured thumb. Cut into 2″ or larger squares, spread each with a little mushroom filling and roll up jelly roll fashion, pinching ends shut and tucking underneath. Bake according to package directions and serve hot with clear beet soup (see above).

SAVORY EGG or SAUERKRAUT PIE *(kulebiak)*: This is also an excellent accompaniment for clear beet soup. Open a pkg of refrigerator crescent-roll dough. Place dough sheet on floured board and with floured thumb press down to obliterate manufacturer's perforations. Run filling down center of dough sheet and fold parallel sides over it to overlap. Pinch seam to seal. Also pinch together any other openings that appear in dough where perforations had been. Place seam-side down on baking sheet, tuck ends under, brush with beaten egg and bake according to pkg directions or to a nice golden brown. Let cool at least 30 min at room temp before slicing and serving. For the filling, combine 1½ c cooked rice, 5 chopped hard-cooked eggs, and 2 chopped onions sautéed in 2 T butter or oil until lightly browned. Combine ingredients with 1 beaten uncooked egg (or liquid egg substitute like Egg Beaters), 1–2 heaping T chopped fresh or frozen dill and salt and pepper to taste. NOTE: A sauerkraut and mushroom filling (with all moisture squeezed out) may be used in place of the rice and egg filling (see page 49).

CLEAR MUSHROOM SOUP *(zupa grzybowa czysta)*: If you have cooked bolete mushrooms for ear-dumplings (see page 40), an easy way to prepare this soup is simply to combine the leftover mushroom liquid with 5 c vegetable stock. Season with a little salt and pepper and (optional) a few drops of Kitchen Bouquet to deepen the color and serve over cooked egg noodles or cooked lasagna noodles, cut into 1″ squares. If you have no leftover mushroom stock, rehydrate and cook 1 oz dried boletes. When tender, slice into strips or dice and add, together with the mushroom stock, to 5 c vegetable stock. Season with salt and pepper. OPTIONAL: Garnish with a little freshly chopped parsley.

CLEAR MUSHROOM SOUP, EASY *(czysta zupa grzybowa najłatwiejsza)*: Dissolve 2 mushroom cubes in 3 c boiling water, add to 3 c vegetable stock and bring to boil. Darken with ⅛ t Kitchen Bouquet and season to taste with a little pepper and lemon juice. Serve over noodles. Garnish with chopped parsley if desired.

MUSHROOM-BARLEY SOUP *(zupa grzybowa z kaszą perłową)*: Soak ½ c pearl barley in 2 c cold water 2 hr, then add 2 T butter and cook in same water until tender. Rehydrate and cook 1 oz dried mushrooms (preferably boletes), slice thin or chop. Add barley, 3 med potatoes, peeled and diced, and the mushrooms and their stock to 6–7 c vegetable stock and simmer until potatoes are done. Make a roux from 2 T flour and 2 T butter or margarine and fry until golden. Dilute with a little water to form a smooth paste and stir into soup. Simmer 3–4 min. Season with salt, pepper and about 1 t lemon juice and garnish with a little chopped fresh parsley.

MUSHROOM-RYEMEAL SOUP *(żurek wigilijny)*: Rehydrate and cook 3–4 dried mushrooms. Slice cooked mushrooms into strips or dice and add together with mushroom stock to 3 c vegetable stock. (OPTIONAL: Cook

2–3 diced potatoes in soup.) Add 2 c liquid rye-sour (*żur*), bring to boil, and remove from heat. Fork-blend ½–¾ c sour cream with 1 T flour until smooth and stir 1 c hot soup into mixture, 1 T at a time so sour cream doesn't curdle. Slowly stir sour-cream mixture into soup and slowly bring to gentle boil, stirring constantly. Season with salt, pepper and several pinches marjoram.

RYEMEAL-MUSHROOM SOUP, EASY (*żurek wigilijny najłatwiejszy*): Whisk 2–3 heaping T *żur* powder with 5 c strained vegetable stock and 1 c milk until smooth. Bring to boil, reduce heat and simmer several min. Add 1 mushroom cube or 1 t mushroom extract and season to taste with salt, pepper, several pinches citric acid and a sprinkling of marjoram.

POTATO-MUSHROOM SOUP (*kartoflanka z grzybami)*: Cook 4–5 diced potatoes in 5 c vegetable stock together with 3–4 rehydrated, cooked, dried mushrooms, sliced or diced, and the mushroom stock until done but still firm. In 2 T butter, margarine or oil sauté 2 med chopped onions until tender and slightly browned. Add onions and 1 c ryemeal-sour to pot and bring to boil. Remove from heat. Fork-blend ½ c sour cream with 1 T flour until smooth and stir 1 c hot soup into mixture, 1 T at a time so sour cream doesn't curdle. Pour sour-cream–flour mixture into soup in a slow stream and slowly bring to gentle boil, stirring constantly. Salt and pepper to taste. Garnish with fresh or frozen chopped dill.

POTATO-MUSHROOM SOUP, EASY (*kartoflanka z grzybami najłatwiejsza)*: Prepare 4 c canned cream of potato soup according to directions on label. Add 2 med chopped onions, lightly browned in 2 T butter, margarine or oil, 1 mushroom bouillon cube dissolved in 2 c boiling water and bring to boil. Season with a little freshly ground pepper and several pinches citric acid. Garnish with chopped parsley and/or dill.

YELLOW PEA SOUP, FAST-DAY (*grochówka postna)*: Rinse well and drain 1½–2 c split yellow peas. In pot combine the peas, 2 rehydrated dried mushrooms, diced, and 6 c vegetable stock. (Dice the vegetables used to make the stock and set aside.) Add 1 bay leaf and 6 peppercorns and cook, covered, on low heat about 2 hr, stirring occasionally. (OPTIONAL: After about 90 min, several diced potatoes may be added and cooked in soup until tender.) When peas have all but disintegrated, in saucepan sauté 1 large chopped onion in 2 T butter or oil until soft and slightly browned. Stir in 2 T flour and brown, stirring constantly and gradually adding 1 c soup. Add roux to soup together with diced cooked vegetables and 2 cloves crushed garlic. Simmer briefly. Switch off heat, season with salt, pepper and at least 1 t marjoram and let stand, covered, about 15 min for flavors to blend.

BEAN SOUP, FAST-DAY *(zupa fasolowa postna)*: Overnight soak 1 to 1½ c dried beans (navy, Great Northern, lima or pea-beans) in plenty of room-temp preboiled water. Next day, drain beans and cook in 6 c vegetable stock until tender. (Cooking time depends on the dryness and variety of beans—probably no less than 1 hr, but possibly 2 hr or more.) (OPTIONAL: Toward end of cooking add ½ c diced pitted prunes.) Thicken with roux made from 3 T butter and 2 T flour and simmer briefly. Add 1 crushed clove garlic, 1 t marjoram and salt and pepper to taste. Garnish with chopped parsley. Provide a cruet of vinegar for guests who like their bean soup on the zippy side. This soup is often served with homemade noodles known in English as "egg barley" (below).

EGG BARLEY *(zacierka)*: Sift 1 c flour onto board. Sprinkle with ¼ t salt, mix in 1 small egg and work into a stiff dough. Roll into a ball, grate coarsely and cook several min in rapidly boiling water. Drain and serve with bean or pea soup. The egg barley can also be cooked in the soup, which will thicken it somewhat. VARIATION: Use rye flour for a darker-colored peasant-style egg barley.

SAUERKRAUT SOUP, FAST-DAY *(kapuśniak postny)*: Drain 1 pt sauerkraut, reserving juice. Plunge sauerkraut into pot of cold water and swish around briefly. Drain in colander, press out moisture, chop coarsely and cook in 5–6 c vegetable stock with 2–3 rehydrated bolete mushrooms at least 1 hr, or until sauerkraut loses its crunch. (VARIATION: Instead of mushrooms, a mushroom bouillon cube can be used.) Sauté 1 chopped onion in 3 T butter, margarine or oil until tender and lightly browned. Stir in 2 T flour and brown, stirring constantly. Gradually dilute with 1 c soup liquid, stirring constantly and add to pot. Simmer briefly. Season with salt and pepper and (optional) several pinches caraway seeds. If not as tart as you like, sour to taste with a little reserved sauerkraut juice. NOTE: This soup can also be made with shredded fresh cabbage, soured to taste with vinegar or (better yet) several pinches of citric-acid crystals.

FISH CHOWDER *(zupa rybna)*: This chowder can be made with roughly ½–1 lb small panfish (perch, bluegills, chubs, crappies, bullheads) or using 1 or 2 heads and trimmings (backbone, fins, tail) or a large fish (carp, pike, walleye, whitefish, etc.). Remove and discard eyes and gills. Rinse well and place in pot, add 6–8 c water and 1 t salt and cook 1 hr; drain. If using panfish, force them through a sieve into stock. If using large fish, discard fins, remove all meat from backbones and heads and return to stock. To stock add 2 sliced carrots, ½ small celeriac (or 1 stalk celery) diced, 1 small sliced parsley root,

2 quartered onions, 2 peeled diced potatoes, 1 bay leaf, 6 peppercorns and 2 grains allspice and cook until vegetables are tender. Remove soup from heat. Fork-blend ¾ c sour cream with 2 T flour and 1 T vinegar and gradually stir into soup. Simmer several min longer. Salt and pepper to taste and add 2–3 gratings nutmeg. Garnish with a heaping T finely chopped fresh or frozen dill.

HEMPSEED SOUP, SILESIAN *(siemieniotka, siemianka)*: Rinse 1½ c hempseeds in cold water and drain. Scald with boiling water, bring to boil and drain again. In pot combine hempseeds with 5 c warm water, bring to gentle boil, reduce heat and simmer until seeds begin to burst. Drain, reserving liquid. Transfer hempseeds to sieve and with wooden spoon squeeze out their contents (hempseed milk). Scald seeds in sieve with a little boiling water and continue squeezing out their milk. Transfer partially crushed seeds from sieve to another bowl add a little boiling water, mix well, drain and squeeze them some more. When no more juice can be extracted, discard seed husks left in sieve. Combine hempseed milk (squeezings) with 3 c milk and the reserved stock (in which the hempseeds were cooked). Thicken with 3 T flour dissolved in a little water, add 2 t salt, and 1–2 T sugar. Mix, bring to boil and simmer several min, stirring so it doesn't burn. Remove from heat, add 1 T butter and serve. This is a traditional Christmas Eve soup in Silesia (Śląsk).

COLD FISH DISHES

MARINATED FRIED FISH *(smażona ryba w zalewie octowej)*: If you like pickled herring, you'll love this recipe. It tastes pretty much the same, except that it can be prepared with any fish you happen to have on hand, including those perch you caught while ice-fishing on a nearby lake. Start with about 1½ lb fresh or thawed, freshwater or ocean fillets. (Perch, pike, walleye, fresh [unsalted] herring, panfish, chubs, eel, bullheads, cod and haddock are especially good.) Cut fish into 1½″ pieces, sprinkle with salt and pepper and fry to a nice golden brown on both sides in hot oil about ¼″ deep. (Small fish: smelt, minnows, undersized panfish no more than 3″ in length may be fried whole.) Drain on absorbent paper. Separately, in pot combine 1½ c 6% distilled vinegar, 1½ c water, 3 small thinly sliced onions, 1 thinly sliced carrot, 1 t salt, 1 t to1 T sugar (depending on whether a tart or a more sweet and sour marinade is desired), 6 peppercorns, 3 grains allspice and 1 bay leaf. Bring to boil, reduce heat and let simmer, covered, 2–3 min. Remove from heat and let stand, covered, until cooled to room temp. Place fried fish in crockery bowl or large jar and drench with marinade and onions. Refrigerate at least 24 hr before serving. Serve as you would marinated herring or use it in salads in place of herring. NOTE: Rather than making your own marinade from scratch, you can also use the marinade left over from a jar of store-bought marinated herring, strained, fortified with a little fresh vinegar, brought to boil and cooled.

SMOKED-FISH SALAD *(sałatka z wędzonej ryby)*: Remove skin and bones from roughly 1 lb smoked fish (carp, whitefish, trout, cod, halibut, etc.) and break up into flakes. Place in salad bowl, add 1 finely grated raw carrot, 1 peeled, coarsely grated apple and 1 bunch scallions chopped fine. Sprinkle with juice of 1 small lemon, toss gently to blend ingredients and lace with sauce prepared as follows. Fork-blend ¾ c mayonnaise, ¼ c sour cream, 1 T prepared horseradish, ⅛ t pepper and ½–1 t sugar. Toss, place in lettuce-lined serving dish and garnish with hard-cooked egg slices. Dust with paprika.

FISH IN ASPIC *(ryba w galarecie)*: Soak 2 packets gelatin in 1 c cold water. In 5 c vegetable stock cook 1–2 large fish heads (carp, pike, walleye, whitefish with eyes and gills removed), backbones, tails and fins. Cook about 1 hr, skimming off scum. Drain. (Meat from fish heads and backbone may be used in fish salad above.) In strained fish stock cook 1½ lb fish fillets 5–8 min) or ¾″ fish steaks (10–15 min). They take only a short time to cook and are ready when flesh flakes easily. Remove fish with slotted spoon to deep serving dish. Decorate with sliced carrots (from vegetable stock), lemon slices and parsley sprigs. (OPTIONAL: Sliced hard-cooked eggs, dill-pickle slices, a sprinkling of capers and 2 heaping T drained canned peas also make nice decorations.) Add softened gelatin mixture to hot stock, heating and stirring until dissolved. Add 2 T vinegar to stock and heat. (OPTIONAL: 1 T fresh or frozen chopped dill may be added to stock at this point.) When stock has cooled somewhat, pour over fish. Refrigerate until set and serve with horseradish sauce (see page 46).

FISH IN (SWEET AND TANGY) ASPIC À LA JUIVE *(ryba w galarecie po żydowsku)*: Carp is by far the best choice for this dish. Proceed as above, but do not decorate fish with hard-cooked eggs or peas. After gelatin has dissolved, add ½ c plumped raisins, juice of 1 small lemon, 2–3 T sugar, ¼ t grated lemon zest and a pinch each of ground cloves, cinnamon and ginger. Arrange cooked fish on platter, intersperse with raisins, decorate with carrot slices and drench with stock after it has cooled somewhat. The dish should be deep enough so no part of the fish protrudes above the aspic. Refrigerate until set and serve with horseradish sauce (next recipe). This dish has long been a favorite of many Polish families.

HORSERADISH SAUCE *(sos chrzanowy)*: Fork-blend ⅓ c sour cream, ⅓ c mayonnaise, ⅓ c prepared horseradish, juice of ½ lemon, ⅛ t ground white pepper and 1 t sugar or to taste.

FISH À LA GRECQUE *(ryba po grecku)*: Cut 1½ lb fillets (cod, pike, etc.) at an angle into 2″ pieces, rinse, pat dry and fry in a little oil to a nice golden brown on both sides. Arrange portions on serving platter. Separately, peel, wash, trim and slice into "matchsticks" 2 carrots, a ½″ slice celeriac (or 1 stalk celery), 1 parsley root (or small parsnip) and 3 onions. Brown lightly in several T oil, stirring constantly, stir in 3 T water and simmer on low until fully cooked. Stir in 3–4 T tomato paste and season to taste with salt, pepper, sugar, vinegar. Several dashes paprika and 1–2 t mustard may be added. The sauce should have a nice, sweet, sour and tangy taste. Decorate fish platter with parsley or lettuce and pour cold sauce over fish. Refrigerate at least 24 hr before serving. Despite its name (Greek-style) and presumed foreign origin, this dish has long been a naturalized citizen on the Polish Wigilia table, and it is very good indeed. In some families it is served hot.

FISH ENTRÉES

FRIED CARP *(karp smażony)*: Slice cleaned 2–3 lb carp into 1–1½″ steaks. Intersperse with onion slices, sprinkle with salt, pepper and lemon juice and refrigerate overnight or at least 2 hr. Just before frying, pat fish dry with paper towel. Dip fish in beaten egg, dredge in 50/50 flour–bread crumb mixture, shaking off excess, and fry in hot oil ½″ deep to a nice golden brown on both sides. (NOTE: The egg may be omitted and the moist fish can be rolled directly in flour-crumb mixture.) Drain on paper towels and serve immediately with horseradish sauce. NOTE: Most any available species may be substituted in this and other fish recipes.

PIKE IN HORSERADISH SAUCE *(szczupak duszony z chrzanem)*: Slice cleaned 2–3 lb northern pike into 1½″ steaks, sprinkle with salt and lemon juice and refrigerate overnight or at least 2 hours. Place fish in heavy skillet, drench with 4 c vegetable stock to cover, add 2 T vinegar and cook, covered, until fish is done and flakes readily. Gently transfer fish to platter and keep in warm oven. In saucepan lightly brown 2 heaping T flour in 2 heaping T butter, gradually add 1 c or more stock, stirring until smooth. Stir in ¼–½ c prepared horseradish and ½–¾ c sour cream. Simmer, stirring constantly until thick and bubbly. If too thick, dilute with a little more stock. Season to taste with salt, pepper, lemon juice and sugar. Drench pike with sauce and serve at once.

POACHED FISH *(ryba z wody)*: In 4 c vegetable stock containing 1 T vinegar and (optional) ¼ c dry white wine, cook 2½ lb portion-sized fish (allowing 1 fish per person) until done, 15–20 min. Perch or rainbow trout with heads and tails intact are very nice. The stock should cover the fish during poaching. Carefully remove cooked fish with slotted spoon to platter. Pour off water that collects on platter. Decorate with parsley and serve with melted butter and lemon. Some connoisseurs contend that this is the only way to savor the delicate flavor of good, fresh fish. Poached fish is also highly digestible and recommended for those on restricted diets. NOTE: If poaching fillets, reduce cooking time.

PERCH POLONAISE *(okoń po polsku)*: For the recipe, see Polish Holiday Banquet/Dinner-Party Favorites, page 77.

CREAMED PERCH *(okoń w śmietanie)*: Rinse well, pat dry, salt and dredge in flour 2¼ lb lake perch fillets and brown on both sides in 3 T butter, margarine or oil. Transfer to small Dutch oven, drench with 1 c vegetable stock (homemade or bouillon-cube type), cover and cook on low heat about 15 min. Fork-blend 1 c sour cream with 1 level T flour and pour over fish. Simmer until hot and bubbly. Turn out onto platter and garnish with fresh or frozen chopped dill and/or parsley. Any panfish may be used in this dish, but fillets are highly recommended because bone-in fish drenched in sour-cream sauce would be very messy and hard to eat. (NOTE: The original name of this recipe was *karasie w śmietanie*, but as far as I know the crucian [*Carassius carassius*—a golden brown Old World panfish of the minnow family] is not available in America, hence the substitution.)

BAKED FISH *(ryba pieczona)*: Wash well and dry a whole 2–2½ lb fish (pike, carp or cod is best) with head and tail left on but eyes removed. Sprinkle fish inside and out with salt and a little (1–2 t) vinegar and place fish in well-greased baking dish large enough to accommodate it. Baste top of fish with about 3 T melted butter and pop into preheated 400° oven. After 10 min reduce heat to 325°, baste with 2 T melted butter, sprinkle with water and baste occasionally with pan drippings. If you don't like to baste, fish may be covered with aluminium foil. Bake about 30 min or until done. OPTIONAL: Fork-blend ½ c sour cream with ⅛ t salt, 1 t sugar and 1 heaping t prepared horseradish and pour over hot fish. Bake another 10 min. Insert a cranberry into the visible eye socket and serve.

BAKED STUFFED FISH *(ryba pieczona faszerowana)*: Wash well and dry a whole 2–2½ lb fish (pike, walleye, whitefish, cod, etc.) with head and tail left on but eyes removed. Sprinkle with salt, place lemon slices in cavity and on both sides, cover and set aside. Meanwhile, in 4 T butter or margarine sauté 8–10 oz fresh mushrooms, washed, dried and chopped, adding 1 T or so water so they simmer nicely. Season with salt and pepper. Beat 2 T butter with 2 raw egg yolks until creamy, add ½ c bread crumbs, the mushrooms and 1 T chopped fresh parsley and/or dill. Fold in 2 stiffly beaten egg whites, and salt and pepper mixture to taste. Discard lemon slices, fill fish cavity with stuffing and sew up or skewer. Place fish in well-greased baking dish large enough to accommodate it. Baste top of fish with about 3 T melted butter and pop into preheated 400° oven for about 10 min. Reduce heat to 325°, baste with 2 T melted butter, sprinkle with water and baste occasionally with pan drippings. Add a little water to pan if drippings all evaporate. Bake 30 min or until done. (OPTIONAL: Fork-blend ½ c sour cream with ½ t salt and pour over fish and bake another 10 min.)

TROUT, BUTTER-FRIED *(pstrąg smażony na maśle)*: Rinse 4 dressed rainbow trout (with heads attached), pat dry, sprinkle with salt and pepper, dredge in flour and fry in ½″ deep hot oil on both sides until done to a nice golden brown. Meanwhile, in 2 T butter sauté 8 oz fresh, washed, drained, sliced mushrooms until fully cooked. Turn trout onto lettuce-lined platter, garnish with mushrooms, placing some into cavities, decorate with lemon slices and parsley sprigs and serve.

BEER-SIMMERED FISH *(ryba duszona w piwie)*: Salt 2¼ lb dressed carp, catfish or pike cut into 1″-thick steaks, sprinkle with pepper, ground cloves and 2 T vinegar. Cover and let stand. In skillet melt 3 T butter, add 2 chopped onions and simmer until soft and transparent without browning. Add ½ c beer, heat to boiling and add fish. Cook, covered with tight-fitting lid, on low heat about 30 min. With slotted spoon remove fish to platter and keep in warm oven. Cook sauce down slightly, add ⅓ c light raisins and ½ t grated lemon zest and bring to boil. Pour hot sauce over fish and serve. This dish is sometimes called carp à la juive *(karp po żydowsku).*

CREAM-BAKED PIKE *(szczupak zapiekany w śmietanie)*: Wash and dry 2½ lb northern pike or walleye fillets, sprinkle with juice of ½ lemon, salt well and refrigerate several hr or overnight. Rinse and pat dry. Place 3 T butter, margarine or oil in casserole and heat in preheated 375° oven. Place fillets in casserole and roll in the hot fat to coat all sides. Bake uncovered about 15 min. Meanwhile, in saucepan melt 2 T butter or margarine, add 2 T flour, stirring into a paste. Dilute with ¾ c milk, add ¼ t salt and bring to boil, stirring constantly. Remove from heat, gradually stir in ½ c sour cream and 1 t lemon juice. Heat but do not boil. Pour sauce over fish and bake about 15 min. Exact cooking time will depend on the thickness of your fillets, so check fish for doneness. Dust with paprika and garnish with chopped parsley just before serving.

FISH STEWED IN RED CABBAGE *(ryba duszona w czerwonej kapuście)*: Shred a small head of red cabbage, scald with boiling water and drain. Place in pot, sprinkle with juice of 1 small lemon, 2 t sugar, ½ t salt and ⅛ t pepper and cook, uncovered, several min. In saucepan sauté 1 chopped onion in 2 T butter or oil until golden, stir in 1 T flour and brown slightly, then dilute with ½ c dry red wine. Stir wine-flavored roux into cabbage and simmer 20 min. Meanwhile, cut 2 lb cleaned bullheads or other fish into 2″ pieces and brown on all sides in hot oil. Add to red cabbage and simmer 15–20 min, or until cabbage and fish are fully cooked.

VEGETABLE, PASTA AND GRAIN DISHES

SAUERKRAUT AND MUSHROOMS *(kapusta z grzybami)*: Prepare 1 qt sauerkraut, coarsely chopped, adding 1 oz rehydrated dried mushrooms at start of cooking. In saucepan brown 1 chopped onion in 4 T butter, margarine or oil until tender and lightly browned, stir in 3 T flour and brown lightly. Stir into sauerkraut and cook on low flame, covered, another 30–60 min. Season with salt and pepper, about 1 t sugar and (optional) ¼ t caraway seeds. VARIATION: After roux is added, sauerkraut may be transferred to baking dish and baked 1 hr in preheated 325° oven. For a gourmet touch, add 4 chopped anchovy fillets to sauerkraut before baking.

SAUERKRAUT AND PEAS *(kapusta z grochem)*: Cook 1 c yellow split peas in 2½ c water until tender. Prepare sauerkraut as above, but reduce the amount of mushrooms to ½ oz. A mushroom bouillon cube may be added instead of or in addition to the mushrooms. Add cooked peas. Sauté 2 chopped onions in 3 T oil until tender and lightly browned around the edges, stir in 2 T flour and brown lightly. Add several T sauerkraut liquid from pot, stir mixture into sauerkraut and cook, covered, on low heat at least another hr, stirring occasionally. Like the previous dish, sauerkraut and peas can also be cooked only on the stovetop or transferred to baking dish and baked in oven. Season with 1 t sugar, ¼ t pepper and several pinches of ground caraway and/or marjoram. NOTE: The more time-consuming original recipe called for whole yellow dried peas, which need to be soaked overnight and cooked in the same water the next day until tender.

SAUERKRAUT AND PEAS, EASY *(łatwa kapusta z grochem)*: Prepare 1 qt coarsely chopped sauerkraut, adding 1 bay leaf, 6 peppercorns, and 1 mushroom bouillon cube to the water. Add 1–1½ c drained canned chickpeas or beans (navy, Great Northern, lima or pea-beans). Sauté 2 chopped onions in 3 T oil until tender and just starting to brown, stir in 2 T flour and brown lightly. Dilute with several T sauerkraut liquid from pot and stir mixture into sauerkraut. Cook on stovetop, covered, at low heat or in oven another hr or so. Season with salt and pepper, a little sugar and several pinches marjoram.

SAUERKRAUT AND NOODLES OR POTATO BALLS *(kapusta z łazankami lub kluskami kartoflanymi)*: To any of the above three sauerkraut dishes add 2–3 c hot cooked flat egg noodles or lasagna noodles cut into 1″ squares and serve. To prepare potato balls, set a large pot of lightly salted water to boil. Combine 1 c mashed potatoes with 3 peeled, diced raw potatoes, processed together with 1 quartered onion to batter consistency in food processor. Stir 1 egg into mixture and salt and pepper to taste. Add enough bread crumbs so dough is not wet and mushy. Pinch off pieces of dough and roll between floured hands into cherry-sized balls. Cook in boiling water 5–8 min, testing one for doneness. Drain, rinse with boiling water and serve in hot sauerkraut.

CABBAGE ROLLS WITH MUSHROOM FILLING *(gołąbki z grzybami)*: See *gołąbki* section, page 142.

MUSHROOMS, BATTER-FRIED *(grzyby smażone w cieście)*: Soak 12 large dried bolete mushroom caps of roughly equal size in warm water 1 or more hr or overnight. Add ½ t salt and cook in same water at a gentle boil until fully cooked but still firm. Carefully remove mushrooms, drain and dry on absorbent paper. (Save water in which mushrooms cooked for other purposes: soups, gravies, sauerkraut dishes, etc.) Prepare batter by combining ¾ c flour, ½ t baking powder, ½ t salt, 1 t oil and several dashes pepper. Stir in 1 c milk and 1 beaten egg and whisk until smooth. Let stand 30 min. Dip cooked mushroom caps in batter to cover and fry in ½″ hot oil to a nice golden brown on both sides. Drain on absorbent paper and serve hot. These make nice handheld accompaniments to clear *barszcz* (page 39) in place of *paszteciki* or *uszka.*

CREAMED MUSHROOMS *(grzyby duszone w śmietanie)*: Slice thin 1 lb washed and dried fresh mushrooms. In large skillet sauté 1 finely chopped onion in 2–3 T butter or vegetable fat until golden. Add the mushrooms, toss with spatula to coat all over, add 3 T water, cover tightly, reduce heat and simmer until cooked (15–20 min), stirring occasionally. Salt and pepper. Fork-blend ⅔ c sour cream with 1 t flour, stir into mushrooms and simmer on low 2–3 min. Garnish with chopped fresh dill and/or parsley (optional). Serve over cooked buckwheat groats, boiled potatoes, noodles or rice. VARIATION: This dish will be even tastier if a few cooked, diced, rehydrated boletes are added together with the water in which they cooked (or at least a mushroom bouillon cube dissolved in a little hot water).

CAULIFLOWER POLONAISE *(kalafior ze zrumienioną bułką)*: See Cooked Vegetables and Main-Dish Accompaniments for recipe, page 151.

BEANS WITH BUTTER *(fasola z masłem)*: For this dish you can use 2–3 c dried navy, lima, Great Northern or pea-beans, soaked in plenty of water overnight and cooked in same water the following day until tender. You can also cook frozen lima beans. Still another extremely easy way is to use drained, canned beans (lima, navy, Great Northern, or pea-beans). After draining the canned beans, warm them up in 1 c vegetable stock (homemade or bouillon cube). Drain and transfer hot beans to serving dish, drench with 3–4 T melted butter and season with salt, pepper, savory and/or marjoram. Provide a cruet of vinegar on the side, since some people like their beans on the tart side.

BEANS WITH PRUNES *(fasola ze śliwkami)*: Dice 8–10 pitted prunes, place in bowl, cover with warm water and let stand 1 hr. In 2 T butter sauté 1 chopped onion until tender and lightly browned. Cook prunes in the water they were soaked in until they disintegrate. Add the onions, 1 T vinegar and season with salt, pepper and marjoram. Prepare the beans as directed in previous recipe. Pour stewed prune mixture over hot beans on serving platter.

PIEROGI/FILLED DUMPLINGS *(pierogi)*: *Pierogi* are a classic Wigilia favorite, especially those filled with sauerkraut and mushrooms and other meatless varieties. Look for them in the *pierogi* section, page 145.

THE SWEET DISHES OF WIGILIA

PRUNE-FILLED PIEROGI *(pierogi ze śliwkami)*: See *pierogi* section, page 145.

POPPY-SEED FILLING *(masa makowa)*: Although not a dish in itself, this filling is used in a number of typical sweet Christmas Eve dishes and cakes. In pot combine 3 c poppy seed with plenty of cold water and swish around with hand. Pour off any impurities that float up. Drench with cold water again and drain through fine sieve. Place poppy seeds in pot, scald with boiling water to cover and simmer on low until poppy seeds disintegrate between fingers (about 40 min). Drain in fine sieve, pressing out moisture. Pass through fine strainer of meat grinder twice or through special poppy-seed grinder once. Or process them in food processor several min until puréed. In saucepan melt 3½ T butter, add poppy seeds, 1 c sugar, ½ t grated lemon zest, 3 T honey and ⅓ c plumped raisins and simmer 15 min or so, stirring frequently. About ¼ t vanilla extract and/or several drops of almond extract may added.

PASTRY STICKS AND POPPY-SEED FILLING *(łamańce z makiem)*: With knife, cut ½ c butter or margarine into 2¾ c sifted flour and mix with hand. Add ⅔ c confectioners' sugar, 2 whole eggs and 1 extra yolk, 2 t baking powder, 1 t vanilla extract and 2 T sour cream. Combine ingredients well by hand to blend, knead briefly and refrigerate 15 min. Roll out ⅛″ thick, transfer to greased baking sheet, cut into ½″ × 2″ rectangles and bake in preheated 400° oven about 15 min. Remove from baking sheet immediately. Mound the poppy-seed filling on round serving dish. Stick the cooled pastry sticks into it, porcupine fashion. This is eaten chip-and-dip–style, with the pastry sticks dipped into the poppy seed mixture.

POPPY SEED NOODLES *(kluski lub łazanki z makiem)*: Cook 1 lb wide or medium-wide egg noodles or lasagna noodles according to directions or until tender. (Italian-style al dente doneness leaves pasta a bit too tough and rubbery for Polish recipes.) If using lasagna, after it has cooked, cut it into roughly 1″ squares. Dot hot, freshly drained pasta with a little butter or Butter Buds and stir in 1 c or more poppy seed-filling (above). Toss gently to evenly distribute. May be served warm, room temp or chilled. Some like to pour a little coffee cream over their portions. NOTE: Canned poppy-seed filling may be used instead of the homemade variety.

GRAIN AND POPPY SEED DESSERT *(kutia/kucja)*: This is a typical Wigilia sweet dish of old southeastern Poland (most of which is now in Ukraine). The traditional way was to soak wheat overnight and cook it many hr until tender. Nowadays, bulghur wheat is an easier alternative. Prepare 1–2 c bulghur wheat according to pkg directions. Leave wheat in pot until cooled to room temp. Stir in about ¾ c poppy-seed filling (m/l to taste), 1–2 T honey and ½–1 t vanilla. OPTIONAL: ¼–½ c ground or chopped almonds or walnuts and/or ½ c plumped raisins may be added. VARIATIONS: *Kucja* can also be prepared using 3 c cooked rice or barley in place of wheat.

ALMOND SOUP *(zupa migdałowa)*: Dry out 3 oz blanched almonds and 5–6 bitter almonds on baking sheet in 200° oven. Grind almonds with ¼ c sugar, adding several T milk while grinding so they do not release their oil. Set aside. Scald ¼ c rice with ½ c boiling milk and cook, covered, on low heat until fluffy. Scald ground almond mixture with 1 qt hot milk, add a pinch of salt and cook, covered, on low 15 min. (OPTIONAL: If you do not want gritty almonds in your soup, strain soup and discard ground residue at this point.) Add ¾ c raisins. When they plump, add the rice. This soup can be served hot or cold. OPTIONAL: 1–2 drops almond and/or vanilla extract may be added. A natural child-pleaser, this soup should appeal to all those with a pronounced sweet tooth.

"NOTHING" SOUP *(zupa „nic")*: Gradually heat to boiling 5 c milk containing ½ a vanilla pod. (1 t vanilla extract may be used instead of pod.) Beat 4 egg whites and 1 scant c confectioners' sugar until stiff and season with ⅛ t ground cinnamon. Remove vanilla pod from boiling milk and drop small spoonfuls of egg-white mixture into it. Bring soup to boil and turn over egg-white dumplings. Remove egg-white dumplings with slotted spoon and distribute among your guests' soup plates. Beat 4 egg yolks with ⅓ c confectioners' sugar until fluffy and gradually stir in 1 c hot milk. Pour in thin stream into the hot milk, vigorously whisking the whole time. When soup thickens pour it over the egg-white dumplings in bowls. This is sure to be a favorite with the sweets-lovers in your gang. One Polish-American cookbook translates *zupa „nic"* as "nothing but delicious."

RICE AND FRUIT DESSERT *(ryż ze śliwkami)*: Soak 1 c pitted prunes in 2 c water 1 hr. Add 1 t lemon juice and cook about 15 min or until prunes are nice and soft. Place about 4 c hot rice on serving platter, dot with butter, top with stewed prunes and season with a pinch of cinnamon. If not as sweet as you like, sprinkle with a little confectioners' sugar to taste. Instead of just stewed prunes you can stew mixed dried fruits in this recipe. Or simply top the rice with canned cherry or apple-pie filling or strawberry or cherry preserves, or *powidła* (Polish plum butter).

BARLEY AND PRESERVES *(kasza jęczmienna z konfiturą)*: Dot 4 c hot cooked barley with butter or Butter Buds and spoon over preserves or canned pie filling of choice. You can also serve it with stewed prunes as in rice and fruit dessert (above).

DRIED-FRUIT COMPOTE *(kompot wigilijny z suszu)*: Soak 1 c mixed dry fruit, 3–4 dried figs, diced and (optional) ½ c raisins in 2½–3 c water for 2 hr. Add a little water if all has been absorbed and cook about 15 min.

OPTIONAL: 1 small sliced lemon (which has been scrubbed well before being sliced) and a pinch of cinnamon may be added before cooking. Chill and serve in dessert bowls. NOTE: Christmas Eve compote may be made with prunes alone or prunes and raisins or prunes and figs. It may also be expanded into the traditional twelve-fruit compote (believed to symbolize the Twelve Apostles) incorporating prunes, raisins and other dried fruit: apples, pears, peaches, apricots, cherries, figs, dates and currants as well as fresh orange and lemon slices.

DRINKABLE COMPOTE (*kompot pitny*): Some people enjoy compote as a beverage to help wash down all those hearty Wigilia dishes. Simply dilute your compote to taste with cold preboiled water and enjoy.

NOODLES AND FRUIT (*kluski z kompotem*): Any of the above compotes may be served over cooked, well-drained egg noodles. If the compote liquid is too thin and runny, pour off ½ glass, stir in 1 T cornstarch, return to compote, simmer a few min and then ladle over noodles.

POLISH PANCAKES (*racuszki*): Beat 2 c sour milk or buttermilk with 2 eggs. Beat in 2 c plus 2 T flour until smooth. Stir in 1 t baking powder and 1 t baking soda. (OPTIONAL: Add ½ t vanilla sugar or liquid extract to batter if desired.) Spoon batter into ¼″ deep hot oil, fry roughly 3″ pancakes to a nice golden brown on both sides and drain on absorbent paper. Serve hot, dusted with confectioners' sugar or topped with fruit mixture: preserves, jam, plum butter, syrup or canned pie filling of choice.

POLISH PANCAKES, EASY (*racuszki łatwe*): Use American-style plain or buckwheat pancake mix for this recipe and prepare according to instructions on pkg, but use buttermilk, add ½ t baking soda and add no oil to batter. (OPTIONAL: Add ½ t vanilla sugar or liquid extract to batter.) Into large skillet pour oil to a depth of ¼″ and heat until fairly hot. Spoon batter into hot oil, fry roughly 3″ pancakes to a nice golden brown on both sides and drain on absorbent paper. Serve hot, dusted with confectioners' sugar or drenched with fruit topping as above.

CRANBERRY GEL/JELLY (*kisiel żurawinowy*): In pot combine 2 c raw cranberries, 2 cloves and 1 c water, bring to boil and cook until the skins of the cranberries pop. Discard cloves. Force cranberries through food-mill or metal sieve (a plastic one may melt!), using rubber spatula to scrape scrapings from bottom of sieve into a clean pot. Add 1 c sugar and a pinch of cinnamon (optional) and simmer until sugar dissolves. Dissolve 3 T plus 1 t potato starch in 1 c cold water and add to cranberries. Simmer a few min, transfer to bowl, cover and let stand until cooled to room temp. *Kisiel* (pronounced: KEY-shell) is a traditional Wigilia sweet served in dessert dishes. It may be topped with poppy-seed milk, vanilla sauce or a dollop of whipped cream.

CRANBERRY GEL/JELLY, EASY *(kisiel żurawinowy łatwy)*: Dissolve ¼ c potato starch in 1 c cranberry juice and pour into pot. Stir in another 1–1½ c cranberry juice and gradually heat to boiling, whisking the whole time. Season with a pinch of cinnamon or cloves if desired. Using more cranberry juice will produce a softer and gooier dessert, using less will make it stiffer.

OAT KISIEL/PUDDING *(kisiel owsiany)*: This is another traditional Christmas Eve kisiel. In pot combine 3½ c water, 4–5 T sugar, ¼ t vanilla and ½ c oat flour. (Oat flour can be obtained by whirling rolled oats to a fine powder in food processor.) Slowly bring to boil, stirring frequently, reduce heat and simmer 1–2 min. Pour into dessert dish to cool. VARIATION: For a richer taste, replace some or all of the water with milk. May be served with a dollop of preserves. A traditional topping is poppy seed milk: Combine the liquid obtained by straining canned poppy-seed filling with an equal amount of milk and bring to boil. If too thin, stir in a little cornstarch dissolved in water and bring to boil again.

FRUIT-NUT-VEGETABLE-BEER DESSERT, SILESIAN *(moczka)*: This unusual dish—something between a thick soup, a compote and a fruit pudding—is a speciality of Silesia (Śląsk). Cover 12 oz pitted prunes with warm water and let soak 1 hr, then cook on low heat several min. Place 12 oz broken-up stale honey-spice cake *(piernik)* in bowl and drench with 1 c dark beer. Separately, in 4 c carp or other freshwater-fish stock cook 1 lg celeriac, 1 med parsnip and 1 med parsley root—all peeled and coarsely diced—until tender. Drain, reserving stock. Grind or process beer-soaked honey-spice cakes with cooked vegetables and add to reserved stock. Add ½ c raisins; ⅓ c chopped walnut meats; 21 blanched almonds, slivered; 4 oz dried figs, halved and cut into thin strips; the stewed prunes; and 3 c dark beer. Bring to boil, add ⅓ c sugar and simmer 15 min. Thicken with golden roux made with 2 T flour and 2 T butter. Simmer several min longer. Finally, stir in juice of 1 lemon. Serve in dessert dishes after it has cooled to room temp.

HONEY-SPICE LIQUEUR, OLD POLISH *(krupnik staropolski)*: The Vigil supper is too solemn an occasion for high-powered libation. Some families serve no alcoholic beverages whatsoever at this repast, others limit things to a glass of wine or a nip of a homemade cordial. One favorite is this delicious old honey liqueur which is served hot as a great cheer-enhancer and warmer-upper. For how to prepare it, see Hot Beverages, page 175.

SUGGESTED WIGILIA MENUS

The traditional Christmas Eve supper always begins with the breaking and sharing of *opłatek*. The meal should comprise an odd number of meatless dishes. Here are some suggested menus for everything from the smallest of families to a large parish Opłatek dinner. To provide maximum exposure to the various Wigilia dishes, I have tried to make the suggested menus as different from each other as possible. In actuality, if someone were to visit two dozen Polish homes on Christmas Eve, they would probably find such items as herring in oil, clear beet soup with ear-shaped dumplings, *pierogi*, sauerkraut and mushrooms, fried carp, dried-fruit compote and poppy seed noodles (in eastern Poland—*kutia*) in home after home. There would, of course, be numerous modifications, additions and deletions from one family to the next. NOTE: For Vigil suppers comprising nine or eleven separate dishes (and such was the norm among the Polish upper gentry of yesteryear), simply expand any of the seven-course suppers to include additional selections from the other menus provided. There are plenty of items to choose from.

Three-Dish Wigilia Supper

NOTE: A Polish Christmas Eve supper comprising only three courses was and remains quite rare. It has been included here for the benefit of those who lack the time, stamina and/or ability to prepare anything more involved or are cooking for only two people but would nevertheless enjoy sampling a taste of traditional Wigilia fare.

I.

Creamed herring with boiled potatoes *(śledzie w śmietanie z kartoflami)*
Clear beet soup with rice and egg pie *(czysty barszcz burakowy z kulebiakiem)*
Wheat and poppy seed dessert *(kucja/kutia z pszenicą)*

II.

Herring with apple and pickle *(śledzie z jabłkiem i ogórkiem)*
Clear mushroom soup with noodle squares *(czysta zupa grzybowa z łazankami)*
Polish pancakes with preserves *(racuszki z konfiturami)*

III.

Potato-mushroom soup *(kartoflanka z grzybami)*
Perch polonaise *(okoń po polsku)*
Prune-filled pierogi *(pierogi ze śliwkami)*

Five-Dish Wigilia Supper

I.

Herring in oil *(śledzie w oleju)*
Clear mushroom soup with egg noodles *(czysta zupa grzybowa z kluskami)*
Pike in horseradish sauce *(szczupak duszony z chrzanem)*
Sauerkraut and mushrooms *(kapusta z grzybami)*
Noodles and stewed fruit *(kluski z kompotem)*

II.

Herring in horseradish sauce *(śledzie w sosie chrzanowym)*
Fast-day bean soup with egg-barley *(postna zupa fasolowa z zacierką)*
Fried carp, sauerkraut salad *(karp smażony, sałatka z kiszonej kapusty*
Cheese-filled pierogi *(pierogi z serem)*
Dried-fruit compote *(kompot wigilijny z suszu)*

III.

Christmas eve herring salad *(wigilijna sałatka śledziowa)*
Creamy sour soup with mushrooms *(żurek wigilijny)*
Baked whitefish *(sielawa pieczona)*
Sauerkraut-filled pierogi *(pierogi z kapustą)*
Cranberry jelly *(kisiel żurawinowy)*

IV.

Prune soup with noodles *(zupa śliwkowa z kluskami)*
Cream-baked pike *(szczupak zapiekany w śmietanie)*
Gołąbki with mushroom filling *(gołąbki z grzybami)*
Beans with butter *(fasola z masłem)*
Barley (or rice) and poppy-seed dessert *(kutia/kucja z kaszą jęczmienną lub ryżem)*

Seven-Course Wigilia Supper

I.

Pickled herring with boiled potatoes *(śledzie marynowane z kartoflami)*
Country-style mushroom soup *(zupa grzybowa po wiejsku)*
Fried northern pike *(szczupak smażony)*
Pierogi with cheese and potatoes *(pierogi ruskie–z kartoflami i serem)*
"Nothing" soup *(zupa „nic")*
Poppy seed roll *(makowiec/ makownik/ strucla z makiem)*
Prune and fig compote *(kompot ze śliwek i fig)*

II.

Herring in mustard sauce *(śledie w sosie musztardowym)*
Clear beet soup with mushroom-filled pasties *(czysty barszcz czerwony z pasztecikiem)*
Carp in gray sauce *(karp w szarym sosie)*
Sauerkraut and peas or beans *(kapusta z grochem lub fasolą)*
Groat and cheese pierogi *(pierogi z kaszą gryczaną i serem)*
Poppy-seed noodles *(kluski lub łazanki z serem)*
Drinkable stewed-fruit compote *(kompot wigilijny pitny)*

III.

Herring with pickled mushrooms *(śledzie z grzybkami w occie)*
Clear beet soup with ear-dumplings *(czysty barszcz czerwony z uszkami)*
Trout sautéed in butter *(pstrąg smażony na maśle)*
Creamed mushrooms and buckwheat groats *(kasza gryczana z sosem grzybowym)*
Sauerkraut and potato dumplings *(kapusta z kluskami kartoflanymi)*
Pastry sticks and poppy-seed filling *(łamańce z makiem)*
Oat kisiel/pudding *(kisiel owsiany)*

POLISH CHRISTMAS CAKES

Some families serve Polish Christmas cakes at their Christmas Eve gatherings, while others reserve them for Christmas Day and later. That is why they are being presented here, following the Wigilia section, as a kind of bridge between Christmas Eve and the winter entertaining (post-Wigilia Christmas festivities, New Year's, Three Kings, Carnival) that follows. These traditional cakes are the ideal refreshments to serve at community *opłatek* gatherings, after carol concerts and other Yule-related events being held before Christmas, and that includes community Wigilia suppers. Of course, these cakes have numerous devotees who enjoy them year-round.

POPPY-SEED ROLL *(strucla z makiem, makowiec)*: This is probably the most common typically Polish Christmas cake. For the filling: rinse well 2 c poppy seeds and drain. Place in pot, scald with boiling water and cook 15 min. Remove from heat, cover and let stand till cooled to room temp (better yet—overnight). Drain poppy seeds well and grind 2 or, better yet, 3 times through fine-mesh strainer. Melt 1 T butter in skillet, add ground poppy seeds, 3 T honey, ½ c rinsed, drained raisins, grated rind of 1 lemon and ¼ c chopped candied orange rind. Simmer, stirring constantly, on low heat 10 min and set aside. Add ½–1 t vanilla extract. When cool, beat 2 egg yolks with ¾ c sugar until creamy and stir into mixture. Fold in 2 stiffly beaten egg whites. For the dough: mash 1¾ cakes yeast with 1 T sugar and ⅔ c warm milk. Stir in ⅓ c flour, cover and let rise in a warm place. After about an hr, beat 2 egg yolks with ½ c sugar until creamy and add to yeast mixture together with 2 ⅔ c flour and 1 whole egg. Work ingredients into a dough. Work in 4 T melted butter and knead until smooth and silky. Set aside in warm place to rise. When doubled in bulk, divide dough in two and roll out each piece quite thin, about ¼″ to ⅓″. Spread dough sheets with poppy-seed filling leaving a ¾″ margin round the edges. Roll up and place in baking pan(s) to rise until doubled in size. Bake in preheated 400° oven about 50 min. Dust with confectioners' sugar or glaze with white icing. OPTIONAL: Soft icing may be sprinkled with chopped candied orange peel, slivered almonds, chopped walnuts or poppy seeds.

POPPY-SEED ROLL, ANOTHER WAY *(makowiec inaczej)*: This is a slightly different version of this Old Polish favorite, which requires no laborious kneading. Sift 3 c flour onto breadboard and cut in ⅓ lb butter chopping to achieve a groat-like consistency. Add 2 eggs and 3 yolks, lightly beaten, ½ c sour cream, scant 1 c confectioners' sugar, 1 t grated lemon zest, 1 t vanilla and 1 cake yeast mashed with 1 T sugar. Quickly work ingredients into a dough, adding a little sour cream if it is too stiff to handle. Divide in two and roll each half out into a roughly 10″ × 14″ rectangle. Prepare poppy-seed filling as in preceding recipe or use a commercial poppy seed pastry filling. Spread each rectangle with filling, leaving a ¾″ margin round the edges, and roll up jelly-roll fashion. Transfer to baking pan, cover with cloth and leave in warm place to rise until doubled in size. Bake in preheated 400° oven 40–50 min. NOTE: Instead of or in addition to the vanilla extract, the filling may be flavored with several drops of other extracts such as almond, rum, orange, lemon, etc.

NUT-ROLL CAKE *(strucla orzechowa)*: The rolled-up yeast-dough cake may contain fillings other than poppy seeds. Prepare dough as for first poppy-seed roll recipe (above). In dry skillet, toast ¾ c peeled hazelnuts (filberts) until lightly browned. When cool, chop and set aside. Grind 2¼ c chopped walnut meats and beat with 1 egg and ½ c sugar until smooth. Add the chopped hazelnuts and 1 jg rum (or 1 jg vodka flavored with several drops rum extract) and mix to blend. Spread rolled out dough with mixture and proceed as in first recipe. (OPTIONAL: Dust baked *strucla* with confectioners' sugar if desired.) VARIATION: Almonds may be used in place of the walnuts and filberts to produce *strucla migdałowa* (almond-roll cake).

CHERRY-ROLL CAKE *(strucla z wiśniami)*: Drain 14–15 oz cherry preserves in colander. (NOTE: Be sure to save the drippings, which are great for flavoring vodka, puddings, cakes, ices, etc.) Mix cherries with 2 T grated lemon zest and 2 jg rum. If mixture seems too wet, stir in a heaping T plain bread crumbs. Proceed as for poppy-seed roll above.

APPLE-ROLL CAKE *(strucla z jabłkami)*: Peel and dice 1⅓ lb cooking apples. In pot melt 2 T butter and add the apples, ½–⅔ c sugar, a pinch of cinnamon and ground cloves and cook on med-low heat, stirring constantly, until a uniform filling forms. Set aside to cool. Spread dough with filling. Sprinkle with a heaping T ground vanilla wafers (or plain bread crumbs), roll up and proceed as for poppy-seed roll above. (OPTIONAL: Adding ½ c ground walnuts or raisins to hot apple filling will improve the flavor of your cake.) NOTE: Other thick fruit fillings may also be used to fill the Polish *strucla.*

CHEESE-ROLL CAKE *(strucla z serem)*: Grind (or process to a powder) 14–15 oz farmer cheese. Beat 2 T butter with 4 egg yolks, add ½ c sugar and beat until smooth. Add ½–1 t vanilla extract, 3 T finely chopped candied orange peel and ⅔ c rinsed, drained raisins. Combine with ground cheese, mix to blend ingredients, fold in 4 stiffly beaten egg whites and mix lightly. Proceed as above.

HONEY-SPICE CAKE *(piernik)*: Here is a very basic recipe for a cake often served during the Christmas-New Year season. Heat 1 c honey with 1 t honey-spice–cake seasoning (m/l to taste). Add 1 c sugar and 2 eggs, mix well until blended and gradually add 3 c flour, mixed with 1 t baking soda. Knead well and set aside to rest about 1 hr. Better yet, prepare dough a day ahead. Spread dough on greased baking sheet and bake in 350° oven about 40 min. Cut into squares after it cools.

HONEY-SPICE CAKE WITH WALNUTS *(piernik z orzechami)*: In saucepan brown 2 T sugar, add scant ½ c beer, ¾ c honey and ¾ c sugar, stir well and bring to boil. Add 1 t honey-spice–cake seasoning, cover and let stand till cooled to room temp. Cream ¼ lb butter, stir in 5 egg yolks and 1½ c flour mixed with 2 t baking soda. Mix well. Stir in another 1½ c flour and ¾ chopped walnuts. Fold in 5 stiffly beaten egg whites, mixing gently. Transfer to greased, flour-sprinkled loaf pan(s) and bake about 1 hr in preheated 375° oven. VARIATION: Almonds and/or toasted hazelnuts may be used instead of walnuts if desired. NOTE: All larger honey-spice cakes (baked in pans rather than on baking sheets) may be cut in half lengthwise and spread with fruit filling (plum butter or apricot jam are very good) before replacing top. They can also be glazed with white or chocolate icing.

HONEY-SPICE CAKE, RUM-FLAVORED *(piernik z rumem)*: In saucepan lightly brown ¾ c honey and cool to room temp. Beat 4 eggs and stir into honey, add 2 jg rum, 1 t honey-spice–cake seasoning and 2½ c flour sifted together with 2 t baking powder. Mix well to blend ingredients and transfer to greased, bread-crumb–sprinkled baking pan. Even out top and bake about 50 min in 350° oven.

HONEY-SPICE CAKE, FRUITED *(piernik z bakaliami)*: Heat 1½ c honey to boiling, stir in 1 c sugar, bring to boil, simmer briefly and cool to room temp. Mash 1 cake yeast and dissolve in ½ c warm beer. To honey-sugar mixture add beer-yeast mixture, 1 T butter, 4 beaten eggs and 4 c flour. Beat well. Add 1–2 t honey-spice–cake seasoning, 1½ c southern fruits (figs, prunes, dates, raisins, walnuts in any combination) chopped fine (raisins may be unchopped) and 2 T finely chopped candied orange rind. Mix dough well to combine ingredients evenly. Spread on greased baking sheet and bake for about 40 min in preheated 350° oven. When cool, cut into squares.

CARROT SPICE CAKE, HONEYLESS *(piernik z marchwi bez miodu)*: Scrape, wash and grate fine just over 1 lb carrots. Beat 4 egg yolks with ¼ lb butter, add 1½ c brown sugar, 1–2 t honey-spice–cake seasoning, 2 t baking powder, the grated rind and juice of 2 lemons and 1½ c flour. Mix to combine ingredients. Stir in another 1½ c flour and fold in 4 stiffly beaten egg whites. Transfer dough to greased, flour-sprinkled cake pan and bake about 50 min in preheated 375° oven.

FRUITCAKE, BASIC *(keks)*: Cream ⅔ c butter with 1 c confectioners' sugar, gradually stirring in 5 egg yolks. Add ½ c chopped walnuts, 2 T finely chopped candied orange rind and 1½ c flour sifted with 2 t baking powder, then fold in 5 stiffly beaten egg whites. Mix to combine ingredients and add ⅔ c raisins, rinsed, drained and floured. Transfer dough to well greased loaf pan(s), even out top and make a deep lengthwise slit in dough with knife dipped in melted butter. Bake for about 1 hr at 375°. After cooling and removing from pan, dust with confectioners' sugar. NOTE: Unlike the

English-style fruitcakes common in America, the Polish *keks* is lighter and contains a lower fruit-to-dough ratio. Raisins, prunes, figs, dates and nuts are among the most common *bakalie* (southern fruits) used in Polish fruitcakes. In this and other Polish fruitcake recipes, feel free to use any or all of the above. The most common nuts used are walnuts, almonds or hazelnuts. Feel free to adjust the amount of season according to preference.

FRUITCAKE, COUNTRY-STYLE *(keks wiejski)*: Beat 5 whole eggs and 5 yolks with 1 slightly heaped c sugar until fluffy. Combine 1¾ c flour with 1 leveled T baking powder and stir into egg mixture, beating until smooth. Stir in ¼ c melted butter. Rinse 1 c raisins and 1 c chopped prunes, drain, shake in plastic bag to coat with flour and stir into dough. Add 3 T finely chopped candied orange rind. Mix gently to evenly distribute fruit. Transfer to well-greased loaf pan and bake in preheated 375° oven about 1 hr. Glaze after cooling, if desired.

FRUITCAKE, WARSAW-STYLE *(keks warszawski)*: Beat 5 eggs with 1¾ c confectioners' sugar until creamy. Cream ¾ c butter with 1 t vanilla extract until light and fluffy, then beat in ¼ c milk and ½ t salt. Sift 1½ c flour with 2 t baking powder, add to butter mixture and mix well. Fold in egg mixture and another 1½ c flour. In cornstarch-filled plastic bag place 1 c chopped prunes and figs, ½ c raisins and ¾ c chopped walnuts and shake to coat thoroughly. Fold into dough and mix to distribute evenly. Transfer dough to well-greased, bread-crumb–sprinkled loaf pan and bake in preheated 350° about 50 min.

ALMOND KING CAKE *(ciasto Migdałowego Króla)*: A traditional Twelfth Night (January 6) celebration involves choosing the king or queen of the evening. One portion of cake contains a whole almond, and the one who finds it in his or her serving gets to be the king or queen of Twelfth Night. Any of the honey-spice cakes, fruitcakes or almond-roll cake (in fact even the simplest of package-mix cakes) could serve this purpose. Rather than putting the almond into the cake batter, however, it is more advisable to insert a whole almond into a single portion of baked cake from the bottom (so the insertion is not readily visible). If an almond is baked inside a cake, it may get cut in half or even fall out and get lost when the cake is being sliced.

POLISH HOLIDAY/BANQUET/ DINNER-PARTY FAVORITES

Polonia seems closest to its culinary roots at folksy, family-style events such as fests, picnics, pierogi suppers, kiełbasa dinners and the like. When more formal occasions arise, we tend to put ourselves in the hands of caterers with their scotch, shrimp, roast beef and lobster. Sociologically, that is understandable, since the overwhelming majority of our Polonia is descended from peasant immigrants. But from a cultural standpoint, should that prevent us from exploring the many other lifestyles our ancestral heritage entails? Does that mean we should never dare venture beyond the quaint, the rustic and, some might even add, the corny? I think not! Every aspect of our cultural legacy is out there waiting to be sampled. It may take Polonia's activities chairmen a little extra thought and energy to move beyond the run-of-the-mill functions they are used to holding, but it will be well worth the effort. Besides the cultural and culinary value of diversified socializing, this approach can be psychologically beneficial to our community by promoting the awareness that not everything Polish must be rustic, blue-collar and lowbrow.

Organizing an upscale Polish-style banquet or elegant dinner-party out of the clear blue sky can be a daunting task to individuals and groups that have never ventured into that realm. Hence it is a good idea to tap all available resources. A caterer, maître d'hôtel, chef or even a waiter with past experience in one of Poland's better hotel restaurants or banquet facilities could be an excellent consultant in such matters. Hopefully, the following suggestions will prove helpful to all those who share a broad, imaginative and inclusive approach to our heritage, rather than a narrow and limited one.

This recipe section has been positioned in this chapter to embrace the roughly six- to eight-week-long period (depending on when Ash Wednesday falls in a given year) of post-Wigilia Christmas, New Year's and Carnival merriment. This has traditionally been a time of Polonaise balls, banquets, dinner-dances, mid-winter frolics, masquerade parties and other forms of pre-Lenten socializing. This includes St. Casimir's Day (March 4) fairs and St. Joseph's Day (March 19) socials. But such events are also held at other times of year, including mid-summer balls, testimonial banquets, harvest balls, autumn dinner-dances, Pułaski Day dinners and the like.

We start with the more sophisticated, upscale affairs, to which people come in evening attire and expect something more than beer, *gołąbki* and *hupaj-siupaj* polka dancing. That is not to criticize that style of merriment, in fact this book contains a wealth of information on the many folk and peasant-style aspects of our heritage. However, there is a time and place for everything, and occasionally most everyone likes to get dressed up and enjoy upscale lifestyles in an elegant setting. And is it not to Polonia's advantage to project a rich and diversified image of its ancestral heritage to the rest of the country?

APÉRITIFS, HORS D'OEUVRES

DRINKS, ALCOHOLIC *(trunki)*: Each type of prepoured drink may be placed on a tray or lined up in even rows. This could include ice-cold vodka (straight from the freezer); possibly other flavored vodkas such as Starka, Jarzębiak, Jałówcówka/Myśliwska (Polish gin), Żubrówka, Śliwowica, etc.; French cognac, French brandy (only the brandy from the Cognac region may be legally referred to as cognac), Polish Winiak (a Polish version of wine-barrel–aged brandy); cordials such as Wiśniówka, Wiśniak, Jerzynówka, Malinówka, Miodówka, etc.; wines—dry red, dry white, Polish mead, Hungarian or domestic Tokay; beer—Polish (Żywiec, Tyskie, Okocim, Lech, Piast, EB, Leżajsk, etc.) and domestic, pale and dark (Porter [strong stout], Karmelowe [weak, sweet bock beer])—in Pilsner glasses (it is best to pour out beer as needed since prepoured beer soon loses its frothy head).

BEVERAGES, NONALCOHOLIC *(napoje bezalkoholowe)*: Juices—apart from the stereotypical orange and grapefruit, be sure to include imported Polish blackcurrant, redcurrant, cherry, pear and apple juice; mineral water—Polish (Nałęczowianka, Kryniczanka, Muszynianka, Żywiec Zdrój, Mazowszanka, etc.), French (Perrier), etc.

SALTY SNACKS *(słone przegryzki)*: These can be served with drinks any time—at informal gatherings, during concert intermission, following a lecture, during a social hour or at a full-blown banquet. For a more Polish-Continental touch, include salted walnuts, filberts and almonds instead of or in addition to peanuts, cashews and Brazil nuts. In addition to salty cocktail sticks (thin pretzel sticks), also include Polish-style poppy-seed cocktail sticks *(paluszki z makiem)*. An Old Polish touch would be unsweetened *pierniczki* (honey-spice cakes). Assorted crackers and other snacks will provide variety to the snack tray.

HORS D'OEUVRES, SKEWERED *(koreczki)*: These colorfully attractive shish kebab–style hors d'oeuvres will add a touch of elegance to any event. They may be the main finger food served at a cocktail party or a light appetizer preceding a banquet. Allow 2–3 hors d'oeuvres per person and prepare that many toothpicks or cocktail picks and any of the following:

Meat and Sausage (unsliced): Polish canned ham, other boiled or baked ham, smoked *kiełbasa,* Krakowska sausage, hunter's sausage (skinned), cooked meat (chicken, turkey, beef, pork, veal), firm *pâté,* boiled beef tongue, skinless frankfurters, etc.

<u>Firm Yellow Cheese (unsliced)</u>: Tilsit, Edam, Gouda, Swiss (Emmentaler, Gruyère), brick, farmer cheese, white (not orange-colored!) American cheese or similar (except orange-colored cheddar).

<u>Fish and Seafood</u>: Smoked sprats, sardines, anchovy fillets and/or marinated herring (well-drained on absorbent paper), smoked fish (salmon, trout, carp, whitefish, herring, mackerel, cod, etc.), solid tuna fish, mussels and baby shrimps.

<u>Fruits and Veggies</u>: Cocktail onions, pickled mushrooms, canned button mushrooms, dill pickles (vinegar and/or brined type), gherkins, fresh cucumber, radishes, bell pepper (red, yellow and/or green), rindless lemon wedges, whole raw cranberries, pitted prunes, other dried fruit, raisins, dates, sm seedless grapes, olives (green and black), capers, lg peas (cooked or canned), pickled beets (well drained and patted dry so they don't stain neighboring ingredients), spiced cherries and/or plums (both pitted). <u>NOTE</u>: Do not use fresh apples, which discolor quickly.

<u>Bread</u>: Rye, black bread, French, unglazed *piernik* (honey-spice cake or gingerbread), etc.

<u>Presentation</u>: Cocktail onions, cranberries, small seedless grapes, raisins, peas, mussels and baby shrimp are left whole, all other items should be cut into small cubes or roughly equal size. On each pick, skewer four or five different items. Good combinations might include:

- cocktail onion, smoked fish, cucumber, radish, cheese
- cucumber, chicken, radish, chicken, cranberry
- sausage, dill pickle, bread cube, mushroom, cheese
- cranberry, ham, bell pepper, bread cube, radish
- green olive, turkey, cocktail onion, cheese, black olive
- raisin, cheese, caper, cheese, cucumber
- cocktail onion, sprat, lemon wedge, anchovy, cucumber
- mushroom, tuna, dill pickle, bread, cheese
- spiced plum, mussel, bell pepper, shrimp, green olive
- gherkin, tongue, *piernik* cube, cocktail onion
- spiced cherry, hunter's sausage, beet, black bread, smoked *kiełbasa*
- radish, cooked meat, cranberry, ham, date
- <u>for vegetarians</u>: cocktail onion, cucumber, bell pepper, radish, cranberry
- <u>for meat-lovers</u>: sausage, bread, tongue, cranberry, pâté, mushroom, ham
- <u>for seafood fanciers</u>: smoked salmon, lemon wedge, tuna, caper, mussel
- <u>for cheese-lovers</u>: Swiss cheese, radish, farmer cheese, olive, Edam or Gouda

These are just a few examples. Use your imagination to come up with combinations of your own. Oranges, apples or grapefruits are impaled with the hors d'oeuvres and placed around the room for easy access. Snugly placing the orange, apple, etc., in a vase, bowl or glass will keep it stable.

"TOADSTOOLS" *(„muchomorki")*: A whole plate of something resembling red-capped white-dotted toadstools or several of these decorating platters containing other food is sure to be a conversation piece at the buffet, *święcone* or banquet table. Start with as many peeled, cool, hard-cooked eggs as you need and remove a ½″ slice from the top and a slightly thicker one from the bottom of each so they can stand without wobbling. (Use egg-white trimmings in salads.) Select half as many firm, round, smallish tomatoes whose circumference is larger than the egg tops. "Glue" the eggs to the platter with a dab of mayonnaise, place another dab on top of each egg and gently press the tomato halves onto them to form a toadstool. To ensure the tomato halves won't slide off, fasten to eggs with toothpicks. Using mayonnaise in a tube, squeeze several dots onto each tomato top, creating a toadstool effect. Strew chopped scallions and chopped iceberg lettuce round the base of the toadstools for a grass-like effect.

HORS D'OEUVRES, ROLLED *(ruloniki)*: This is another type of skewered hors d'oeuvre, but instead of impaling cubes of different solid foods on a pick, small rectangles of meat or fish are covered with a thin coat of spread, rolled up and then skewered. Some examples follow:

Ham and Mustard: Cut thinly sliced boiled or canned ham into 1″ by 1½″ rectangles, spread thinly with mayonnaise-based mustard sauce or horseradish sauce, roll up and impale on wooden or plastic picks; a thin slice of radish may be added on top or both on top and beneath the ham roll-up.

Ham and Egg: Cut thinly sliced boiled or canned ham into 1″ by 1½″ rectangles, spread thinly with mayonnaise-based mustard sauce or horseradish sauce, place a wedge of hard-cooked egg (egg may be divided into 4 or 6 wedges) on each, roll up and impale on pick.

Ham, Egg and Anchovy: Cut thinly sliced boiled or canned ham into 1″ by 1½″ rectangles, spread thinly with mayonnaise-based mustard sauce or horseradish sauce, place a wedge of hard-cooked egg and a small piece of canned anchovy fillet on each piece of ham; roll up and impale on picks.

Roast Beef and Horseradish: Cut thin slices of cooked roast beef in 1″ by 1½″ pieces and spread thinly with mayonnaise-based horseradish, roll up and impale on wooden or plastic pick; for extra color and crunch, sandwich your beef roll between two thin slices of radish, or a slice of radish and dill pickle.

Smoked Pork Tenderloin and Prune: Cut thin slices of Polish canned smoked pork tenderloin into 1″ by 1½″ pieces. Place a thin slice of pitted prune on the rectangle, roll up and impale on picks; a large caper or a whole raw cranberry may be impaled on top of the roll.

Smoked Pork Tenderloin and Cheese: Cut thin slices of imported Polish canned smoked pork tenderloin or domestic Canadian bacon into 1″ by 1½″ rectangles; on each place a thin slice of yellow cheese, roll up and impale on picks; top with pitted spiced cherry if desired.

Smoked Salmon, Lemon and Dill: Cut thin slices of smoked salmon into 1″ by 1½″ rectangles; spread thinly with mayonnaise, sprinkle with a little fresh, finely chopped dill and roll up; run pike through a small thin piece (quarter-slice) of rindless lemon before impaling the salmon roll.

Herring and Apple: Drain well and dry marinated herring on absorbent paper and cut into 1″ by 1½″ rectangles; place a small ¾″-long piece of peeled apple on each rectangle, roll up and impale on pick; for added color, impale a small piece of red bell pepper on top of each herring roll. VARIATIONS: Simply follow the general guidelines above and use your imagination to produce a host of different colorful and taste-tempting rolled hors d'oeuvres. To serve, stick the hors d'oeuvres into grapefruits, apples or oranges set out at the bar or around the room. NOTE: If you are serving more than one type of hors d'oeuvre with a similar outer wrapping of ham, beef, pork tenderloin, etc, it is best to embellish one type with a radish slice, another with a slice of pickle, the third with a sliced pickled mushrooms, caper, cranberry, bell pepper, olive, etc. In case you have guests who do not like or cannot eat certain foods, you will know which hors d'oeuvre is which.

HOT HORS D'OEUVRES *(zakąski gorące)*: Hot bite-sized hors d'oeuvres are less common than cold ones for three reasons; 1) At a full-course banquet hot starters are served after the soup course, so many feel there is no sense including hot hors d'oeuvres during the cocktail hour; 2) Hot hors d'oeuvres are more difficult to serve, require cooking and a chafing dish to keep them hot; 3) They can be messy to eat—a drop of fat dripping off a hot hors d'oeuvre impaled on a pick can mean a nasty stain on a guest's best outfit. Nevertheless, they are a nice touch that guests usually enjoy. Try some of the following:

Hot Prune and Bacon: Wrap pitted prunes with 2″ strips of thinly sliced bacon, fasten with wooden picks and bake in 425° oven about 15 min or until bacon browns nicely; keep hot in chafing dish.

Hot Chicken Liver: Trim chicken livers of any veins and membrances and cut into bite-sized pieces, impale on picks with condiments/fruits/veggies, brush with oil and broil on rack 5–6 min or until nicely browned and cooked through; on either side of liver impale peeled apple cubes, pear cubes, pieces of bell pepper, capers or small fresh mushroom caps; keep hot in chafing dish.

Cocktail Pierożki: Hot small bite-sized *pierogi* (pan-browned or boiled *kołduny* or baked *pierożki*) make a nice hot appetizer with an ethnic accent; impale on picks and keep hot in chafing dish.

Cocktail Kiełbasa: Brown rounds of skinned or skinless smoked *kiełbasa*, impale on picks and keep hot in chafing dish; provide mustard and horseradish.

Cocktail Wieners: Tiny bite-sized cocktail wieners, browned in fat and kept hot in chafing dish are another possibility; provide a mustard pot nearby.

Cocktail Meatballs: Follow any of the meatball recipes in this book but use mixture to form tiny, cherry-sized (one-bite) meatballs, roll in flour and brown in hot fat until cooked through, drain on absorbent paper, impale with picks and keep hot in chafing dish.

Broiled Mushrooms: Choose rather small (bite-sized), fresh, store-bought mushrooms of roughly equal size; wipe with damp cloth, pat dry, cut off stems even with cap and reserve for some other use. Salt and pepper mushrooms, brush with oil and broil on rack on both sides to a nice golden brown; impale with picks and serve in chafing dish.

Stuffed Broiled Mushrooms: Proceed as above, but choose slightly larger mushrooms and chop their stems fine and brown in butter with a little finely chopped onion; for 16 mushrooms, mix fried stems with 2–3 T bread crumbs, 1 small egg, a little chopped dill and/or parsley and salt and pepper; mound portions of mixture on stem side of mushroom caps, drizzle with a little oil and broil filled-side up about 10 min.

CANAPÉS, OPEN-FACE SANDWICHES *(kanapki, tartinki)*: In general, canapés are served at less formal affairs that do not include fancy hors d'oeuvres. They can be a snack served after a meeting or conference or even the culinary mainstay following meetings and club functions or at house parties. Sometimes a simple hot dish (e.g., *bigos*) might follow, or the only other refreshments served could be cakes and tea or coffee. Prepare 2 or 3 kinds of bread, light and dark, such as cocktail rye, similar-sized slices of white bread, *rogale* (Polish crescents), *baguettes* (thin French bread) or any firm bread cut into squares or other shapes (using pastry cutter). The canapés should be either bite-sized (1–1½″ in diameter) or slightly larger, but generally should not exceed 2″. Start by thinly spreading canapé bread with butter, margarine and/or mayonnaise. Divide into four batches and sprinkle one batch with finely chopped fresh dill, another with parsley, the third with chives and place a small piece of Boston lettuce on the remaining bread. Then proceed to create canapés by adding some of the following:

- ✦ Slice of hard-cooked egg, radish slice, dollop of mayonnaise, caper, dusting of paprika
- ✦ Cucumber slice, hard-cooked egg slice, anchovy, dollop of mayonnaise, sprinkling of chopped parsley
- ✦ Ham, red and green bell-pepper strips, dollop of horseradish-flavored mayonnaise, cooked (or canned) peas
- ✦ Roast pork loin, mushroom slice, spiced plum half, bell-pepper strips
- ✦ Smoked sprat, dollop of mayonnaise, rindless lemon wedge, caper
- ✦ Thin slice of tongue, cucumber slice, radish slice, mini-dollop of horseradish, ½ cranberry (pressed into horseradish)
- ✦ Thin slice of cooked meat (roast beef, pork, veal, turkey, chicken), dill pickle strip, red bell-pepper strip, small tomato wedge, dollop of mayonnaise, caper; sprinkling of chopped chives
- ✦ Thin slice of smoked *kiełbasa* (skinned), marinated mushroom, red bell pepper, gherkin, dollop of mustard-flavored or horseradish-flavored mayonnaise
- ✦ Pâté, dill-pickle and bell-pepper strips, dollop of mayonnaise (plain or horseradish-flavored), piece of prune
- ✦ Cucumber slice, marinated herring, tomato wedge, mayonnaise, sprinkling of chopped dill
- ✦ Smoked salmon (lox), cucumber slice, radish slice, dollop of mayonnaise, lemon wedge (inserted into mayonnaise), sprinkling of chopped dill
- ✦ Yellow cheese, strips of red, green and yellow bell pepper, dusting of paprika
- ✦ Ham thinly spread with mustard-flavored mayonnaise, hard-cooked egg slice, strip of cheese, bell-pepper strips

NOTE: The canapé toppers should not extend beyond the rim of the bread slices. This is but a small sample. Be creative and improvise unique combinations of your own.

CANAPÉ SPREADS *(pasty kanapkowe)*: In addition to canapés assembled from solid ingredients (as above), various savory spreads both facilitate the preparation of canapés and add variety to your hors d'oeuvre tray. Many kinds of spreads are commercially available. After applying a layer to slices of canapé bread, all you need to do is decorate them with any of the veggies listed above. You can also make your own customized mayonnaise-based canapé spreads using items you may already have on hand. Simply grind the solid ingredients and mix together with the mayonnaise (or other creamy binders) and seasonings to a nice, spreadable consistency.

- ✦ 1 c ground boiled ham, 1–2 hard-cooked eggs, 1 T mustard, 1 T horseradish, 2 t lemon juice and 1 heaping T mayonnaise m/l
- ✦ 1 c ground smoked Polish sausage (skinned), 1 lg or 2 med dill pickles, 1 sm onion, 2 T horseradish and 1 heaping T mayonnaise m/l
- ✦ 1 c ground cooked meat or beef tongue plus the ingredients listed in either of the above combinations
- ✦ ¾ c ground ham, sausage, cooked meat or tongue, 1 hard-cooked egg (optional), 4 radishes, 1 dill pickle, 1 sm onion, ½ peeled cooking apple, 1 T chopped parsley, 1 T chopped chives, 1 T chopped dill and enough mayonnaise to get a spreadable consistency
- ✦ 1 c ground bologna, frankfurters or knackwrust; 1 onion, 2 dill pickles, ½ peeled cooking apple, 1 hard-cooked egg, 2 T mustard, 1 heaping T mayonnaise m/l
- ✦ ½ c ground marinated herring (drained well and dried before grinding), 2 hard-cooked eggs, 1 small onion, ½ peeled tart cooking apple, 1 heaping T mayonnaise m/l
- ✦ ¼ lb chicken livers sautéed in 2 T butter or oil with 1 chopped onion (drained well before grinding), 1 hard-cooked egg, salt, pepper and a pinch of ginger, 1 heaping T mayonnaise m/l to bind ingredients into a nice spread
- ✦ 1 c ground hard-cooked eggs, 2 T fresh chopped dill, 1 T chopped chives, 1 t chopped parsley, 1–2 t mustard, 1 T sour cream, several dashes paprika, salt and pepper (rather generously) and just enough mayonnaise for a thick spread;
- ✦ 1 c ground farmer cheese or dry cottage cheese, ½ c soft butter m/l, 2 cloves crushed garlic, 2 T chopped chives, several pinches ground caraway, salt and pepper

NOTE: For future reference, take note of which appetizers disappeared first and which were left over. Next time you'll know what your guests prefer.

STARTER/APPETIZER COURSE

Unlike the above-mentioned canapés, snacks and other hors d'oeuvres, which are nibbled while standing or seated to the accompaniment of apéritifs, *przystawki* (starters) are a bona fide sit-down course served at table. Typically salad plates and the appropriate flatware are laid out, and bread (rye, wheat, light, dark) and bread rolls plus unsalted butter are provided. Seasonings and condiments (see below) should also be available.

This course is not meant to fill up on but to socialize and enjoy good food and drink in a pleasant, relaxing and often entertaining atmosphere. A good rule of thumb for the cold starter course is to have one cold meat offering (this could be a pâté, aspic dish or assorted cold-meat platter), one cold fish item (e.g., herring or fish in aspic), hard-cooked eggs (in sauces, deviled) and at least one salad plus relishes, condiments, bread and butter. At more sumptuous affairs, there may be several different cold fish, meat and egg dishes and numerous salads. At simpler gatherings, a single starter may be offered (e.g., smoked salmon, individual molded aspics, a cold roast). Check the Wigilia section for a wide range of herring and other fish dishes and the Easter section for various egg and meat dishes.

Since in Polish tradition this is the traditional "drinking course," clear and flavored vodka, other spirits (preferably served in crystal carafes) as well as wine and/or mead (in the original bottles) should be placed on the tables. If there are no waiters to do the pouring, it is the duty of the gentlemen at individual tables or stretches of a single table to make sure glasses are kept filled. The starter course may be served family-style (platters on the table for guests to help themselves), or prepared individual portions (everyone gets an identical sampling of cold dishes) are placed before guests, or waiters bring food on platters round to individual guests and dish it out according to their preference.

SEASONINGS *(przyprawy)*: A well-provided starter course should include the seasonings that allow individual diners to custom-season the dishes to their own particular tastes. A nice touch are crystal (cut-glass) sets that include not only shakers for salt and pepper, but also paprika, Turkish pepper (cayenne) and possibly other seasonings like marjoram, which is widely used in Polish cookery. Cruets may be provided for vinegar, oil, Maggi (or similar liquid seasonings: Winiary, Knorr, etc.) and red-pepper sauce (Tabasco, etc.).

CONDIMENTS, RELISHES, PICKLES *(dodatki)*: Typical Polish condiments include mustard and horseradish, relishes such as *ćwikła*, and various pickles. (NOTE: By pickles are meant not only dill pickles [pickled cucumbers] but other marinated vegetables such as pickled mushrooms, pumpkin and peppers, mixed pickled salads and spiced fruits.) The main thing at an elegant banquet or dinner-party is the presentation. These meal enhancers should never be set out in their original store-bought jars but should be transferred to crystal or china serving bowls or compartmentalized serving dishes.

HERRING IN HORSERADISH MAYONNAISE *(śledzie w majonezie chrzanowym)*: Prepare salt herring from scratch (see page 37), or use store-bought marinated herring. If using marinated herring out of a jar, drain and discard onions and spices. Cut 3 c herring into 1″–1½″ pieces, plunge into cold water briefly and allow to drip dry in sieve. Line serving dish with Boston lettuce and arrange herring thereon. Fork-blend ½ c mayonnaise, ¼ c sour cream, 1 heaping T prepared noncreamed horseradish (m/l to taste), 1 t mustard, juice of ½ a lemon and 1 t confectioners' sugar. Pour over herring. Chill at least 1 hr before serving. (OPTIONAL: Decorate herring with hard-cooked egg slices and sprinkle with finely chopped chives.) NOTE: Many other herring dishes suitable for Polish banquet spreads are found in the Wigilia section.

EGGS IN CAPER SAUCE *(jaja w sosie kaparowym)*: Fork-blend ½ c mayonnaise with ¼ c sour cream. Season with salt, pepper and ¼ t sugar. Add 5–6 chopped gherkins, (or 2 dill pickles), 1 heaping T drained capers and 1 t caper liquid. Place 12 shelled, hard-cooked egg halves cut-side down on lettuce-lined platter and drench with sauce. NOTE: If capers are on the large side, they may be chopped.

EGGS IN MAYONNAISE *(jaja w majonezie)*: If you don't want to fuss making a special sauce, a very easy but quite tasty embellishment to hard-cooked eggs is a dollop of store-bought mayonnaise. An eye-appealing touch of color and flavor twist can be added to this simple dish by garnishing each dollop of mayonnaise with one or more of the following: finely chopped chives and/or dill; a dusting of paprika; several capers; finely chopped dill pickle (this will approximate tartar sauce!); a thin radish slice (inserted into the mayo); half an olive, etc. NOTE: For other ways of presenting hard-cooked eggs, see Easter section.

COLD SMOKED-MEAT PLATTER *(półmisek wędlin)*: Line an elegant, large, oval or round platter with leaves of Boston lettuce. Artistically arrange thin slices of imported Polish canned ham (and/or other boiled or baked ham), Polish canned pork loin and Polish canned Canadian bacon, either in flat overlapping slices or in rolls, down the center of platter. Alternating the pink ham and Canadian bacon with the whitish loin will make for a nice color contrast. Run overlapping slices of slices of *krakowska* (sausage) down both sides and trim edge of platter with thin rounds of cooked fresh *kiełbasa,* smoked *kiełbasa* or hunter's sausage, or alternate rounds of any two or all three. Imaginatively arranged pieces of thin *kabanosy* will add variety to the platter. Decorate platter with sprigs of parsley, pickled mushrooms, gherkins, grape tomatoes, bell-pepper rings or strips (green, yellow and/or red) and/or radish roses (see next entry).

RADISH ROSES *(różyczki z rzodkiewek)*: Cut thin "petals" round the sides of each radish by making a thin slice straight down from top to bottom, taking care to leave the petal attached at bottom. Keep radishes in bowl of very cold water containing ice cubes for about 30 min. The petals should unfold, creating a rose-like effect.

COLD ROAST-MEAT PLATTER *(półmisek zimnych mięs)*: On lg lettuce-lined platter run different types of cold cooked meats in rows. This could include roast pork loin *(schab pieczony),* boiled beef tongue *(ozór wołowy gotowany),* roast veal *(pieczeń cielęca),* roast beef *(pieczeń wołowa),* larded beef roast *(sztufada),* beef tenderloin *(polędwica wołowa),* roast turkey *(indyk pieczony)* and/or smoked turkey slices. Trim platters with spiced cherries and/or plums, spiced crabapples and dill-pickle spears. NOTE: Balance your time and know-how on the one hand, and your financial means on the other. Many ready-to-serve meats are available at better delicatessens, sausage shops and other Polish or European-style outlets. If you prefer to prepare these meats from scratch, recipes are presented below or found elsewhere in this book (except smoked turkey, which is strictly a deli item).

PORK LOIN, ROAST *(schab pieczony)*: Mince and mash 2–3 cloves garlic into a paste with 1 t salt and rub into 3 lb boneless pork loin. Place in roasting pan, cover and let stand at room temp 2 hr. Remove loin, dust with flour (through sieve) and brown in hot fat on all sides to seal in juices. Place loin in roaster, fat-side up on rack and sprinkle with caraway seeds, pepper and marjoram. Roast, uncovered, at 450° for 15 min, then reduce heat to 350°. Add 1 c water to pan and baste occasionally with drippings that form. Roast about 90 min or until liquid that comes out of meat when pricked is white, not pinkish. Remove from oven and cool to room temp. Refrigerate overnight and slice cold.

BEEF TENDERLOIN, COLD *(polędwica wołowa na zimno)*: Mince and mash 2–3 cloves garlic with ½ t salt. Trim a 1½ lb beef tenderloin of surface fat and connecting tissue and rub all over with garlic paste. Heat 4 T lard or oil in heavy skillet. Through sieve dust meat on all sides with flour, shaking off excess. Brown tenderloin on all sides to form a nice crust that will seal in the juices. If you like beef rare, that is all the cooking you'll need. If you prefer it better done, simmer in covered skillet over low heat another 3–5 min. When cooled to room temp, refrigerate until ready to use. To serve, slice thin and arrange on platter. Polish plum sauce or horseradish sauce are nice accompaniments.

BEEF TONGUE, COLD, BOILED *(ozór wołowy na zimno)*: Cook a beef tongue in water covering it by 2–3 inches, add 1 T salt and cook 2 hr. Add 1 portion soup greens (see page 30), 10 peppercorns, 1 bay leaf, 2 cloves and 3 grains allspice and cook another hr or until fork-tender. Remove white skin under cold running water and set tongue aside to cool. When cooled to room temp, cover with plastic wrap and refrigerate overnight. Arrange on platter trimmed with spiced cherries and/or plums and sprigs of parsley. Each slice may be topped with a grating of fresh horseradish root on platter. NOTE: The tongue stock makes a nice base for the clear beet soup or other soups of choice.

TURKEY SLICES, COLD *(indyk na zimno)*: If you do not have the time to roast a turkey, fully cooked light- and dark-meat turkey is available at your favorite deli. Order it sliced the way you want. Smoked turkey breast is also available. Add to your cold-meat platter or serve on separate platter with an orange shell of tangy cranberry-currant sauce at center. Cold turkey is often decorated with drained compote (canned) or spiced fruits: cherries, peaches, apricots, plums and pears.

TURKEY PÂTÉ *(pasztet z indyka)*: Into bowl crumble 3 stale kaiser rolls (or equivalent amount of other white buns or bread), add 2 c milk and set aside to soak. Grind the meat from 2 cooked turkey drumsticks and thighs and an equal amount of cooked white meat together with the soaked rolls and 2 raw turkey livers at least twice. Three times is even better, because a good *pasztet* should have a smooth, creamy texture. When ground mixture stops coming out, add a stale slice of white bread to grinder to force out any remaining filling. Beat 2 eggs until creamy and work into meat mixture by hand. Continue kneading with your fingers until it is uniformly blended. Mixture should be on the soft and mushy side. If it is on the stiff side, work in a little skim milk until absorbed. If it is too soggy, work in some bread crumbs. Season to taste with salt, pepper, ¼ t ground nutmeg and a pinch of marjoram. Transfer mixture to vegetable-sprayed nonstick rectangular pan in which pâté should be no higher than 2 inches. Smooth top of mixture, cover with strips of uncooked bacon and bake in preheated 350° oven about 60 min. When cooled to room temp, cover with aluminum foil and refrigerate until ready to serve. Slice ¼″ thick and serve cold with horseradish sauce or tartar sauce.

COLD MEATS IN ASPIC *(zimne mięsa w galarecie)*: Aspic dishes have been popular in Poland since the Middle Ages and fully deserve to receive more prominence across Polish America. They keep cold meats tender and juicy and add a sparkle of elegance to any buffet or banquet table. The roast pork loin, larded beef roast, beef tongue, turkey slices and pâté can all be served in aspic (only beef tenderloin usually isn't). The degreased tongue stock (above) or other meat stock is good. Soak 4 packets unflavored gelatin in 1 c cold water. Bring 4 c stock to boil, add soaked-gelatin mixture and stir to dissolve. Add 1 T vinegar, 1 T dry white wine and ½ t Maggi. Arrange sliced cold meat in a deep platter so it will not protrude above the aspic.

Drench meat with room temp gelatin liquid and refrigerate until fully set. Meat may be decorated with hard-cooked egg slices, cooked carrot slices, several T drained canned peas and carrots, tomato wedges, spiced cherries and/or plums, etc., before being drenched with gelatin. Serve with horseradish sauce or tartar sauce.

TURKEY IN MALAGA ASPIC *(indyk w maladze)*: This simple but elegant starter is at home even at the poshest banquet. Bring 2½ c strained, degreased meat stock to boil with 2 beaten egg whites (to clarify). Strain through cloth, squeezing out liquid. Soak 2½ packets unflavored gelatin in ⅓ c water for 5 min and dissolve in hot stock. Add ½–⅔ c Malaga (wine) and season to taste with salt, pepper and juice of 1 sm lemon. When liquid has cooled somewhat, pour a little into a large, deep platter and chill until set. Arrange turkey slices on platter, interspersing them with whole grapes, orange wedges, well-drained canned fruit (sliced peaches, cherries, pears). Drench platter with remaining gelatin mixture to cover and chill until set.

HAM HORNS, STUFFED *(rożki z szynki nadziewane)*: An attractive (and economical!) way to serve sliced boiled ham is to spread each slice with a little green pea salad (below) or other vegetable salad of choice (see Easter section) and roll up into a horn (open at one end and closed at the other. Arrange ham horns with thin ends pointing towards center of a circular lettuce-lined platter, leaving enough room at center for an orange shell, which can serve as a distinctive container for horseradish sauce or other sauce. With scissors, you can cut out a zigzag design around the rim of the orange shell.

GREEN PEA SALAD *(sałatka z zielonego groszku)*: Combine 4 c well-drained canned baby peas with 3–4 chopped radishes, 2 chopped scallions, 2 chopped vinegar-type dill pickles and 1 T chopped dill. Add 4 chopped hard-cooked eggs and toss gently so as not to crush peas. Lace with sauce made by combining ¾ c mayonnaise, ¼ c sour cream, salt, pepper, sugar and lemon juice to taste. Mound on serving dish and decorate with tomato wedges.

TOMATOES, SALAD-STUFFED *(pomidory nadziewane sałatką)*: Select rather small, firm tomatoes of equal size. Cut off tops and carefully scoop out pulp, taking care not to damage walls. (NOTE: Freeze tomato pulp for future use in soup, *bigos*, stews, etc.). Fill hollowed-out tomatoes with green pea salad (see above). Tops may be replaced, or salad can protrude slightly out of tomatoes. VARIATION: Other mayonnaise-type salads may be used instead of green pea salad.

EGG SALAD *(sałatka jajeczna)*: In salad bowl combine 3 med cold, cooked potatoes, diced; 4–5 hard-cooked eggs, chopped; 4–5 scallions, finely chopped; and 1 T finely chopped parsley and/or dill. (OPTIONAL: For a gourmet twist, add 1 heaping T capers.) Toss ingredients and lace with about ¾ c mayonnaise or mustard sauce (see Easter foods). Garnish with finely chopped chives. VARIATION: For added color and crunch feel free to add some diced radishes and/or dill pickles to your egg salad. NOTE: Look for other suitable starter salads in the Wigilia and Easter sections.

MIXED-VEGETABLE/BEAN/POTATO SALADS *(sałatki jarzynowe)*: Other widely enjoyed salads suitable for the cold starter course are found in the Wigilia, and Easter sections.

SOUP COURSE

Considering the variety of dishes normally served at Polish banquets or dinner-parties, the soup course should provide a light and refreshing interlude between courses. Clear soups served in small quantities (1 c) in special twin-handled *bulionówki* (bouillon) are usually preferred. A favorite is clear red *barszcz*, generally accompanied by hot *paszteciki* (savory filled pastries) or salty pastry fingers. Broth or bouillon as well as clear mushroom soup are also appropriate. This can also be a smallish portion of one of the more elegant soups eaten with a spoon. But thick, hearty soups would not normally be served at a banquet, unless it was a theme party (old-style harvest dinner, country/peasant celebration, soup festival, etc.) highlighting a rustic, down-home motif. Tripe (*flaki*), a favorite with many, is presented among the hot starters (below).

NOTE: Suitable selections for everything from a gourmet banquet to more down-to-earth festivities are found in the Traditional Polish Soups, page 123. Also, be sure to check the soups in the extensive Wigilia and Easter sections.

HOT STARTER/FISH COURSE

This course, which was once common on the Polish banquet scene, is now encountered mainly at only the most sumptuous of feasts, often held in palatial settings. It was sometimes referred to as the fish course, because hot fish dishes traditionally preceded the main roast course, but other light, hot entrées such as mushroom, egg or even meat dishes could also be served. The hot starter is a short course, meaning that it is usually not served with potatoes, cooked vegetable and salad the way the main course is, but often only with bread and rolls plus condiments and relishes. However, sometimes certain dishes in sauces take well to a bed of rice or groats.

For a wide selection of suitable fish dishes, consult the Wigilia section. Stuffed eggs in shells is an appropriate hot entrée. *Bigos* is another possibility, although it can also be served at other times—a meal in itself at supper parties, a stick-to-the-ribs energizer during hunts, sleigh rides and other cold-weather activities or most any time. Tripe with marrow/suet dumplings could also be offered. Almost any of the main-course meat dishes could double as a hot starter if served in smaller quantities (on a salad plate) without the usual main-course side dishes. For a down-home country touch, a small plate of *pierogi* (no more than three per person) or a small *gołąbek* might be appreciated by many. Only a few hot-starter recipes are presented below, because they can be found elsewhere in this book. For an extensive collection, see *Polish Heritage Cookery.*

PERCH POLONAISE *(okoń po polsku)*: In 4 c vegetable stock cook 2 lb lake perch fillets until done (only a few min). Remove cooked fillets with slotted spoon to platter and keep warm in oven. In saucepan melt 3 T butter and switch off heat. Add 4–5 finely chopped hard-cooked eggs and toss to coat evenly with butter. Add 2–3 T finely chopped fresh dill and salt and pepper generously. Toss to blend ingredients. Sprinkle fish with lemon juice and top with hard-cooked egg topping. Serve immediately. (OPTIONAL: A finely minced onion may be sautéed in the butter before eggs are added.) NOTE: Walleye or other freshwater fillets may be substituted for the perch.

TROUT, BUTTER-FRIED *(pstrąg smażony na maśle)*: Rinse 4 dressed rainbow trout (with heads attached), pat dry, sprinkle with salt and pepper, dredge in flour and fry in ½″-deep hot oil on both sides until done to a nice golden brown. Meanwhile, in 2 T butter, sauté 8 oz fresh, washed, drained, sliced mushrooms until fully cooked. Turn trout onto lettuce-lined platter, garnish with mushrooms, placing some into cavities, decorate with lemon slices and parsley sprigs and serve.

EGGS STUFFED IN SHELLS, HOT *(jaja faszerowane w skorupkach)*: This tasty egg entrée is always a big hit and is well worth the effort. With a little practice, its preparation is a snap. Start with 8–10 cold, hard-cooked eggs. Hold egg against cutting-board and tap it lengthwise with a sharp, thin-bladed, preferably heavy, nonserrated-edge knife. With swift cutting motion cut through to cutting-board, shell and all. With small spoon gently scoop out yolk and white and set aside, taking care not to break the shell. Carefully remove and discard any loose, jagged shell fragments that adhere to eggs or rim of shells. Set shells aside. Simmer 2 finely minced onions in 2 T butter until tender and golden. Grind or chop eggs fine and combine with onion. Add 1–2 heaping T finely chopped fresh dill (now available year-round in the produce department of better supermarkets), 1 heaping T finely chopped chives, and salt and pepper to taste. Mix ingredients well. (OPTIONAL: For a softer filling, work in 1 T sour cream.) Fill shells with mixture pressing it down very gently so as not to damage them. Sprinkle tops generously with bread crumbs, pressing them in gently. These can be refrigerated overnight until ready to serve. To serve, fry stuffed eggs, open-side down, in 2 T butter or margarine until a golden crust forms on the bottom and top of shells are hot to the touch. Serve at once with bread and marinated vegetables.

MUSHROOMS, PAN-FRIED *(grzyby/pieczarki z patelni)*: Fresh milky-cap mushrooms *(rydze)* are the best for pan-frying in butter, but they may be difficult to find, so champignons (the white store-bought variety) may have to do. Wipe 1¼ lb mushrooms with damp cloth or wash under running water, dry well and trim off any hardened stem ends. NOTE: For a truly elegant dish use only the caps and reserve the stems for other uses (soups, sauces, drying). Brown the mushrooms caps on both sides in 2 T hot butter, add 2 more T butter, sprinkle with salt and freshly ground pepper and simmer a bit longer. Turn out onto platter and sprinkle with pan drippings. Decorate platter with parsley sprigs and grape tomatoes and serve with Polish rye and/or French, Italian or Vienna (white) bread. NOTE: Portobello mushrooms are superb!

MUSHROOMS, CREAMED *(grzyby w śmietanie)*: See Vegetable, Pasta, and Grain Dishes for recipe, page 50.

TRIPE *(flaki, flaczki)*: This is a traditional Polish favorite, esp. at Mardi Gras functions, weddings and other such festivities, including outdoor fests and picnics. Although technically a soup, this thick, hearty pottage may be served as a hot appetizer, hence its inclusion in this section. Since raw beef tripe requires up to 4 hr of cooking to become tender, a better alternative may be the fully cooked tripe sold at meat markets and delis. Cut 2½ lb cooked tripe into thin strips 2″–3″ long. Scald with boiling water to cover and cook 10 min, then drain. Combine tripe with 6¾ c beef stock and a portion of soup greens (see page 30), sliced into matchsticks and cook on med until vegetables are tender. Dissolve 3 T flour in 1 c of slightly cooled stock and return to pot, simmer briefly. Season to taste with salt, pepper, marjoram, ginger, paprika and several gratings of nutmeg. Many people like their *flaczki* on the spicy side, so provide some Tabasco, similar red-pepper sauce or cayenne pepper on the side. For Warsaw-style tripe, serve grated yellow cheese on the side for sprinkling over the soup. Serve with good rye bread and/or suet dumplings (see below) with ice-cold vodka on the side. NOTE: When short of time, consider heat and serve tripe available at Polish delis. "Flaki Zamojskie" (Zamość tripe), imported from Poland in jars, only requires reheating and is quite tasty as is. Freeze-dried Polish-style *flaki* are also marketed as a "cup of" type product (add boiling water to carton, stir and eat), but these are barely passable.

SUET or MARROW DUMPLINGS *(pulpety z łoju lub szpiku)*: This is the classic accompaniment for Polish-style tripe. These dumplings may be made with beef suet and/or marrow. First set a pot of lightly salted water on to boil. Trim away any veins or membranes from about ½ lb beef suet and/or marrow and grind fine. Mix well with 2 eggs and, when mixture is smooth, gradually stir in ⅔–1 c plain bread crumbs and 1 T finely chopped fresh parsley. Salt and pepper and mix well. Pinch off cherry- or walnut-sized pieces and roll between floured palms into oblong dumplings. Cook in boiling water about 5 min. Remove with slotted spoon and serve with tripe soup.

TRIPE, CHICKEN-STYLE *(flaczki z drobiu)*: This recipe has been created for those who either: 1) cannot easily obtain real tripe, 2) may feel squeamish about eating cow stomachs, or a combination of both. Simply boil a chicken until tender, remove from bone and cut into 1½″-long matchsticks. Cut soup vegetables into matchsticks as above and cook in chicken stock. When tender, add chicken and season as above.

BIGOS, MEAT AND SAUERKRAUT RAGOUT *(bigos)*: This is one of several recipes found in this book for that classic of Old Polish cookery, *bigos*—a savory ragout containing meat, sausage, sauerkraut, cabbage, prunes, apples and many other ingredients and seasonings. In English it is often referred to as hunter's stew. Since many steps are involved, the procedure will be taken point by point.

1. Rehydrate 2–4 oz dried boletes, dice or slice into strips and set aside.
2. In roaster combine 1–2 lb beef rump roast, 1–2 lb pork shoulder roast, 2 turkey drumsticks and thighs, 1 duck, 3 onions, 1 bay leaf and 3 grains allspice. Sprinkle with salt, pepper, marjoram and caraway seeds, add 2 c water and bake in 350° oven 90–120 min, or until meat comes away from bone easily. Turn meat over during baking and replace liquid that evaporates. Set aside to cool.
3. When meat is cool enough to handle, remove from bones and dice into cubes of roughly equal size.

4. In open pan containing 2 c water, bake 1 lb fresh *kiełbasa* in 350° oven 60 min.
5. Place cut meat into container to measure and use the same amount of sauerkraut which should be prepared the usual way (see Basic Ingredients and Procedures).
6. Shred 1 sm head cabbage, scald with plenty of boiling water to cover by 2″ and cook 20 min from the time boiling resumes. Drain.
7. In baking pan or pot combine the meat, sauerkraut, mushrooms, cabbage, baked fresh *kiełbasa*, sliced into rounds, and 1 lb sliced smoked *kiełbasa*, skinned.
8. Toss ingredients to mix and bake 2 hr at 325°, stirring occasionally to bring bottom ingredients to top and vice-versa. Note: *Bigos* may also be simmered on low heat in a lg stovetop pot, but must be stirred frequently to ensure even cooking and prevent burning. A scorched pot bottom often imparts a bitter taste to the entire batch of *bigos*.
9. Add ½–1 c diced, pitted prunes, 2 apples, peeled and diced, 3–4 T tomato paste, and ½ c dry red wine or 1 c dark beer (Polish porter, Guinness stout, bock, etc.). Cook another hr or so.
10. Leave in oven or on stovetop until cooled to room temp and refrigerate overnight.
11. Next day, reheat, adding some water if *bigos* is not moist enough. If it is too soupy, some liquid may be poured off and 2 T flour m/l can be stirred in. Season if required with salt, pepper and marjoram. Simmer at least another hr before serving.

Note: *Bigos* improves in flavor with each reheating and bigos-lovers insist that the tastiest are the last scrapings from the bottom of the pan days after it first cooked.

POLISH HOLIDAY/BANQUET/ DINNER-PARTY ENTRÉES

The term entrée has traditionally meant the hot course served before the roast, however in American usage it usually now means the main course. In the following section, it is being used the American way to mean a meal's principal hot course.

The main, hot course at traditional Polish sit-down dinners and banquets was called *pieczyste* (the roast course). It was preceded by cold starters, soup and at sumptuous, festive meals—possibly also a hot starter course, sometimes referred to as the fish course. Below you will find a selection of typically Polish hot meat courses suitable for everything from post-Wigilia Christmas/New Year's entertaining and gourmet banquets to nameday or birthday parties, Sunday dinner at the in-laws', First Holy Communion parties and family-style weddings.

Clear red *barszcz* with *paszteciki* or salty pastries is suitable at most any such get-together. Check Traditional Polish Soups for other suggestions, including cold *barszcz (chłodnik)* for hot-weather entertaining and creamed mushroom soup in autumn. A hearty homemade broth with egg noodles is not only a great warmer-upper during the colder months but is the all-time favorite for most homier, family-centered occasions.

This section presents some of the most typically Polish ways of preparing chicken, duck, turkey, goose, beef, pork, veal and game. The typical party would feature one such hot dish, but more sumptuous affairs might set out two or more. For hot fish dishes, see the Wigilia section entitled Fish Entrées, page 46.

ROAST TURKEY POLONAISE *(indyk po polsku)*: Wash and pat dry an 8–12 lb turkey. Rub inside and out with salt and let stand at room temp, covered, 2 hr. Crumble 12–15 slices stale French bread (or equivalent amount of *chałka*, kaiser rolls, buns, etc.) into bowl and drench with 2 c milk. Mix and let soak. When soggy, grind with raw turkey liver and 5–6 raw chicken livers. Add 4 egg yolks, beaten until creamy with 4 T soft butter and 1 T sugar; 1 c drained, presoaked raisins; 1 c ground blanched almonds; and 3–4 T chopped parsley. Season with salt and pepper, ¼ t grated nutmeg and 2 pinches or so ground cloves. Mix well. Gently fold in 4 beaten egg whites and toss very gently. Mixture should be moist and soggy, as it firms up during roasting. If it is very wet, add ¼–½ c bread crumbs. Fill cavity loosely and sew bird up. (NOTE: This quantity is about right for a 10-lb turkey, so adjust the amount to the size of your bird.) Tuck ends of drumsticks under skin flaps and place in roaster. Rub all over with butter and place thin wide strips of salt pork on breast and drumsticks. (VARIATION: Rub turkey all over with salad oil instead of using butter and salt pork.) Roast, uncovered, in 450° oven 20 min to sear, then reduce heat to 350°. Drench turkey with 2 c boiling water and baste frequently with pan drippings. Roast 20–25 min per lb. When done, remove from oven and let stand at least 15 min before carving. NOTE: The pan drippings make an excellent gravy: combine with equal amount of water and stir in 2 T flour per c liquid. Heat to boiling, beating with whisk and season with about 1 t Maggi and several twists of the peppermill. Serve turkey with mashed potatoes and lingonberry-apple sauce, cranberry-pear sauce or similar.

TURKEY SLICES IN GRAVY *(indyk w sosie)*: You can whip up this simple but elegant dish in no time if you have leftover sliced turkey in your freezer. You can also get ready-to-eat roast turkey at your deli. In pot combine 1 can condensed cream of mushroom soup, 1 c sour cream and 1 mushroom bouillon cube dissolved in 1 c boiling water. Heat, stirring frequently, until you get a smooth sauce. Season with several twists of the peppermill. Add a little boiling water if it is too thick. Reheat the turkey slices in gravy until heated through. Serve with egg noodles, rice or mashed potatoes and a vinaigrette-laced cucumber salad.

GOOSE, BRAISED WITH APPLES AND PRUNES *(gęś duszona z owocami)*: Wash a cut-up 6–7 lb goose and rub all over with salt, pepper and marjoram. Wrap in foil and refrigerate overnight. Next day, place goose in Dutch oven, scald with boiling water, bring to boil, reduce heat and simmer, covered, 1 hr. Pour off water. Add fresh boiling water reaching ½ way up the goose, cover, and cook on low heat about 60 min. Turn goose over, add 12 oz pitted prunes, 2 peeled, cored, diced apples, 2 chopped onions and 2 cloves crushed garlic, cover and cook on low heat until meat is tender. Sprinkle with a little ginger and ground cloves before serving. Pan liquid may be thickened with a little flour and simmered (several min) to get a nice gravy. Serve with mashed potatoes and a salad. NOTE: A heaping T raisins and/or mixed dried fruits may be added with prunes and apples. VARIATION: Instead of braising a cut-up goose, a whole bird can be stuffed with rice, apples and prunes and roasted (see next recipe).

ROAST GOOSE WITH RICE STUFFING *(gęś nadziewana ryżem)*: Cut off wings and rump from 6–10 lb goose and freeze together with neck for *czernina* (goose and/or duck soup). Rub bird inside and out with 2 cloves crushed garlic, salt, pepper and marjoram, place on rack in roasting pan, cover and let stand at room temp 2 hr or overnight in fridge. Next day, combined 4 c slightly undercooked rice; ½ c presoaked pitted prunes, diced; ¼ c presoaked dark raisins; and 3 peeled, cored cooking apples, cubed. Sprinkle mixture with salt, pepper, marjoram and a little chopped fresh parsley and fill goose cavity. Prepare m/l depending on size of goose, whose cavity should be loosely filled. Sew up neck and tail opening and tie legs together with string across tail end. Roast, uncovered, in preheated 450° oven 20 min, then reduce heat to 375° and roast from 2½ to 4 hr or until fork-tender. During roasting prick with fork here and there to let out excess fat and baste bird with drippings. If top browns too quickly, cover with foil. Whole peeled potatoes may be added to roaster during last 30 min to cook in drippings. A typical accompaniment is braised red cabbage. VARIATIONS: Goose may be stuffed with peeled, cored apple halves, apple halves and pitted prunes, buckwheat groats or other poultry stuffings given for turkey and chicken. In addition to winter entertaining, goose is traditionally served on St. Martin's Day (November 11).

ROAST DUCK WITH APPLES *(kaczka pieczona z jabłkami)*: Wash a 4–5 lb duck and pat dry. Rub inside and out with salt, pepper, marjoram and (optional) 1 clove crushed garlic. Let stand at room temp 2 hr, in covered roasting pan. Stuff tightly with unpeeled, cored quarters of tart cooking apples. Cut off protruding fat at neck end and sew up neck and tail openings. Place duck on rack in roasting pan and roast in preheated 450°oven 10–15 min, turning over to sear on all sides. Reduce to 350°, sprinkle with 2 T water, prick with fork to release fat and roast 1½–2 hr or until fork-tender. Baste with pan drippings frequently. To get a crisp skin, briefly turn heat up to 450° towards the end of roasting. Since the apple stuffing shrinks considerably, prepare additional apples on the side. Place 2–3 additional peeled apple quarters in pan, drench with several T duck pan drippings, sprinkle with marjoram and bake in same oven the last 45 min. Mix separately cooked apples with those with which the duck was stuffed and serve in serving dish. If making up portions, dish out a heaping spoonful of hot apple mixture on each dinner plate and place a portion of roast duck on top. VARIATION: Mix about ¾ c whole-style canned cranberry sauce (or orange-flavored cranberry sauce) into the apple quarters with which the duck is stuffed.

ROAST DUCK WITH PRUNES *(kaczka pieczona ze śliwkami)*: This is a take-off on the above recipe that combines apples and prunes, both of which beautifully complement roast duck. Preheat oven to 475°. Rub a well-rinsed, dried 4–5 lb duck with salt, pepper, marjoram and 2 cloves mashed garlic. Place in covered roasting pan and let stand at room temp 1 hr. Fill cavity with peeled apple halves or quarters tightly (unlike bread stuffing which expands, apples shrink during roasting) and sew up. Return to pan and pop into oven. After 15 min reduce heat to 350°. Sprinkle duck with about ½ c water and then baste occasionally with pan drippings. After 1 hr, add 1 c pitted prunes to drippings and bake another 45–60 min or until fork-tender. Serve with mashed or boiled potatoes or rice, garnishing them with the cooked prunes.

APPLES WITH LINGONBERRIES, BAKED *(jabłka pieczone z borówkami)*: Either of the above roast duck recipes can also be served with a baked apple on the side. Remove core from 6 large cooking apples. Fill opening with lingonberry jam (or whole-style canned cranberry sauce). Place in pan in water 1½″ deep and bake in 350° oven 30–40 min or until done.

Serve with roast duck, allowing 1 apple per person. It can also accompany other roast poultry.

ROAST STUFFED CHICKEN, POLONAISE *(kurczę pieczone po polsku)*: Soak 2 broken-up stale bread rolls (kaiser, hamburger, French bread, etc.) in milk to cover until soggy. Process or grind together with 3 raw chicken livers. Combine mixture with ¼ lb raw ground veal, 1–2 eggs, 1–2 T soft butter or margarine. Work well by hand until fully blended. Season with salt, pepper, a dash of nutmeg, 1 heaping T finely chopped fresh dill and (optional) 1 t finely chopped parsley. Mix well. Rinse well 2½–3 lb broiler and pat dry. Rub inside and out with salt and stuff just before roasting. (NOTE: For fluffier stuffing, add the beaten yolks first and then fold in the stiffly beaten whites.) The exact amount of stuffing depends on the size of your bird. The general rule of thumb is to allow about ¾ c stuffing per lb of chicken. Sew up, tying legs together. Rub chicken all over with a little oil, sprinkle with pepper and paprika and rub in. Bake in preheated 375° oven 75–90 min. Baste occasionally with pan drippings. Serve with *mizeria* and new potatoes.

ROAST CHICKEN WITH BABKA-RAISIN STUFFING *(kurczę nadziewane babką)*: This is a tasty way to use up leftover *babka, chałka* or plain coffee cakes, or holiday egg breads. Wash and pat dry a 3–4 lb broiler or roaster (chicken). Rub inside and out with salt and pepper and let stand, covered, at room temp 1 hr. Meanwhile, in bowl place 2–3 c crumbled stale yeast-raised egg-bread or coffee cake (without icing, fruit filling, cheese, etc.). (NOTE: The exact amount depends on the size of your fowl, but the general rule of thumb is to allow ¾ c stuffing per lb of chicken.) Drench with 1 to 1½ c milk. When soggy, add 2 lightly beaten raw egg yolks, ⅓ c raisins (rinsed and drained), 2 T soft butter and mix well with hand. Mixture should be moist and soggy, but if it appears too wet, stir in 1 T or so bread crumbs. Season with salt and pepper to taste and several gratings of nutmeg. Fill chicken with dressing, sew up openings and fasten wings and legs close to body with skewers or by tying. Rub all over with 2 T butter or oil, place on rack in roasting pan and sear in 450° oven 15 min. Add 1 c boiling water to pan, reduce heat to 350° and bake about 2 hr or until tender, basting occasionally (every 10–15 min) with pan drippings. Serve with potatoes cooked in pan drippings during last 30 min of roasting and a crispy green salad. Lingonberry or cranberry sauce is always a good accompaniment for poultry.

OTHER POULTRY STUFFINGS *(inne farsze do drobiu)*: Any of the above poultry as well as other birds not listed (guinea fowl, pheasant, etc.) can also be stuffed with other fillings. As a general rule of thumb, about 3 c bread or grain stuffing is enough to stuff a 4 lb chicken, leaving room for it to expand during roasting. Adjust the proportions to the size of your bird. But apple stuffings shrink (if they do not contain bread), so you need not leave any space and can snugly fill cavity with as much as will fit. NOTE: These stuffings are suitable for other things such as filled dumplings, savory pastries and pies (like *kulebiak*), *gołąbki*, etc.

Rice and Mushroom Stuffing *(farsz ryżowy z pieczarkami)*: Coarsely dice 8–12 oz fresh, washed, drained mushrooms and sauté in 2–3 T butter with 1 chopped onion until cooked, stirring frequently until pan liquid evaporates. Mix with 3 c cooked, slightly underdone rice, add 1–2 T chopped parsley and/or dill, and salt and pepper to taste. (OPTIONAL: For a stuffing that holds together better, stir in 1 whole egg.) Good for stuffing chicken or turkey as well as duck, goose and game birds.

Rice and Egg Stuffing *(farsz ryżowy z jajkami)*: Sauté 2 chopped onions in 3 T butter until soft and golden and combine with 3 c slightly undercooked rice, 3–4 chopped hard-cooked eggs. Add 2–3 T chopped fresh dill, and salt and pepper generously. For a firmer stuffing, stir in 1 raw egg. This stuffing is ideal for roast chicken but can be put to other uses as well. Next to classic dill-flavored bread and liver stuffing for chicken polonaise, this is one of the author's favorites.

Buckwheat-Mushroom Stuffing *(farsz gryczany z grzybami)*: Rehydrate ½ oz dried mushrooms and cook until tender, cooking to reduce liquid. Set aside. In small amt of water cook the bird's heart and gizzard (cleaned and trimmed of veins) until tender. To what little liquid remains add coarsely chopped bird liver and 2 t butter, bring to boil and cook 1 min. Coarsely grind mushrooms and giblets and combine with 3 c slightly undercooked buckwheat groats. Add 1 T chopped fresh dill, and salt and pepper to taste. (NOTE: Any remaining liquid from the mushrooms and giblets can be added to the gravy.) This stuffing is traditionally used to fill geese and suckling pigs, but there's no reason why it couldn't be used for roast chicken, duck or turkey. NOTE: Feel free to used cooked barley or fine-milled Kraków buckwheat (*kasza krakowska*) in any of the stuffings calling for rice or regular buckwheat groats.

CHICKEN-BREAST CUTLETS *(kotlety z piersi kurczaka)*: Pound 4 skinned and halved chicken breasts to between ⅛″ and ¼″ thick. Sprinkle with salt, pepper and (optional) hunter's seasoning, dredge in flour, dip in egg wash and roll in bread crumbs, shaking off excess. Fry in several T hot butter to a nice golden brown (several min per side), drain on absorbent paper and serve immediately. Dress portions with parsley sprigs and lemon wedges. Serve with rice or potatoes and *mizeria* or lettuce. NOTE: Around the turn of the century, chicken-breast cutlets, regarded by some as a healthier alternative to the traditional *schabowy* (breaded pork cutlet), were gaining in popularity on both sides of the Atlantic.

CHICKEN-BREAST CUTLETS IN WALNUT BREADING *(kotlety z piersi kurczaka w orzechowej panierce)*: Pound 4 skinned and halved chicken breasts to between ⅛″ and ¼″ thick. Sprinkle with salt and pepper. Mix 3 beaten whites with 4 T potato flour, dip cutlets in mixture and roll in about 1 c ground walnuts. Fry in butter as above. NOTE: You can also roll cutlets in ½ c ground walnuts mixed with ½ c bread crumbs.

CHICKEN KYIV/KIEV* *(kotlet de volaille)*: Pound 4 skinned, halved chicken breasts until ¼″ thin. Sprinkle cutlets with salt and pepper, chopped fresh dill and/or parsley. Cut a ¼ lb stick of cold butter in half and cut each half into 4 sticks. Place a small stick of butter at the end of each cutlet and roll up, tucking in sides. Refrigerate at least 1 hr. Bread cutlets in flour, egg wash and bread crumbs and brown on all sides in plenty of hot butter. Reduce heat and cook another 4–6 min to a nice golden brown. Do not overcook. If properly done, the melted butter will flow out the minute someone cuts into their cutlet.

CHICKEN ESCALOPES/ESCALOPES DE VOLAILLE *(eskalopki z kurczaka)*: This is an elegant take-off on chicken-breast cutlets. Cut each chicken-breast half into 3–4 pieces, pound thin and shape edges with flat of knife blade into scallop-shell-shaped cutlets (or ovals). Bread in regular or walnut breading and proceed as above. Allow 3–4 escalopes (the equivalent of 1 chicken-breast cutlet) per serving.

CHICKEN TENDERS, BREADED *(panierowane polędwiczki z drobiu)*: Lightly pound 1 lb chicken tenders (the juicy tenderloin-like strips of meat found in chicken breasts of which there are 2 per chicken), salt and pepper, dredge in flour, dip in egg wash and roll in bread crumbs. (OPTIONAL: Before rolling in crumbs, sprinkle each tender with a pinch of finely chopped fresh dill.) Fry in hot oil on both sides to a nice golden brown—this will take only a min or so. Allow 3–4 tenders per serving. VARIATION: Prepare chicken tenders in walnut breading as above.

PORK CUTLETS, BREADED *(kotlety schabowe)*: By rights this homey favorite belongs among the family-style dishes, but since it is probably Poland's single most popular main course, I have decided to include it among the banquet and dinner-party entrées. Cut bones away 6 center-cut pork chops

---

*Since the former Polish city of Kijów is now the capital of free Ukraine, its Ukrainian spelling has been listed ahead of its Russified version. The French-loving Poles have avoided the problem entirely by using the French term: *de volaille*.

or slice boneless center-cut pork loin 1″ thick and pound with meat mallet pound on both sides until ¼″–⅓″thick. Sprinkle with salt, pepper and a pinch of marjoram and/or garlic powder if desired. Dredge in flour, dip in egg wash and roll in fine, plain bread crumbs. Gently press breading into cutlets so it stays put during frying. Fry to a nice golden brown on both sides in hot lard, vegetable shortening or oil, drain on paper towel and serve immediately. OPTIONAL: For those who like their cutlets tender and juicy, place fried cutlets in baking pan, add 2–3 T pan drippings, cover tightly and let simmer in 350° oven 20–30 min. For super-tender cutlets, place on rack in pan, add 1 c boiling water, cover with foil and keep in 325° oven 1 hr. Serve with boiled, dilled or mashed potatoes and braised cabbage or sauerkraut. (Not apple sauce!)

ROAST PORK LOIN WITH PRUNES *(schab pieczony ze śliwkami)*: Rub a 4–5 lb pork loin with salt, pepper, marjoram and 1–2 cloves crushed garlic, place in roaster, smother meat with 2 sliced onions, cover and let stand at room temp 1 hr. Remove loin, pat dry, sprinkle with flour and brown on all sides in hot oil or lard to seal in juices. Return to roaster. Brown onions in the pan drippings and return to roaster. Add 1 c water and bake in 375° oven 1 hr. Meanwhile, soak 2 c unpitted prunes in water to cover 20 min, drain and add to roaster. Bake another 90 min or until tender but not overcooked. Cut the loin in half to make sure it is no longer pink inside. Serve with rice (for an Old Polish touch, make it saffron rice!) and a green salad or (during autumn and winter) a grated carrot, apple, horseradish salad.

ROAST PORK WITH PRUNES *(pieczeń wieprzowa ze śliwkami)*: This is a more economical version, since pork shoulder costs less than pork loin. Rub a 4–5 lb tied, rolled, boneless pork shoulder roast all over with salt, pepper, marjoram and 1–2 cloves crushed garlic. Place on rack in roasting pan and roast in 325° oven about 25 min per pound, basting occasionally. To drippings in pan add 3 quartered onions and 1–2 c unpitted prunes, and baste meat with ½ c dark beer. Bake until meat is fork-tender. Serve with rice, mashed or boiled potatoes and a crispy green salad.

PORK TENDERLOIN STUFFED WITH PRUNES *(polędwiczki wieprzowe nadziewane śliwkami)*: Split pork tenderloin lengthwise without cutting through. Spread meat out on board butterfly fashion and pound thicker places with mallet to even them out. Sprinkle with salt, pepper, garlic powder and marjoram, spread surface with 1 c or so whole or chopped pitted prunes, roll meat up and fasten with skewers or tie with string. Dust with flour, shake off excess and brown on all sides in hot lard or oil. Place on rack in open roasting pan, add 2 c water to pan and bake in 350° oven 80 min or until tender, basting occasionally. Let stand several min before removing skewers or string and slicing. Combine pan drippings with enough water to make 3 c. Add 1 crushed beef bouillon cube, 1 T white dry wine and 2 t cider vinegar and bring to boil. Thicken with a little flour and simmer briefly. Season with salt, pepper and marjoram if necessary. Serve with rice or buckwheat groats *(kasza gryczana)* or rice and a crispy salad.

BEEF TENDERLOIN STEAK *(befsztyk z polędwicy)*: Trim 2¼ lb washed, dried beef tenderloin of any membranes and sinews. Sprinkle with salt and pepper, dust with flour and brown on all sides in 3–4 T hot oil until a nice crust forms. Remove from skillet, cool to room temp, wrap in plastic wrap and refrigerate until ready to use (several hr or overnight). When ready to serve, slice into 1″–1½″ rounds and fry in very hot fat on one side until crusty, then turn over, reduce heat and fry on other side, covered, to desired doneness (from 1 min for rare to several min for well-done). Serve at once with dilled new potatoes in summer and puréed potatoes at other times, lettuce salad and vegetables Polonaise.

BEEF TENDERLOIN STEAKS *(befsztyki z polędwicy)*: Trim 2¼ lb beef tenderloin as above, but cut into 1½″ steaks. Flatten with palm of hand but do not beat with mallet, and even out edges with flat of knife into nice rounds or ovals. Sprinkle with pepper but do not salt (as this can make the meat tough!) and cook in 3–4 T hot fat several min on each side to desired degree of doneness. When frying is nearing completion, sprinkle steaks with salt and place a small ball of horseradish butter (see below) at the center of each steak. It should melt partially but still be visible when served. Serve with potato balls and a crispy green salad. VARIATION: Tenderloin steaks may be brushed with oil and charcoal grilled to desired doneness

HORSERADISH BUTTER *(masło chrzanowe)*: Fork-blend ½ c soft butter with 1 T freshly grated horseradish (or 2 T well-drained, prepared horseradish). Chill in fridge. When needed, use melon scoop to scoop out balls of horseradish butter. NOTE: For other flavored butters, substitute 1–2 T chopped dill, parsley or chives (or a combination of any 2 or all 3) or 2 T prepared mustard for the horseradish.

BEEF ROAST, LARDED *(sztufada)*: Shred 1 portion soup greens (see page 30) plus 2 onions in processor. Mix with ½ c cider or wine vinegar, ½ c dry red or white wine, 4 T oil, 1 crushed bay leaf, 1 t freshly milled black pepper and 3 bruised or crushed grains allspice. Place 4 lb rolled beef rump in glass or earthenware container and smother all over with vegetable mixture. Cover and refrigerate 24 hr. Remove meat, dry and lard with 3″ lardoons (see Basic Ingredients and Procedures, page 25) sprinkled with pepper and paprika (also salt if unsalted fatback is used for larding). Dust with flour and sear on all sides in hot fat. Place roast in roasting pan, smother with vegetable mixture, add 1 c water and bake, covered, at 325° for 2 hr or until fork-tender. When cooled to room temp, refrigerate, as it slices best when cold. When ready to serve, reheat. For a nice gravy, sieve the hot vegetables and drippings, add enough water to get a pourable sauce, bring to boil, salt and pepper to taste. On platter, drench the hot sliced roast with the gravy. NOTE: This roast can be chilled, sliced when cold and served as a cold starter.

BEEF ROAST, HUSSAR-STYLE *(pieczeń wołowa po huzarsku)*: Wash and beat 2½ lb beef round tip or boneless rump roast. Sprinkle with salt, dust all over with flour and brown on all sides in hot fat to form a crust. Transfer to roaster, add the browning fat, ½ c water, cover and bake in 325° oven 1½ to 2 hr or until nearly done. Meanwhile prepare filling: combine ½ lb onions, grated, with 1 c bread crumbs (rye bread crumbs are esp. good in this dish) and ¼ c butter, and salt and pepper generously to taste. Transfer roast to cutting board, and cut ¾ of the way down at 1½″ intervals. Fill the openings with onion-bread stuffing, press roast back together tightly, fasten with skewers, return to roaster and bake another 30 min or so. Let stand, covered, 15 min or so after removing from oven. Slice roast so that each portion contains a layer of filling enclosed by meat. VARIATIONS: Instead of onion-bread stuffing, fry 6 oz finely chopped fresh mushrooms in 3 T butter with 1 chopped onion, stir in 1 heaping T bread crumbs and 1 T chopped parsley, season with salt and pepper. Serve with potatoes of choice and braised sauerkraut, white cabbage or red cabbage. A grated vegetable salad is also a good accompaniment.

BEEF ROAST, PLAIN-COOKED *(pieczeń wołowa naturalna)*: This is a good way to cook roast beef that can later be warmed up for serving with any of the sauces given in the Hot Sauces and Culinary Polonizers section, page 189. Wipe 4–5 lb solid or rolled beef roast with absorbent paper, sprinkle with salt, pepper and flour, place fat-side up (if fat is visible) in roaster and pop into 500° oven to sear. After 20 min reduce temp to 300° and bake 25–30 min per lb, basting occasionally. When tender, let stand 15 min before slicing. Serve with gravy of choice. NOTE: Pan drippings may be combined with any of the gravies in Hot Sauces and Culinary Polonizers.

ROAST BEEF, BRAISED *(pieczeń wołowa duszona)*: Sprinkle washed, dried 4–5 lb beef roast with salt and pepper, dust with flour and brown in hot fat on all sides. Transfer to Dutch oven, add boiling water to half-cover meat, cover tightly and simmer about 4 hr. Turn meat over several times. Use drippings as gravy base. NOTE: For pot roast (*pieczeń wołowa duszona z jarzynami*), during last 45 min add several diced carrots, 1 small celeriac, sliced, several sliced parsnips and/or turnips and 6–8 whole small onions. Serve with mashed potatoes or groats.

VEAL ROAST *(pieczeń cielęca)*: Slice 2 cloves garlic into 6–8 vertical slivers. In a 2½ to 3 lb veal leg, rump, loin or boneless shoulder roast, make as many incisions as you have slivers of garlic. Sprinkle meat with salt, pepper and paprika and rub seasonings into all surfaces of roast. Sear the meat all over in hot fat until a brown crust forms on the outside and place in uncovered roasting pan on rack in a preheated 350° oven. Place several thin rashers of pork fatback on meat, add 1½ c water to roaster and roast about 2 hr or until done. Cool to room temp and refrigerate overnight. To serve, slice cold roast about ¼″ thick and reheat in pan drippings. Use pan drippings to make a sauce, including any of those in the Hot Sauces and Culinary Polonizers section, page 189. Serve with potatoes or rice, peas or spinach and a sour cream-laced salad. NOTE: Sliced, cold veal roast is a delicious cold meat for your starter course.

VEAL ROAST, HUNTER'S STYLE *(pieczeń cielęca na dziko)*: Rub a 3-lb veal leg roast all over with 1 t crushed or coarsely ground juniper. In saucepan combine ⅔ c vinegar, ⅔ c water, several cloves (2–3 each), peppercorns and grains allspice, and 1 large sliced onion. Bring to boil and simmer, covered, on low heat 10 min. Scald meat with marinade, cover and refrigerate 2 days. Rinse, salt, lard with ¼ lb (preferably frozen) seasoned lardoons (see page 25). Roast 45 min in 450° oven, basting with butter and pan drippings that form, then reduce heat to 375° and cook another 75 min or until done. Cool to room temp, refrigerate and slice when cold. Heat and strain pan drippings and combine with 1 c sour cream fork-blended with 1 heaping t flour. Simmer until bubbly, salt and pepper to taste and reheat sliced veal roast in gravy. Serve with mashed potatoes or pasta, peas and carrots and a green vinaigrette salad. NOTE: Beef roast can be prepared the same way.

VEAL CUTLET, BREADED *(sznycle cielęce)*: Pound 2½ lb boneless veal cutlets (or veal round steak cut into portion-size pieces) to a thickness of ¼″. With flat of knife shape each into an oval cutlet. Salt and pepper, bread in flour, egg wash and bread crumbs, and fry in hot fat until golden on both sides. Reduce heat, add 1½ T butter and cook until done on low heat. Serve with mashed potatoes garnished with chopped chives, peas and lettuce salad. NOTE: The Poles erroneously call breaded veal cutlets served with a fried egg on top "*po wiedeńsku*" (Viennese-style)—something the people of Vienna have never practiced. That's actually a German way of serving these, but it's a very tasty way indeed, especially suited to down-home, family-style dinners.

VEAL MEATBALLS IN SOUR-CREAM SAUCE *(klopsiki cielęce w śmietanie)*: Soak 1 stale, broken-up bread roll (about 1½ oz) in 1 c milk until soggy. Run through meat grinder. Mix with 1¼ lb ground veal, add 1 egg and work by hand until well blended and smooth. Salt and pepper to taste and (optional) add 1 t–1 T chopped fresh dill. Roll into walnut-sized balls, dredge in flour and lightly brown on all sides in 3 T butter. Whisk together 1½ c meat stock, ¾ c sour cream and 1 t or more flour until smooth and drench meatballs with mixture. Cover and simmer on low 30 min. Season sauce to taste with salt, pepper and lemon juice. Serve with mashed potatoes, rice or noodles and a noncreamed salad. VARIATION: Instead of meat stock, make sauce with 1 mushroom bouillon cube dissolved in 2 c water, ½–⅔ c sour cream and 1 T flour.

TURKEY MEATBALLS IN SOUR-CREAM SAUCE *(klopsiki indycze w śmietanie)*: Substitute ground turkey (white or dark meat or some of each) for the ground veal in the preceding recipes and proceed as above. Just before serving garnish sauce with a little chopped fresh parsley and dill. Bilberry or cranberry sauce makes a nice accompaniment.

HARE POLONAISE, IN SOUR CREAM *(zając po polsku w śmietanie)*: Wash and pat dry 1 dressed hare or jack rabbit (esp. the saddle and hind legs), place in crockery container and drench with buttermilk (about 1 qt) to cover. Cover and keep in cool place 1–2 days. Discard buttermilk, rinse and wipe hare, rub in 5–6 ground juniper berries and some ground pepper and lard with ¼ lb frozen fatback sticks. Return hare to washed crockery container, smother with 2 onions, 1 carrot and 1 parsley root—all sliced—cover and keep in cool place or refrigerate several hr or overnight. Discard vegetables, place hare in baking pan, sprinkle with salt, dot all over with butter (about ¼ c) and add 1 broken-up, washed, uncooked dried mushroom. Bake at 400° 90 min, basting frequently with pan drippings, and adding a little water if they evaporate. When hare is fully cooked, fork-blend ¾ c sour cream with 1 t flour and pour over hare. Reduce heat, cover and let simmer another 15 min. Then leave in oven another 15–20 min for flavors to blend. The traditional accompaniments are braised beets and mashed potatoes. NOTE: This and the remaining game dishes presented are ideal for banquets, dinner-dances and other gatherings with a hunting (or autumn) motif.

ROAST PHEASANT *(bażant pieczony)*: Rub dressed pheasant inside and out with salt and about 1 T crushed spices (peppercorns, juniper, allspice, basil, sage and grated zest of 1 lemon. Place in bowl or crockery container and drench with marinade containing ⅓ c each: vinegar, white wine and water.

Cover and refrigerate several hr or overnight. Wipe pheasant and lard with ⅛ lb frozen lardoons (see index). Place 1 quartered onion, 1 cut-up carrot and 1 parsley root in cavity and bake in 375° oven 75–90 min or until fork-tender, basting with butter and pan drippings. Serve with mashed potatoes and cranberry sauce or Old Polish cranberry-apple-horseradish sauce: stir together 1 c whole-style canned cranberry sauce with 1 c applesauce, 1 heaping t horseradish and a little lemon juice.

ROAST VENISON *(pieczeń sarnia)*: Rub a 2½-lb venison leg roast (preferably from a younger deer, since older specimens can be tough!) all over with salt and drizzle with juice of 1 lemon. Lard with ⅓ lb frozen fatback sticks, cover and let stand at room temp 2–3 hr. Fry until golden 2 chopped onions in 1 heaping T butter. Place meat in roaster, pour the onions and drippings over it and bake in 350° oven for about 25 min per lb of meat, basting occasionally with 1 c dry red wine and the drippings that form. Strain pan drippings and add enough stock to make 1 c. Transfer to saucepan, stir in ½ c whole-style canned cranberry sauce or cherry pie filling. Simmer briefly and pour over sliced venison on platter.

HUNTER'S BIGOS *(bigos myśliwski)*: Since we are discussing game dishes, it is only fitting that we close this entrée section with the traditional Polish ragout associated with the hunt. For a more hunt-oriented version of Poland's national dish, soak 1 oz dried bolete mushrooms in 1½ c water several hr, then cook in same water until tender, chop, return to liquid and set aside. Drain 3 qt sauerkraut, reserving liquid, rinse in cold water, drain again, squeeze dry and chop coarsely. Place in pot with 1 bay leaf, cover with cold water and cook, uncovered, about 60 min, stirring occasionally. Transfer drained sauerkraut to baking pan and add some or all of the following: 2 qt various cooked cubed meat (beef, venison or other game, pork, veal, turkey, duck), 3 c smoked Polish sausage (or other deboned, cubed smoked meat like ham, ribs, hocks), the mushrooms and their liquid, 1 c chopped, stewed tomatoes, 1 c chopped, pitted prunes, ½ c dry red wine, 2 cloves crushed garlic, 2 large cooking apples, diced. Toss ingredients to blend and bake, uncovered, in 350° oven 30 min. Mix again, cover pan and bake another 2 hr at 325°. After switching off heat, leave *bigos* covered in oven until it cools to room temp. Refrigerate overnight. Reheat at 325° for 90 min before serving. If *bigos* appears too moist, dust with 1 or more T flour, mix well and bake another 15 min. If the *bigos* is not as tart as you want, stir in a little reserved sauerkraut juice. Season with salt, pepper, marjoram and crushed juniper. Serve with mashed or boiled whole potatoes or rye bread.

ZRAZY (COLLOPS, ROLL-UPS)— A FAVORITE POLISH ENTRÉE

This delicious meat dish has been a Polish favorite for centuries. The Polish word *zraz* can be variously translated into English as a rasher, slice, collop or fillet and refers exclusively to meat (never bread, cheese, etc.). It starts with a fairly thick slice of boneless meat, usually beef, that is pounded thin and cooked until tender in its own pan drippings, along with other ingredients, seasonings, etc. When rolled up it is called a *zraz zawijany*. In English, such meat roll-ups are sometimes referred to as beef olives or veal birds.

Unlike *pierogi, kiełbasa* and *gołąbki*, *zrazy* are still relatively unknown across Polish America, but fully deserve to be popularized, hence this special section devoted to their preparation. Since *zrazy* is a dish most everyone (regardless of nationality) enjoys the first time they try it, it would make a delicious and elegant entrée on Polonia's upscale banquet scene. But pounded fillets and roll-ups are also at home at more casual family dinners, parish suppers or even outdoor food concessions. The rolled-up variety are a bit complicated to prepare, but perhaps that is a challenge our Polish-American restaurants, catering sector, delis and frozen-food industry should consider taking up. Collops and roll-ups are usually paired up with two other very Polish accompaniments: buckwheat groats and beets. *Smacznego!*

STEAK ROLL-UPS, BASIC PROCEDURE *(zrazy zawijane, przepis podstawowy)*: Trim 2¼ lb round steak, top sirloin or other boneless cut and slice into ½″ × 3″ pieces. Pound until thin (under plastic wrap to avoid splattering) or have your butcher run the slices through his tenderizer. Spread each piece with filling of choice (see below) and roll up tightly. Fasten each with toothpick or tie with strong thread. (HINT: Protruding toothpicks make it difficult to evenly brown the roll-ups in fat. Trimming toothpicks to meat level [so they don't protrude] makes them difficult to remove from the cooked roll-ups. Thread is also messy to remove. One solution is the following: Roll up, leaving a 1″ end flap exposed and beat the flap nearly to a pulp. It should now stick to the roll-up almost like glue. The hot browning fat should seal the seam, so the thread or toothpicks can be dispensed with.) Dredge roll-ups in flour, shake off excess and brown on all sides in hot fat. Transfer to baking pan, add 2 chopped onions (optional) and drench with 2½–3 c beef stock. Simmer on low in heavy covered skillet or in oven 45–60 min, or until tender. Serve with pan sauce or thicken it with flour and (optional) sour cream to get a thick gravy.

STEAK ROLL-UPS, STANDARD *(zrazy zawijane popularne)*: Spread pounded beef slices with mustard, top with a strip of onion, a dill-pickle stick and a stick of uncooked bacon, roll up and proceed as above. NOTE: The additives should be stick-shaped and not exceed the width of the beef slice so they can be rolled up tightly and not protrude out the sides. This is one of the most popular varieties of steak roll-ups in Poland today. VARIATION: A stick of black or rye bread may be included in each roll-up.

STEAK ROLL-UPS ANOTHER WAY *(zrazy zawijane inaczej)*: Sauté 2 chopped onions in 3 T fat briefly (they need not be fully cooked). Stir in just enough bread crumbs to form a soft filling. Garnish with a little chopped parsley and/or dill. Salt and pepper. Spread pounded meat slices with mixture and proceed as above. NOTE: Bacon or fatback drippings, with or without the bacon or fatback nuggets, are excellent in this recipe. This is an inexpensive but quite tasty version of this old Polish favorite.

STEAK ROLL-UPS WITH DRIED MUSHROOMS *(zrazy zawijane z grzybami)*: Chop fine 1 oz cooked, rehydrated dried bolete mushrooms. Sauté 2 chopped onions in 3 T fat briefly, stir in the chopped mushrooms and just enough bread crumbs to form a soft filling. Add 1 T chopped parsley, salt and pepper, and mix well. Stir in 1 T or so mushroom liquid if mixture seems too dry. Spread meat slices with mixture and proceed as above. Drench with the water in which the mushrooms were cooked and enough beef stock to make 2½ to 3 c. An elegant Polish banquet entrée.

STEAK ROLL-UPS WITH FRESH MUSHROOMS *(zrazy zawijane z pieczarkami)*: Briefly sauté 8 oz chopped fresh (wild or cultivated) mushrooms and 2 chopped onions in several T oil or other fat. Salt and pepper, add 1 T chopped parsley and/or dill and just enough bread crumbs to get a soft filling. Proceed as above. Drench with 2½ to 3 c mushroom-cube bouillon and cook as indicated.

BEEF COLLOPS IN SOUR CREAM *(bitki wołowe w śmietanie)*: Whether you choose the generic description above or use a fancier term like "braised steak fillets Polonaise," this dish is likely to be a big hit with your guests. Trim 2¼ lb round steak, top sirloin or other beef cut, slice into 1 or 1½" squares and pound thin (between sheets of plastic wrap) or have butcher run pieces through tenderizer. Sprinkle with salt and flour and brown in hot fat on both sides. Add 2 sliced onions and continue browning briefly. Cook in same skillet on stovetop or transfer to baking pan. Drench with 2 c beef stock or mushroom-cube bouillon and simmer, covered, 1 hr or until tender. Fork-blend ½–¾ c sour cream with 1 heaping T flour and pour over meat. Simmer several min longer. After switching off heat, let stand 10 min or so for flavors to blend. Garnish with chopped parsley and/or dill.

BEEF COLLOPS WITH MUSHROOMS *(bitki wołowe z grzybami)*: Trim 2¼ lb round steak, top sirloin or other beef cut, slice into 1½″ squares and pound thin. Sprinkle with salt and flour, brown in hot fat on both sides and set aside. In same skillet (adding a little butter if necessary) lightly brown 8 oz fresh sliced mushrooms and 2 chopped or sliced onions. Combine the browned meat with mushrooms and onions, drench with 2 c mushroom bouillon (from 1 mushroom cube) and simmer 1 hr or until tender. Stir in ½–¾ c sour cream fork-blended with 2 T flour. Add 2 sliced onions and continue browning briefly. Cook in same skillet on stovetop or transfer to baking pan. Drench with 2 c beef stock or mushroom-cube bouillon and simmer, covered, 1 hr or until tender. Fork-blend ½ c sour cream with 1 heaping T flour and pour over meat. Simmer several min longer. Salt and pepper to taste. After switching off heat, let stand 10 min or so for flavors to blend. Garnish with chopped parsley and/or dill if desired. Serve over groats, pasta or potatoes.

BEEF TENDERLOIN FILLETS À LA NELSON *(zrazy po nelsońsku)*: 2¼ lb beef tenderloin is normally used in this gourmet speciality, but more reasonably priced round steak is also good. Rehydrate and cook 1 oz dried bolete mushrooms and reduce liquid to ½ c. Slice mushrooms into strips. Peel about 12 med oblong potatoes of roughly equal size, slice ¼″ thick, scald with boiling water, add 1 t salt and cook until still underdone. Drain. Cut the tenderloin into 1″ slices, remove any connective tissue and pound meat lightly to a thickness of about ⅓″. Sprinkle meat with a little salt, dust with flour and brown in 4 T hot fat (preferably butter) on both sides. It should still be rare on the inside. Set meat aside and in the same drippings (adding a bit of butter if more fat is needed) fry 2–3 sliced onions until tender. In well-buttered baking dish arrange in layers the meat, potatoes, onions and mushrooms (top layer should be potatoes), seasoning layers with freshly ground pepper. Fork-blend 1 c sour cream and the mushroom liquid with 1 T flour and pour over contents of pan. Bake, covered, in 400° oven about 20 min or until tender. (OPTIONAL: The dish may be sprinkled with 1 jg Madeira [wine] before baking.) This dish is often served in the same casserole in which it was baked. This is one of several hearty but elegant Polish beef and potato dishes named after Britain's legendary naval commander, Horatio Nelson (1758–1805).

VEAL ROLL-UPS *(zrazy zawijane cielęce)*: Cut 2¼–lb veal round steak into 8 pieces and pound on both sides into ⅛″ to ¼″-thick cutlets. Pepper each cutlet, season with a pinch of garlic powder and place a slice of pork fatback, bacon or boiled ham on each. Roll up and tie each roll-up with strong thread or fasten with picks. Dredge in flour and brown on all sides in several T hot fat. Add 2 finely minced onions and let them simmer until transparent. Transfer roll-ups, onions and drippings to baking dish. Add 2 c meat stock, cover and bake at 350° for 1 hr or until tender. Remove thread or picks before serving. Serve with rice or dilled potatoes and tomato salad. VARIATION: This dish can also be made with any of the fillings suggested for beef roll-ups.

BREADED PORK ROLL-UPS *(zrazy wieprzowe zawijane)*: Slice a 1¼–lb piece of center pork loin into 8 pieces. Pound each piece into a thin rectangle, then proceed in one of the following ways.

- Thinly spread meat (leaving a ½″ border along the edges) with *powidła*, sprinkle with marjoram, place a slice of skinned smoked sausage (*Podwawelska, Krakowska, Zwyczajna*) along 1 of the narrower ends and roll up.
- Thinly spread meat (leaving a ½″ border along the edges) with Polish-style mustard, cover pork with a thin slice of imported Polish or other boiled ham and roll up.
- Spread meat with the same sauerkraut-mushroom filling indicated for sauerkraut and mushroom *pierogi* (see page 147) and roll up.

Salt and pepper pork roll-ups, bread and fry in hot fat seam-side down to seal seam. Brown on all sides, reduce heat, cover and simmer on low 20–25 min, turning to ensure even cooking. NOTE: For very tender roll-ups, transfer to baking dish and keep in 325° oven for another 60 min. Serve with braised red cabbage or sauerkraut salad (in the first two cases) and accompany the sauerkraut-filled roll-ups with a grated mixed vegetable salad (carrot, apple, celeriac, horseradish) or *ćwikła.* Potatoes are a good combination with all three varieties.

BREADED CHICKEN ROLL-UPS *(zrazy zawijane z kurczęcia)*: Pound 4 skinned and halved chicken breasts on both sides into 8 cutlets ¼″ thick and do any of the following:

- Spread with thin layer of *powidła* and a sprinkling of pepper and marjoram.
- Place a thin slice of boiled ham on the cutlet and spread with a thin layer of lingonberry or cranberry jam.
- Simmer several finely chopped fresh mushrooms with 1 small finely chopped onion in 1 T butter until nicely browned; add 1 T bread crumbs and season with salt, pepper and 1 T chopped dill and/or parsley and, when cooled, spread thinly over cutlets.
- Soak several pitted prunes in water to cover until plump, then cook several min until fully cooked but not falling apart; drain well, chop prunes and spread over cutlets; season with salt, pepper and marjoram.

Roll cutlets up from wider towards narrower end. Salt and pepper, bread in flour, then egg wash, and then bread crumbs and place seam-side down in hot butter or oil to seal. Brown on all sides, then reduce heat and simmer another 4–6 min. Drain on absorbent paper and serve at once, with rice (plain or saffron-flavored for an Old Polish gourmet accent) and a green salad.

POLISH MARDI GRAS PASTRIES

No social get-together during the season of pre-Lenten merriment—whether a small house party or a glittery ball—would be complete without those seasonal favorites *pączki* and *chruściki* (or *faworki*). Many people enjoy them at other times of year as well. Here are a few recipes for those who want to try their hand at preparing them from scratch. They are also available at Polonian bakeries, pastry shops, delis and groceries.

PĄCZKI, LARGE POLISH DOUGHNUTS *(pączki duże)*: Mash 1¾ oz fresh yeast with 2 T sugar and dissolve in 5 T milk. Set aside to rise. Cream 4 egg yolks and 2 whole eggs with 6 T sugar and grated zest of half a small lemon. Add yeast mixture, 7 c flour, ½ t vanilla sugar or extract, 1½ c milk, 1 t salt and knead ingredients to combine. Add 2 T rum and knead again. Gradually add 9 T melted butter and continue kneading until fully blended, then set aside in warm place to rise. When dough doubles in bulk, divide into 4 parts. Roll out each part on floured board to a thickness of ⅓″. In sieve drain 1½ c cherry preserves. (Use the drippings to flavor tea, vodka, cake, pudding or ice cream.) Cut dough into rounds with glass or biscuit-cutter and place some drained cherry preserves at center, cover with another round and pinch rounds together with fingers and roll snowball-fashion into balls. Place *pączki* on flour-sprinkled surface, cover with cloth and set aside in warm place to rise. After they double in size, turn them over. Heat lard or oil in a fairly wide pan. It is hot enough if a piece of dough floats to top immediately. Brush excess flour off *pączki* and fry in hot fat deep enough so they can float freely. When one side is browned, turn them over and brown the other side. Transfer *pączki* to absorbent paper and dust with confectioners' sugar.

PĄCZKI, SMALL POLISH DOUGHNUTS *(pączki mniejsze)*: Mash 2 cakes yeast, dissolve in 1½ c prescalded lukewarm milk and set aside. Cream ½ c room-temp butter with ½ c sugar until fluffy. Stir in 3 egg yolks beaten with 1 whole egg, 1 t salt and ½ t grated nutmeg. Beating constantly, gradually add the yeast-milk mixture and 4½ c flour. When dough is fully blended, let rise in warm place until doubled in bulk. Punch down, knead and let rise a second time. Roll dough out on floured board about ½″ thick and cut into rounds. Place a spoonful of thick rose-petal jam at center, fold each round in half and pinch edges together. Shape snowball-fashion into balls and let them rise on floured surface. Fry in hot deep fat, turning only once. Remove to absorbent paper and glaze with white icing. Before icing sets, sprinkle each *pączek* with a little finely diced candied orange rind.

FILLING PĄCZKI *(nadziewanie pączków)*: *Pączki* may be filled with preferably thick fruit fillings such as *powidła* (plum butter), jam, drained preserves (e.g., cherry, plum, strawberry, apricot) or commercial fruit-flavored pastry fillings. The most elegant *pączki* are filled with rose-petal jam or rose-hip preserves. The important thing is that the filling must not be runny (liquid), because the dough surrounding it will not cook properly. Such a jam should first be cooked down until thick and cooled before spooning it onto the dough rounds. A single candied cherry, sugared prune or other non-wet fruit may be inserted into each *pączek* before closing it. Almond paste *(marcepan)* or rose-flavored ground walnuts are other possibilities. Apparently under the influence of bismarcks, jelly doughnuts and other non-Polish pastries, in Polonia *pączki* are sometimes filled with custard. But, when all is said and done, it is an undeniable fact that *pączki* cook most evenly when fried without filling. Plain, unfilled *pączki* convey an atmosphere of old rural Poland and are recommended for peasant-style Mardi Gras doings. However, if you prefer filled *pączki,* after they have been drained on absorbent paper and cooled, a dollop of fruit jelly (cherry and strawberry are very good!) may be inserted with a thin pastry-filling syringe. (In a pinch, a medical syringe with a thick needle may be used.) Then, glaze with icing or dust with sugar if desired.

PĄCZKI, GOURMET WARSAW DOUGHNUTS *(pączki wyborne warszawskie)*: Beat 12 egg yolks with 1 t salt at high speed until mixture is thick and piles softly (about 7 min). Separately, add 2 pkg active dry yeast to a bowl containing ¼ c warm water to soften. Cream ⅓ c room-temp butter or margarine, gradually adding ½ c sugar, until fluffy. Stir 1 c flour into yeast mixture. Add 3 T rum and ½ c prescalded whipping cream, then beat in another 1 c flour and stir in another ½ c of whipping cream. Beat in another 1 c flour and the yolk mixture, beating about 2 min. Gradually beat in 1½ c flour and continue beating until air blisters appear in dough. Cover dough with plastic wrap and place in a warm place to rise. When doubled in bulk, punch down, cover again and when it rises again, punch it down. Roll dough out on floured board ¾″ thick. Cut into 3″ rounds. Place a spoonful of very thick jam or preserves at center of half the rounds. Brush edges of rounds with water and top with remaining rounds. Pinch edges together to seal and shape snowball-fashion into balls. Cover *pączki* and keep in warm place until doubled in bulk (about 20 min). Fry *pączki* in hot (365°) fat to a nice golden brown on both sides. Transfer to absorbent paper and sprinkle with cinnamon sugar if desired.

MINI-PĄCZKI *(pączuszki)*: These tiny *pączki* are sure to be a hit. Simply tear off plum-sized pieces of risen *pączki* dough, roll into balls and fry in hot fat. These smaller *pączki* should cook in no time, so be sure to test one for doneness so they are not overcooked. After draining on paper and cooling, serve as is or glazed, garnished with chopped candied orange peel or dusted with confectioners' sugar. NOTE: One drawback of these tiny *pączki* is that they tend to absorb more fat.

PĄCZKI, COUNTRY-STYLE *(pączki wiejskie)*: After your *pączki* dough (prepared in any of the ways suggested above) has risen twice, tear off pączki-sized pieces and roll them into a ball snowball-fashion. Fry as above on both sides and drain on absorbent paper. When they cool, serve just as they are—unfilled, unglazed and unsugared. These plainer, more irregularly shaped *pączki* would be more typical of what rural-dwelling Poles once enjoyed during the pre-Lenten season. NOTE: If, after you have prepared them, you regret they're unfilled, you can remedy the situation using the syringe method described in Filling Pyczki (see page 98).

FAVORS, ANGEL-WINGS *(faworki, chruściki)*: These delectable but highly fragile, fried and sugar-dusted pastries are another traditional treat of the Polish pre-Lenten party scene. Possibly due to the difficulty in spelling and pronouncing *chruściki* (their most common name among Polonia), over the years English-speaking Americans have come up with an entire litany of names: favors, favorites, crisps, angel wings, bow-knot pastries, carnival cookies, crullers, cracklings and kindling. But whatever they're called, they are usually a hit. To prepare them, sift 2 c flour onto board. Make well at center and deposit therein 5 egg yolks, 1 T butter, 2 T sour cream, a pinch of salt and 1 T 6% distilled vinegar or 190-proof grain alcohol. (OPTIONAL: ½ t vanilla or rum extract may be added if desired.)Work into a dough and knead well (about 15 min) until dough is glossy and full of small holes when cut in half. Beat dough with rolling pin on all sides—the more air forced into the dough, the lighter the pastries will be. Roll out as thin as possible on light floured board, sprinkling top of dough sheet with a little flour. With pastry-wheel or knife cut dough sheet into 1–1½″ strips, then cut strips at an angle into 5″ pieces. Cut a 1½″ vertical slit down center of each piece and gently pull one of the ends through the slot to form a bow. Heat at least 1½ lb lard or shortening (or oil) in deep pan or electric skillet to 350°. Deep-fry to a light golden brown on both sides and remove to absorbent paper. Fry in batches so they are not crowded and can float freely. When slightly cooled, dust with confectioners' sugar.

FAVORS, BAKING-POWDER TYPE *(faworki na proszku)*: Fork-blend ¼ sour cream, combine with 2⅓ c flour and heap on board. Make a well in center and drop into it 6 raw egg yolks, 2 pinches salt 2 t baking powder and 2 T grain alcohol or 100-proof vodka. Combine ingredients and work into a uniform dough. Knead well until dough is smooth and air blisters appear. Roll out thin on lightly floured board and cut with pastry wheel or knife into 2″ × 5″ strips (for larger *faworki*) or 1½″ × 4″ (for daintier ones). Make a vertical slit in each strip and pull one of the ends through it to form a bow. Gently brush any excess flour from *faworki* and deep-fry in about 2 lb hot 350° lard or shortening (or oil) to a light golden brown, turning once. Transfer to absorbent paper and dust with confectioners' sugar when slightly cooled.

CARNIVAL ROSES or ROSETTES *(róże karnawałowe)*: This is the fanciest version of *faworki* known. These unusual pastries, which blossom into an opening flower when fried, often graced the most elegant Mardi Gras balls and banquets of yesteryear. Is the effect achieved worth the extra effort? You be the judge! To prepare these exquisite fried pastries, start by combining 3½ c flour with 2 T soft butter, 3 T sour cream, 6 raw egg yolks, 1 T grain alcohol or 100-proof vodka and a pinch of salt. Work into a dough, knead well and beat with rolling pin until air bubbles appear. Roll out as thin as possible and cut with glasses or biscuit-cutters of different sizes into an equal number of 1½″, 2″ and 2½″ rounds. Cut 6 slits round the edge (towards center) of each round and form each rosette by placing the largest on bottom, dabbing a little egg white at center, sticking on a medium-sized round, dabbing with egg white and topping with the smallest round. Press down at center with thumb to stick rounds together. Fry like *faworki* in hot fat on both sides and transfer to absorbent paper. Dust with confectioners' sugar and place a cherry (from drained cherry preserves) at the center of each.

KINDLING PASTRIES *(chrusty)*: This more rustic, less pampered and less expensive version of *faworki* would have been more typical of the kind of pre-Lenten treats enjoyed in the countryside of yesteryear at *zapusty* festivities. Combine 2 c flour with 2 T soft butter, 2 T sugar, 1 egg, 1 T vinegar and ⅓–½ c sour cream. Work ingredients into a uniform dough and knead well. Roll out on floured board slightly thinner than ¼″ thick. Either cut into 2″ × 5″ strips, make a vertical slit in each strip and pull one of the ends through it to form a bow; or cut into irregular strips and pieces without making a slit at center. Twist into whatever shape you want (or leave as is) and deep-fry in hot lard to a light golden brown on both sides. NOTE: If you want to re-create the authentic atmosphere of old-time, peasant-style, pre-Lenten festivities, do not dust with powdered sugar. Any kind of manufactured sugar was once out of the reach of most Polish peasants. If you decide to dust your peasant-style *chrusty* with confectioners' sugar to make them more appetizing, by all means go ahead! It was also not uncommon for even peasants of the most modest means to splurge at certain times, including Christmas, Easter, weddings and *zapusty.*

THE LEAN FOOD OF POLISH LENT

Here are some of the dishes the people of Poland prepared to tide them through the 40 long days of Lent, when *żur* and herring became dietary staples. Perhaps some of these might be worth introducing on Polonia's Lenten scene. One or more of these soups, herring and boiled potatoes and fried fish could be featured at parish or club suppers held during that period.

RYEMEAL SOUP, LENTEN *(żur postny)*: This tart soup, a Lenten staple in Old Poland, was totally meatless, unlike the Easter *żur* made with sausage stock. In crock or glass jar combine 1 c rye flour or 1 c rolled oats or 1 part of each, add several rye-bread crusts or 1 slice rye bread and 1–3 cloves crushed garlic and drench with 4 c preboiled lukewarm water. Cover mouth of container with cheesecloth fastened with rubber band and let stand in warm (75°–80°F) place 4–5 days, or until liquid becomes pleasantly tart. To make your soup, combine 4 c vegetable stock (traditional or made from bouillon cube) with about 2 c ryemeal sour and bring to boil. Simmer briefly and season with salt, pepper and marjoram. Thicken with 1 T flour dissolved in a little cold water, if desired. VARIATION: 1–2 rehydrated cooked bolete mushrooms (or other dried) mushrooms may be diced and added together with their liquid to pot. NOTE: ryemeal sour *(żur)* imported from Poland is available in jars at Polish-American delis and specialty food shops.

RYEMEAL SOUP, EASY LENTEN *(żur postny łatwy)*: In pot combine 6 c water, enough vegetable bouillon cubes to make 3 c bouillon, 1 mushroom bouillon cube or 1 t liquid or powdered mushroom extract and bring to boil. Dissolve 3–4 T *żur* powder (see Basic Ingredients and Procedures, page 33) in 1 c water and add to pot. Simmer briefly. Sour to taste with 2–4 T white vinegar or several pinches citric acid crystals. Season to taste with salt, pepper, marjoram and 1–2 cloves crushed garlic. Serve with rye bread or a dish of mashed potatoes, garnished with chopped onions fried in a little oil, on the side.

GARLIC SOUP "OUT OF THIN AIR" *(zupa postna na gwoździu)*: Mince and mash 2–3 cloves garlic with ¼ t salt. Place garlic paste in soup bowl, drench with 1½ to 2 c boiling water and enjoy. A pinch of pepper and a drop or two Maggi seasoning (as well as a pinch of chopped parsley and/or dill) may be added. This unusual soup can be made one bowl at a time as needed, so you needn't prepare a whole pot. It may be eaten with rye bread on the side or stale rye-bread cubes or oil-fried rye-bread croutons in the bowl. NOTE: The humorous Polish name of this soup suggests it is cooked with little more than a carpenter's nail for flavoring and lacks the meat or sausage stock on which the Poles' favorite non-Lenten soups were based.

BREAD AND WATER SOUP *(zupa chlebowa na wodzie)*: For each serving cut 1–2 slices rye bread into cubes and fry in 1 T oil to a nice golden brown on all sides. Salt and pepper hot croutons, place in soup bowl and scald with 1½ to 2 c boiling water. May be served with boiled potatoes (garnished with oil-fried chopped onions) on the side.

BREAD SOUP, FAST-DAY *(zupa chlebowa, postna)*: Proceed as in preceding recipe but drench the rye-bread croutons with hot vegetable stock (made with traditional soup greens or vegetable bouillon cubes).

BREAD AND GARLIC SOUP *(zupa chlebowa z czosnkiem)*: Prepare the above bread soup but add 1–2 cloves crushed garlic mashed with a little salt before drenching the croutons with hot vegetable stock. A pinch of chopped dill and/or parsley will improve the flavor and color. (OPTIONAL: A heaping T or two diced or crumbled farmer cheese or dry cottage cheese may be added to each bowl of this and the preceding two soups.)

BEER SOUP, LENTEN *(postna polewka piwna)*: In pot place 1½ c rye or whole wheat bread (or some of each) with crust removed and crumbled or torn into small pieces. Add 1 qt beer, 1 c water, 3 T margarine, ¼ t salt, 1 t sugar and ½ t bruised caraway. Bring to boil and simmer 2–3 min. Strain, forcing bread through sieve into another pot. Bring to boil again and season additionally to taste with salt and pepper if desired. Serve over cubed farmer cheese and dry rye-bread cubes or oil-fried croutons. NOTE: This soup was once eaten by many mainly during Lent, because in Old Poland beer was considered a beverage rather than an intoxicant that should be given up when fasting.

BEER SOUP, OLD POLISH *(staropolska polewka piwna)*: Beat 5 raw egg yolks with ½ c sugar until white and stir in ¾ c sour cream. Heat mixture while whisking the whole time and gradually add 1 qt beer. Add a pinch of cinnamon and a pinch of ground cloves and continue heating and whisking until mixture thickens. Serve hot with some diced farmer cheese added to bowls. NOTE: Unlike the lean Lenten beer soup in the preceding recipe, this rich and creamy version is typical of the less-than-serious "fasting" of Polish gentry of yesteryear.

SAUERKRAUT SOUP, FAST-DAY *(kwaśnica postna)*: Prepare 12 oz sauerkraut, chop coarsely, place in pot, add half a bay leaf and 3 grains allspice, cover with 6 c vegetable stock and cook until tender (at least 1 hr, preferably longer). Separately cook 4 med potatoes. When cool, dice and set aside. In 3 T oil fry 2–3 chopped onions to a nice golden brown. To soup pot add 1 oz diced cooked dried mushrooms, the fried onions, diced potatoes, 1 clove crushed garlic and ¼ t caraway seeds. (OPTIONAL: If you prefer a thicker soup, stir in 1 or so T flour dissolved in ½ c water.) Bring to boil, simmer briefly and salt and pepper to taste. Serve with unbuttered rye bread on the side. VARIATIONS: Raw potatoes may be cooked in soup after sauerkraut is tender. Another way is to serve hot boiled or mashed potatoes on the side, garnished with fried onions (rather than adding the potatoes and fried onions to the soup).

BUTTERMILK AND POTATOES *(maślanka z kartoflami)*: Cold or room-temp buttermilk is often served in a bowl and eaten with a spoon like a Lenten soup to wash down a plate of boiled potatoes on the side. The potatoes may be garnished with a little chopped dill and/or butter or margarine or even chopped onions browned in oil, but no pork cracklings, bacon bits or meat drippings of any kind!

OTHER FAST-DAY SOUPS *(inne zupy postne)*: Any of the meatless soups listed in the Wigilia section are appropriate for Lent. However, in general they should not contain such rich ingredients as sour cream and butter or only very little. Any soup made with meatless vegetable stock is also suitable with the above provision.

HERRING *(śledzie)*: Any of the herring presented in the Wigilia section are suitable. Rigorous fasters may prefer to prepare only herring marinated in vinegar or oil for Lent rather than those laced with rich sour cream and/or mayonnaise. The choice is yours. Herring and boiled potatoes are a typical Lenten meal.

FISH DISHES *(potrawy rybne)*: Any of the fish dishes found in the Wigilia section are suitable for Lent. However, to reflect the true spirit of Lent, plain and unembellished dishes are preferable. A typical Lenten meal might comprise fried fish with boiled potatoes and sauerkraut salad (see Wigilia section for the recipes).

CABBAGE ROLLS, LENTEN *(gołąbki postne)*: Meatless cabbage rolls suitable for Lent are included in this book's special *gołąbki* section.

ONION CAKES *(kołaczyki z cebulą)*: Mash ½ cake yeast with ½ t sugar and dissolve in ¼ c lukewarm milk. When it rises, combine in bowl with 1¾ c flour, 3 to 3½ T butter, 2 raw egg yolks and ⅓ t salt. Combine ingredients well and knead until dough no longer sticks to bowl or hands. Set aside to rise in warm place until doubled. Form small 3″ buns or cakes and place them on greased baking sheet 2″ apart to rise (about 30–45 min). Meanwhile, in sieve, scald 2–3 thinly sliced med onions with boiling water. Drain until dry and simmer until tender in 3–4 T butter or margarine but do not brown, stirring frequently. Sprinkle onions with ½ t sugar and several twists of a peppermill. When cakes double in bulk, make a depression at center of each cake with bottom of juice glass or similar object and brush with lightly beaten egg whites. (OPTIONAL: Sprinkle cakes with caraway seeds.) Fill depressions with onion mixture and bake in 400° oven 20 min or to a nice golden brown. Check for doneness with toothpick.

POTATO-RYE MUSH DUMPLINGS, FAST-DAY *(prażucha postna)*: Peel 6–7 med potatoes, cut each into 4 pieces, place in pot, scald with boiling water to cover and cook until slightly underdone. Add 1 c rye flour or ordinary enriched (wheat) flour, sprinkle with ½ t salt and continue cooking until potatoes fall apart. Mash potatoes and flour together to a uniform consistency. If too thick, stir in a little boiling water. With wooden spoon scoop "dumplings" from the mush onto serving platter. Garnish generously with chopped onions browned in oil. VARIATION: Garnishing the dumplings with melted butter and sugar is the preferred topping of children. NOTE: On nonfast days, this dish is usually garnished with fried salt pork nuggets or onions fried in lard or bacon drippings.

NOODLES AND CHEESE, LENTEN *(kluski z serem postne)*: In lightly salted water cook 16 oz egg noodles of choice until tender. (NOTE: The Polish way is to cook noodles and other pasta until soft; Italian-style al dente doneness is too chewy and rubbery for Polish tastes so you may have to cook them a bit longer than directed on pkg.) Drain well, dot with butter or margarine (about 2 T) and stir in 16 oz grated or crumbled farmer cheese. Dry cottage cheese and farmer cheese may be whirled to a powder in food processor but do not overprocess because the whey may separate from the cheese. Salt and pepper to taste. NOTE: On nonfast days, noodles and cheese are often garnished with pork-crackling nuggets. If you are a food hobbyist, try serving this dish with your own homemade cheese (see following recipe).

WHITE CURD CHEESE, HOMEMADE *(twaróg domowy)*: Set a large flameproof baking dish in a warm place (on or next to radiator, near heating duct or furnace). Add 1 gal whole milk and stir in 1 c fork-blended sour cream. Let stand in warm place until fully clabbered (1–3 days). To keep out dust and insects, cover with cheesecloth. When clabbered, gently transfer to stove and heat on very low heat until curds float up to top. Switch off heat. Do not stir or disturb. Let stand until cooled to room temp. Strain through fine cheesecloth-lined sieve, reserving the liquid (whey) that drips out. When dripping stops, cover curds in sieve with saucer or dish and weight it down with something heavy (a qt jar of water) to extract more moisture. When dripping stops, twist cheese into a tight ball through cheesecloth and refrigerate. Use in any dish calling for farmer cheese or in the whey soup below.

WHEY SOUP *(polewka z serwatki)*: Pour 6 c whey (liquid left over from homemade cheese above) into pot and heat. Dissolve ¼–½ c flour in 1 c milk and add to whey. Bring to gentle boil, reduce heat and simmer, stirring constantly. Salt to taste. Crumble homemade cheese into soup bowls and drench with hot soup. Serve with boiled potatoes on the side. VARIATION: This soup may also be sweetened with several T sugar.

OTHER LENTEN DISHES *(inne potrawy postne)*: The peasant cookery of Old Poland usually involved a plain dish of boiled vegetables, potatoes, groats, noodles, dumplings or *pierogi* embellished with a fatty garnish (*okrasa* or *omasta*). This could be fried salt pork or bacon bits and their drippings, melted lard or butter, pan drippings or other rendered fat. This was done away with during Lent, and the only permissible *okrasa* was plain oil or onions fried in oil. Well-to-do families (who incidentally were often less rigorous about Lenten fasting) included melted butter as a fast-day garnish. Examples of typical Lenten meals could include a plate of hot cooked or canned (drained) navy beans garnished with oil-fried onions, boiled potatoes dotted with butter, butter substitute or margarine, buckwheat groats with fried mushrooms and onions and boiled noodles or potato dumplings with fried chopped onions.

ŚWIĘCONE—THE POLISH EASTER FEAST

Święcone, the Polish Easter Feast, literally means "blessed things," "consecrated stuff" or "hallow fare," from the tradition of blessing Easter food on Holy Saturday. Both the blessed food itself and the Easter meal is known as

Święcone. Sometimes *Święcone* is translated as Easter breakfast, brunch or lunch, but in actuality these festive foods are served throughout the two-day Polish Easter holiday (Easter Sunday and Monday) and beyond. Many are regularly featured on Polonia's Dyngus Day and *Święconka* scene. Those still relatively unknown in Polish America deserve to be explored all the more! NOTE: The inclusion of any of the dishes, sauces and cakes in this section is not to suggest that they are confined only to the Easter season. Most of them are also served at banquets, dinner-parties, Mardi Gras festivities, First Holy Communion gatherings, nameday get-togethers and other festive occasions throughout the year.

POLISH EASTER SOUPS

EASTER RYEMEAL SOUP, TRADITIONAL *(żurek wielkanocny)*: To prepare this soup the traditional way, you will need ryemeal-sour (*żur*), whose preparation is explained in Basic Ingredients and Procedures, page 33. To make your soup, in pot combine 2 c water in which fresh or smoked *kiełbasa* were cooked, 1–2 rehydrated, cooked, diced dried mushrooms and their water, 2 c plain water and 2 c or more ryemeal sour—depending on tartness desired. Thicken with 1 heaping t rye flour (or regular enriched flour), bring to boil, reduce heat and simmer several min. Season with salt, pepper and marjoram. Serve hot *żur* over sliced hard-cooked eggs and diced cooked meat (ham, sausage, roasts) in bowls. In the Kraków area, the *żur* is served with a side dish of hot mashed potatoes garnished with *skwarki* (crunchy fried salt-pork nuggets). NOTE: ryemeal-sour *(żur)* imported from Poland is available at Polish-American delis and specialty food shops.

EASTER RYEMEAL SOUP, EASY *(żurek wielkanocny łatwy)*: In pot combine 2 c water in which fresh or smoked *kiełbasa* was cooked, 3 c plain water and ½ mushroom bouillon cube. Cook until bouillon cube dissolves. In 1 c cold water dissolve 2–3 T homemade *żur* powder (see Lenten Ryemeal Soup, Easy, page 101) and stir into soup. Simmer several min. Sour to taste with 2–3 T white vinegar or several pinches citric acid crystals. This soup should have a definitely tart edge but should not be excessively sour. Add 1 T marjoram and 1–2 cloves crushed garlic. Taste soup before adding any salt and pepper, as the *kiełbasa* water may have already seasoned it sufficiently. Serve as in preceding recipe over hard-cooked eggs and diced sausage. In some parts of Poland (including the Kraków region), a serving of mashed potatoes garnished with crunchy fatback nuggets is often served on the side.

<u>EASTER RYEMEAL SOUP, EASY, ANOTHER WAY</u> *(żurek wielkanocny łatwy inaczej)*: Combine in soup pot the following ingredients, allowing for each serving 1 c water, 1 c degreased *kiełbasa* water (see page 116), 1 slightly heaped T rolled oats and ½ slice crumbled-up rye bread. Bring to boil, reduce heat and simmer 10 min. Strain, forcing as much of the cooked oats and bread through strainer with wooden spoon as possible, scraping strained mixture clinging to bottom of sieve into pot. Taste soup, since the *kiełbasa* water may have provided it with enough salt and pepper already. If not, salt and pepper to taste. Add 2–3 cloves mashed garlic, several pinches marjoram and sour to taste with sour salt (citric-acid crystals). The soup should have a tart edge to it but should not be mouth-puckeringly sour! Into each bowl place 5–6 thin rounds of cooked *kiełbasa* and ½ a sliced hard-cooked egg, drenching them with hot soup. Serve with rye bread.

<u>WHITE EASTER BARSZCZ, TRADITIONAL</u> *(biały barszcz wielkanocny tradycyjny)*: This is an eastern Polish variant of *żurek*. You may make it with ryemeal-sour (homemade or the imported bottled variety). Or, you may first prepare a rye-bread–sour by drenching 6 slices stale rye bread in glass jar or crock with 1 qt preboiled lukewarm water and keeping in warm place several days until it tastes nicely tart and tangy. Skim off and discard any mold that forms at top. It is not harmful (penicillin comes from bread mold!), but it is unsightly. In pot combine 4 c meat stock with 2–3 c strained rye-bread–sour. Bring to boil and simmer several min. Remove from heat. Fork-blend 1 heaping T flour with 1 c sour cream until smooth. Add about 1 c hot soup to flour-cream mixture, a spoonful at a time, stirring vigorously. Stir cream mixture into soup in a thin stream and simmer several min longer. Add 2–3 cloves crushed garlic. Serve over hard-cooked eggs, diced *kiełbasa* and ham. Provide prepared horseradish for your guests to add extra zing to their *barszcz* if they wish. <u>VARIATION</u>: Instead of meat stock, white *barszcz* may be made with *kiełbasa* water (as above) or by cooking 2 to 2½ c diced sausage, ham, roasts, etc. together with 1 bay leaf and 1 large onion in 5 c water, covered, for 1 hr. Then proceed as above.

<u>WHITE EASTER BARSZCZ, EASY</u> *(biały barszcz wielkanocny łatwy)*: In pot combine 3 c water in which fresh or smoked *kiełbasa* was cooked, 2 c cold water and 1 c bouillon made from a bouillon cube. Bring to boil and remove from heat. In 1 c milk dissolve 1 heaping T flour and stir into soup. Simmer several min. Season with heaping T prepared horseradish, salt, pepper, marjoram and 2–3 T white vinegar or more (or several pinches citric acid crystals) to get the tart flavor you want. Serve over hard-cooked eggs and diced cooked meat (ham, sausage, roasts) in bowls. Some people also add cubes of farmer cheese and rye bread to hot soup in bowls.

EASTER BEET BARSZCZ *(wielkanocny barszcz burakowy)*: Scrub but do not peel 4 med beets (about 2 lb) and bake in preheated 350° oven 90 min or until a fork goes in easily. In pot containing 3–4 c water in which Polish sausage was cooked, add 3 c plain water and 1 portion soup greens (see page 30), diced. Cook until vegetables are tender. Peel cool baked beets, grate, dice or slice thin, add to pot together with 2 or more c beet-sour or dill-pickle brine (to give the soup a tart edge) and 2 cloves crushed garlic. Bring to boil and simmer several min. Remove from heat. Fork-blend ¾ c sour cream with 1 heaping T flour until smooth, adding about 1 c hot soup a spoonful at a time and stirring constantly. Stir flour mixture into soup pot and simmer several min longer. Salt and pepper to taste if needed. Serve with rye bread or boiled potatoes on the side.

BEET SOUP, CLEAR *(czerwony barszcz czysty)*: This clear, tangy soup, served in a twin-handled barszcz cup or large teacup, would be nice at an Easter brunch with a gourmet twist. You can find the recipe on page 39. It is usually served with pastry sticks or *paszteciki* (filled pastries), page 193.

HARD-COOKED EGGS, SAUCES AND SALADS

EGGS, HARD-COOKED *(jaja na twardo)*: Eggs to be hard-cooked should begin at room temp so they don't crack during cooking. Place eggs in pot and fill with cold water to cover by at least 1″. Add a T or so salt. Remove and discard any egg that does not touch the bottom of water-filled pot. If it floats up, it is not very fresh. Bring water to boil and immediately reduce heat to a gentle simmer. Cook 10–12 min (depending on size of eggs). Cool immediately in cold water, as that prevents the yolk from darkening and eggs will be easier to shell.

HARD-COOKED EGG SAUCES AND CONDIMENTS *(dodatki do jaj na twardo)*: Bowls of shelled, whole, plain hard-cooked eggs may be placed at intervals on your Easter brunch table, allowing diners to enjoy them with the condiments (salt, pepper, horseradish, *ćwikła*, mustard) or sauces of their choice. This approach would be good to convey a rustic, down-home mood. For a more gourmet-style presentation, serve the eggs on a bed of lettuce (Boston lettuce is the closest to Polish-style lettuce readily found on the American market), laced with sauces. Please consider the following:

- Eggs may be served whole or halved, in the latter case—either cut-side up or down.
- Garnish each egg with just a small dollop (spoonful) of sauce or literally drench the eggs with it.

- ✦ You can also put just a dab on the eggs (many people nowadays are dieting!), and serve extra sauce on the side in a sauceboat or serving bowl.
- ✦ Eggs in white or light-colored sauces can be garnished with finely chopped chives or garden cress for added color and flavor.
- ✦ Easter means greenery, so use your imagination in trimming platters with sprigs of parsley, tufts of dill or twigs of box (*bukszpan*—a small-leafed evergreen). A few radish roses will add a touch of color (see page 72).
- ✦ Although a wide variety of sauces are presented below, probably no more than 2 or 3 different types of hard-cooked eggs in sauces would be served when entertaining at home; at community events 3 or 4 should be sufficient.
- ✦ At a community buffet, it might be not be a bad idea to label the sauces, since sour cream sauce does not differ much from horseradish sauce and other light-colored toppings.

EASTER-EGG CROSS *(krzyż wielkanocny z jaj)*: This arrangement is mainly for visual effect and is typical of the treatment lavished on the Święconka table in the prosperous Polish homes of yesteryear. A rectangular serving dish or tray is best, but a round one can be used as well. Count the number of eggs needed to make a cross. You will need only half the number if you serve egg halves. Place the required number of cold, peeled, hard-cooked eggs in a bowl or jar and drench them with beet juice (from canned or pickled beets). Weight down with a plate to keep them submerged and refrigerate overnight. Remove, drain on dry paper towels. If using egg halves, place them on platter cut-side down. If using whole eggs, cut a thin slice (⅛″) off the bottom of each egg to make them more stable. (Chop the egg trimmings and add to any of the salads presented in this book.) Form a cross with the red eggs and surround them with either plain hard-cooked eggs or drenched with a white or light-colored sauce.

EASTER-EGG LAMB *(baranek z jaj)*: The same principle applies here too, but it will take more effort and artistic flair to create something resembling a lamb. You will need only a few beet-colored eggs for the red cross of the lamb's banner. A rather large platter or tray is needed. Fill the serving platter with eggs (whole or halved). Use plain eggs for the lamb and drench the eggs outside its outline with green sauce. The banner should be white with beet-red eggs forming the cross. Decorate with greenery as above.

HORSERADISH, PREPARED *(chrzan tarty w occie)*: Prepared horseradish is the basic condiment of the Polish Easter table—either plain, creamed or used to flavor various sauces. Polish and domestic bottled, prepared horseradish is commercially available, so shop around until you strike on the variety whose taste and potency are to your liking. Personally, I prefer the plain grated horseradish not containing powdered milk or other dairy additives, since it is so easy to add your own sour cream or sweet cream just prior to serving. See Traditional Polish Condiments, page 176, if you want to try your hand at making your own.

HORSERADISH SAUCE, CREAMY *(sos chrzanowy śmietankowy)*: Combine 1 c sour cream with 1 heaping T of homemade prepared horseradish (see page 177). Season to taste with salt, sugar and lemon juice or vinegar. VARIATION 1: Fork-blend ½ c prepared horseradish with ½ c heavy cream. Season to taste with salt, sugar and lemon juice or vinegar. VARIATION 2: Beat 1 c cold whipping cream until stiff and fluffy and stir in 1 heaping T or more prepared horseradish. Season as above.

HORSERADISH-MAYONNAISE SAUCE *(sos chrzanowy na majonezie)*: Depending on the potency of your horseradish and how zingy you want your sauce to be, fork-blend 1 heaping T prepared horseradish or more with ¼ c sour cream (or plain low-fat yogurt) and ¾ c mayonnaise. Season to taste with salt, vinegar (or lemon juice) and sugar. Use to garnish hard-cooked eggs and cold meats.

EASTER SAUCE *(sos do święconego)*: Fork-blend ½ c dairy sour cream with ½ c mayonnaise, add 1–2 chopped hard-cooked eggs and ½–¾ c mixed finely chopped vegetables: dill pickle, chives, pickled mushroom, and radish. Stir in 1 heaping t to 1 T freshly grated horseradish or prepared horseradish and season to taste with salt, confectioners' sugar and lemon juice or vinegar.

EASTER SAUCE, LOW-FAT *(sos do święconego chudy)*: Substitute light sour cream (or plain, unsweetened low-fat or no-fat yogurt) and light mayonnaise for the normal-fat-content products in the preceding recipe.

TARTAR SAUCE *(sos tatarski)*: In Polish tradition, this sauce is right in its element on the Easter table, since it is used mainly as a topping for hard-cooked eggs, pâté and other cold meats. It is also used with cold fish dishes (aspic dishes, marinated fish, etc.), but (unlike Anglo-mainstream practice) not on hot fried fish, for which Poles regard horseradish sauce as a more suitable accompaniment. To make your own tartar sauce, see page 177.

MUSTARD SAUCE, COLD *(sos musztardowy zimny)*: Depending on how mustardy you want your sauce to be and how sharp a mustard you are using, fork-blend ½ c sour cream (or plain low-fat yogurt) and ½ c mayonnaise with 1 heaping t to 1 heaping T mustard, preferably brown Polish-style or Düsseldorf type. If using a very sharp Dijon type, reduce the amount slightly to taste. Season with salt, vinegar and sugar to taste. NOTE: This and the other creamy sauces presented here can be used both over hard-cooked eggs as well as cold meats.

SOUR CREAM-MUSTARD SAUCE *(sos musztardowy ze śmietaną)*: Fork-blend 1 c sour cream (or 1 part sour cream and 1 part plain low-fat yogurt) with 1 slightly heaped or heaping T brown prepared mustard, adding a little salt, sugar and lemon juice to taste. Use on hard-cooked eggs and cold meats.

CREAMY HORSERADISH *(chrzan śmietankowy)*: Fork-blend 1 part prepared horseradish with 1 part unwhipped whipping cream, seasoning to taste with a little lemon juice and sugar. Excellent over hard-cooked eggs, ham and other cold meats.

GREEN SAUCE *(sos zielony)*: Fork-blend ⅓ c sour cream (or plain low-fat yogurt) and ⅓ c mayonnaise with 1 t brown prepared mustard or prepared horseradish. Stir in ¾ c finely chopped greens in any proportion you like, including chives, scallions, dill, parsley, fresh basil and fresh spinach. Capers and finely chopped dill pickles may also be added to sauce. Spoon sauce over hard-cooked eggs.

EGGS IN MAYONNAISE *(jaja w majonezie)*: Fork-blend 1 c mayonnaise with 1 level T brown prepared mustard and a little salt, sugar and lemon juice to taste. A heaping t sour cream or plain yogurt will perk up the flavor. (OPTIONAL: Several dashes of paprika will improve the color, and a dash or 2 of Tabasco will provide added zing.) Spoon sauce over hard-cooked eggs.

EGGS IN SPRING SAUCE *(jaja w sosie wiosennym)*: Combine ⅔–1 c finely chopped spring greens (scallions, radishes, chives, parsley, dill, garden cress) with ½ c mayonnaise and ½ c sour cream. Season with 1 t prepared horseradish, 1 t lemon juice, ¼ t salt and several dashes of pepper. Spoon sauce over hard-cooked eggs as above.

DEVILED EGGS, MUSHROOM-STUFFED *(jaja nadziewane pieczarkami)*: In saucepan sauté 4 oz finely chopped fresh mushrooms and 1 finely chopped med onion in 2 T butter or margarine until fully cooked (about 15 min), stirring frequently. Peel 6 hard-cooked eggs cut in half lengthwise and remove yolks. Mash yolks and combine with cool mushroom-onion mixture. Stir in 2 T sour cream and 3 T finely chopped fresh parsley. Mix well, salt and pepper to taste and use mixture to stuff whites.

DEVILED EGGS, SAUSAGE-STUFFED *(jaja nadziewane kiełbasą)*: Cut 6 shelled, hard-cooked eggs in half lengthwise and gently remove yolks. Set aside whites. Grind or process cooked yolks with ¼ lb skinned smoked

Polish sausage and 1 small quartered onion. To mixture add 1–2 t brown mustard, ¼ t paprika and 2–3 T mayonnaise or sour cream (or a little of each). Mix well and salt and pepper to taste. Stuff egg whites with mixture, rounding off tops with spoon. Into the top of each each, insert a thin radish slice or radish cross. (Cut thin small radish slices halfway through, fit 2 slices together to form a cross and insert in top of each deviled egg.) Serve on lettuce-lined platter and trim its rim with overlapping radish slices. These may be garnished with finely chopped chives. (OPTIONAL: Garnish eggs with a little freshly grated yellow cheese [Swiss, Gouda, brick, white American or other similar type].)

SPRAT-STUFFED DEVILED EGGS *(jaja nadziewane szprotkami)*: Peel 6 hard-cooked eggs and cut in half lengthwise. Scoop out yolks and set aside whites. Mash yolks thoroughly with 4–5 well-drained smoked Baltic sprats (sardine-like canned fish) or sardines. Add 1 T grated onion and 1–2 t lemon juice and mix in 3 T mayonnaise. Mix until smooth and fill whites with mixture. Decorate tops with thin rindless lemon wedges and thin strips of mild pickled red peppers. VARIATION: Well-drained, finely chopped tuna fish may be used in place of sprats or sardines.

EGGS IN HOT HORSERADISH SAUCE *(jaja w sosie chrzanowym na ciepło)*: Melt 2 T butter in saucepan, sprinkle with 2 T flour, stir to combine and dilute with a little water to get a smooth paste. Stir ¾ c sour cream and 1 heaping T prepared horseradish. Dilute with a little hot water or stock and continue simmering until sauce is thick, bubbly and pourable. Season with salt, white pepper and a little lemon juice and sugar. Serve at once over hot (freshly cooked) hard-cooked eggs.

EGGS STUFFED IN SHELLS, HOT *(jaja faszerowane w skorupkach)*: This is one of Poland's culinary classics, at Easter time and other occasions as well. I have never met an American (Polish or otherwise) who did not take to this delicacy. For the recipe, see Polish Holiday Banquet/Dinner-Party Favorites.

BEET AND HORSERADISH RELISH *(ćwikla z chrzanem)*: See Traditional Polish Condiments, page 178, for different ways of preparing this typically Polish relish—a "must" on the traditional Easter table.

BILBERRY-HORSERADISH SAUCE *(borówki z chrzanem)*: See Traditional Polish Condiments, page 180, for recipe.

MIXED VEGETABLE SALAD *(sałatka jarzynowa)*: There is an infinite variety of *sałatki* of this type. One version goes as follows: in salad bowl combine 4 c diced, cooked, cold potatoes, 2 cans drained peas and carrots,

2 cans drained navy beans, 4 diced dill pickles, 1 bunch chopped scallions, 1 bunch diced radishes, 2–3 peeled, cored, diced apples and 4–6 diced hard-cooked eggs. Toss ingredients gently, season with salt and pepper, garnish with 3 T chopped fresh parsley and lace with just enough mayonnaise to thinly coat ingredients. Feel free to juggle ingredients as desired.

MIXED VEGETABLE SALAD, PINK *(sałatka jarzynowa różowa)*: This is simply a variation of the above mixed vegetable salad, but it will add a nice color contrast to your *Święcone* table. Proceed as for mixed vegetable salad but replace peas and carrots with 2 c drained, canned beets, diced. Toss ingredients gently until the salad becomes uniformly pink. VARIATION: Instead of canned beets, stir in several heaping T *ćwikła,* which will not only give the salad a pinkish hue but added zing as well.

SPRING-ONION SALAD *(surówka ze szczypioru)*: See Typically Polish Salads, page 158.

LEEK SALAD *(sałatka z porów)*: Remove green tops from 3 leeks. (Freeze greens for soup.) Trim off "whiskers" at bottom of root if still attached. Cut leeks in half lengthwise and wash well under running water to remove any imbedded grit. Cut each half in half lengthwise which should give you 12 leek sticks. Place them on cutting board side by side and dice fairly fine. Place in bowl. Add 1 stalk celery, diced fine, and 1–2 peeled cooking apples, diced fine. Season with salt, pepper, sugar and lemon juice, toss and lace with mayonnaise.

RADISH SALAD *(surówka z rzodkiewki)*: See Typically Polish Salads, page 158.

POTATO SALAD WITH VINAIGRETTE DRESSING *(sałatka kartoflana z winegretem)*: In salad bowl combine 4 c diced, cooked, cold potatoes, 2 finely chopped shallots, 2 finely chopped scallions, 1 heaping T capers and (optional) 1–2 diced dill pickles. Fork-blend ⅓ c vinegar (white distilled wine vinegar or cider vinegar) with ½ c salad oil, 1 t prepared brown mustard, several dashes of garlic powder, ⅛ t pepper, ¼ t ground caraway and 1 t sugar. Pour over salad and chill well before serving.

BEAN SALAD *(sałatka fasolowa)*: In salad bowl combine 2 c canned, drained navy beans, 1 c lima beans, 1 c pinto beans, 1 c kidney beans, 1 peeled diced cucumber, 3 chopped dill pickles, 1 bunch chopped scallions, 1 diced green bell pepper and 2 cloves crushed garlic. Toss gently. Drizzle with juice of 1 large lemon and 3 T salad oil. Season with salt, pepper, basil and a little sugar and vinegar for a tangy, sweet and sour flavor. (OPTIONAL: Stir in 1–2 heaping T mayonnaise.)

MEATS—COLD AND HOT

COLD-MEAT PLATTER *(półmisek zimnych mięs)*: On oval or rectangular serving platters arrange an assortment of sliced cold meats. Boiled ham, baked ham, *polędwica* (Canadian bacon), *kabanosy* (thin dry sausage), *myśliwska,* (hunter's sausage), *krakowska* (Kraków sausage), smoked *kiełbasa*, cold sliced roasts (pork loin, veal, beef), boiled and baked slab bacon, boiled beef tongue, stuffed veal breast and *pasztet* (pâté) are traditional favorites and smoked turkey breast is becoming increasingly popular. *Studzienina*, also known as *galareta z nóżek* and *zimne nogi* (jellied pig's trotters and/or calf's feet) is another Easter classic. Many of these items are now available at delicatessens and sausage shops in Polish neighborhoods. NOTE: Be sure to artistically arrange the platters. On a large platter you can run 3 parallel rows of sliced meats. Each row should contain one variety of overlapping slices. Thin rounds of *kiełbasa* can rim the platter, and don't forget the parsley sprigs and radish roses (see page 72) for color. An Easter egg may be placed in a bed of greenery at one end of the platter. On a circular lettuce-lined platter, place half an orange shell at center and fill it with any of the above sauces. Arrange the sliced cold meats around it and trim the platter as above. Think festive, be artistic and use your imagination—that's the Polish way!

PIG'S FEET/PORK TROTTERS, JELLIED *(galareta z nóżek wieprzowych/zimne nogi/studzienina)*: Singe 6 split pig's feet (pork trotters or pig's knuckles) over flame to remove any remaining bristle. Wash well, place in pot, cover with cold water and bring to boil. Simmer several min, then pour off water. Add fresh cold water to cover (2½ qt, m/l) and 1 T salt, bring to boil once again and reduce heat. Skim off any scum that forms at top. Add 8 peppercorns and 1 bay leaf and cook on low heat 2 hr. Add 1 portion soup greens (see page 30) and cook another 2 hr or until meat falls away from bone. When meat is nearly ready, add 2–3 cloves crushed garlic. Remove pork feet. Drain stock, discarding vegetables and spices. (OPTIONAL: The carrot may be saved, diced and added to the aspic for better color.) Remove the meat from bones, discard bones and dice meat. Transfer meat to glass or crockery pans and drench with stock. For individual aspics, divide the meat among as many teacups or individual molds as needed and evenly distribute the stock. Chill in fridge until set. Before turning out, scrape off and discard the congealed fat at top of containers. VARIATION: Placing first diced hard-cooked eggs in container, then the meat and finally the stock will give your aspic a touch of

Easter. (In this recipe 2–4 hard-cooked eggs may be used.) Provide cruets of vinegar, lemon juice, a 50–50 vinegar-lemon juice mixture or prepared horse-radish for guests to season their jellied pig's feet to taste.

KIEŁBASA, HOMEMADE SMOKED *(kiełbasa domowa wędzona)*: Dice 11 lb pork butts into ⅓″–½″ cubes. (VARIATION: The meat may be coarsely ground instead of diced.) Mix 7 T salt with 1 t salt-peter and combine with diced meat. Mix, even out the top of meat, pressing down lightly and let stand in cool place or refrigerate covered overnight. Sprinkle mixture with 2 t ground black pepper, 2 t marjoram, 2 t sugar and 4–6 cloves garlic, minced. Work by hand, letting mixture squish between fingers, until it feels sticky. Stuff hog casing with mixture, twisting into links every 13″ or 14″. Hang up outdoors or in well-ventilated place indoors at 35°–50° for 1–2 days to air-dry. Then smoke in cold smoke for 48 hr.

KIEŁBASA, FRESH HOMEMADE *(biała kiełbasa domowa)*: Dice 9 lb pork butts into ½″ cubes. (VARIATION: Meat may be chopped fine or coarsely ground instead of being diced.) Sprinkle 2 lb raw hamburger, ground round steak or ground veal with 5–6 T salt, 1½ t ground black pepper, 1½ t marjoram and 6 cloves finely minced garlic, and work seasoning into ground meat. Then combine with diced, chopped or ground pork. Work by hand, gradually adding 1 c cold meat stock or water and continue working until liquid is completely absorbed. Stuff hog casings with mixture, twisting into 12″–13″ links and tying them with white twine. Cook by boiling, baking or pan-baking (see following directions). (OPTIONAL: Several pinches dry mustard and ground coriander may be added to mixture before stuffing casings.) NOTE: Additional sausage-making ideas are found in *Polish Heritage Cookery*.

KIEŁBASA, FRESH BOILED *(biała kiełbasa gotowana)*: Place 3 lb fresh *kiełbasa* in pot of cold water which should cover it by at least 1″. Add 1 bay leaf, 1 beef bouillon cube and 1 large quartered onion and cook on low to a gentle boil. Simmer on low, covered, 30–40 min. Let stand in hot liquid another 10 min before serving. Pork must be fully cooked so make sure it is no longer pink inside. If so, cook a while longer.

KIEŁBASA, FRESH BAKED (1) *(biała kiełbasa pieczona)*: Arrange 2–3 lb fresh *kiełbasa* in a single layer in baking pan. Cover with cold water and bake in 350° oven. Turn sausage over when half the water has evaporated. It is ready when all water disappears and sausage begins to brown, 60–75 min.

KIEŁBASA, SMOKED BAKED *(kiełbasa wędzona pieczona)*: Proceed as in previous recipe, using smoked *kiełbasa* instead of fresh.

KIEŁBASA, FRESH PAN-BAKED *(biała kiełbasa z patelni)*: Heat 1 T oil or lard in heavy skillet. Into it place 2 lb fresh Polish sausage (or as much as will fit) in a concentric coil to cover the skillet's entire surface. When it browns on 1 side, prick sausage at 1″ intervals with toothpick. When the liquid that flows out evaporates, turn sausage over, let it brown and then prick surface. When liquid steams away, reduce heat, cover with tight-fitting lid and simmer on low until fully cooked (45–60 min). VARIATION: Before covering sausage with lid, intersperse with 1–2 thinly sliced onions (cut onions in half, then slice each half thin). A little liquid may also be added to pan.

KIEŁBASA, FRESH BAKED (2) *(biała kiełbasa pieczona)*: Preheat oven to 400°. Place 2½ lb fresh *kiełbasa* in one layer in baking pan greased with 1 T lard or butter. Cut 2 onions into quarters and slice each quarter quite thin, spreading onions on and around the *kiełbasa*. For a more garlicky taste, add 2–3 cloves crushed garlic. Pop into oven and bake 15 min, then reduce heat to 350° and bake another 40–45 min. With toothpick, occasionally prick sausage to releases excessive fat. NOTE: A little water may be added.

KIEŁBASA, FRESH BEER-BAKED *(biała kiełbasa duszona w piwie)*: Place 3 lb fresh *kiełbasa* in single layer in baking pan. Drench with 2 c beer and enough water to barely cover the sausage. Bake in preheated 375° oven 30 min. Smother with 4 thinly sliced onions and bake another 30 min. Cut into 4″–5″ portions and serve.

KIEŁBASA, FRESH, COOKED, SERVED HOT *(biała kiełbasa na gorąco)*: The traditional Polish way is to limit cooking on Easter Sunday and serve mainly cold foods or precooked ones that are merely warmed up. This arrangement might also be a convenient solution at various community events where kitchen facilities are limited. Cut the refrigerated precooked (boiled or baked) *kiełbasa* into 2-inch pieces and reheat it in a vegetable-sprayed non-stick skillet until heated through and lightly browned on all sides.

KIEŁBASA, FRESH, COOKED, SERVED COLD *(biała kiełbasa na zimno)*: This is a nice addition to the cold-meat platter, and the ⅛″–¼″ thick rounds of this sausage are a great platter-rimmer. It should be prepared at least a day ahead and refrigerated until needed. Place 4 lb fresh *kiełbasa* in pot, add enough boiling water to cover the *kiełbasa* by at least 3 inches, add a large quartered onion, ½ a bay leaf and 2 grains allspice, bring to boil, reduce heat and simmer, covered, about 1 hr. Leave sausage in water until cooled to room temperature. After removing sausage from liquid, wipe it with paper towel and refrigerate overnight tightly covered with plastic wrap. Also cover and refrigerate the water you cooked the *kiełbasa* in. Next day, discard congealed fat and use *kiełbasa* water to prepare *żurek* (see page 18).

KIEŁBASA AND SAUERKRAUT *(kiełbasa zapiekana w kapuście)*: Drain 2–3 qt sauerkraut and rinse in cold water. Drain, press out moisture, chop (optional), place in pot, scald with boiling water to cover, add 1 bay leaf and cook, uncovered, 45–60 min. Drain and transfer to baking pan. Cut baked fresh and/or smoked *kiełbasa* prepared as above into 2″ or 3″ pieces and mix with sauerkraut. Season *kiełbasa* pan drippings with 1 t liquid Maggi seasoning and add to sauerkraut. Bake in 350° oven 90 min or so. Leave in oven 30 min after switching off heat. Taste improves with each reheating.

BOILED BACON *(boczek gotowany)*: Place 2¼ lb slab bacon, fresh or smoked, into pot. Add 1 portion soup greens (see index), 1 bay leaf, several peppercorns and grains allspice and water to more than cover. Bring to boil, reduce heat, skim off scum and simmer 80–90 min or until fork-tender. Remove bacon, pat dry and refrigerate overnight. Serve cold, sliced thin with typical Easter accompaniments. (NOTE: The degreased stock makes a good soup base.)

BAKED BACON *(boczek pieczony)*: See page 133.

POLISH EASTER CAKES

EASTER BABKA, TRADITIONAL *(babka wielkanocna)*: Mash 1 cake yeast with 1 T sugar, stir in 1 c lukewarm milk and 1 c flour. Mix, cover with cloth and let stand in warm place to rise (about 15 min). Beat 5 egg yolks with ¼ t salt on low speed, add ¾ c confectioners' sugar and 2 T vanilla sugar (or 1 t vanilla extract) and beat on high speed until thick and fluffy. Sift 3 c flour into bowl, add yeast and egg mixtures, mix to blend and work by hand until smooth and glossy. Gradually add ½ c melted butter and keep kneading until air blisters appear and dough no longer sticks to hands. Add 1½ c rinsed, dried raisins and knead to distribute them evenly. Cover with cloth and let rise in warm place until doubled in bulk (about 1 hr). Fill generously buttered and flour-dusted babka pan only ½ full, cover with cloth and let rise again. When doubled, bake in 375° oven about 45 min. It is done when a wooden pick comes out clean. When cool, remove from pan and glaze with icing (mix together ⅔ c confectioners' sugar, 1 t rum or vanilla extract and 2–3 T boiling water).

EASTER BABKA, EASY *(babka wielkanocna łatwiejsza)*: Mash 1 cake yeast with 1 c sugar. Add 3 whole eggs, beaten, ¾ c butter dissolved in 1 c very warm milk, 3 c flour, 1 t vanilla extract and ½ c raisins. Mix well to blend ingredients, but do not knead. Fill well-greased babka, brioche, Turk's head, Bundt or other tube pan with dough, but it should be only ⅓ full. Cover with cloth and let stand in warm place until doubled in bulk (about 2 hr). Bake about 1 hr in preheated 350° oven. It is fully baked when a wooden pick comes out clean. Dust with confectioners' sugar or glaze with icing (see preceding recipe).

LEMON BABKA *(babka cytrynowa)*: Proceed as with "Easy Easter Babka" above, but add grated rind of 1 lemon to dough. After it is baked, glaze with icing made with ⅔ c confectioners' sugar, juice of 1 lemon and 1 T or so boiling water.

BABKA, BAKING POWDER-RAISED *(babka łatwa na proszku)*: Cream 1 c plus 1 T butter or margarine with 1¼ c sugar. Continue beating while gradually adding 4 eggs, alternately with 1½ c flour mixed with 3 t baking powder. Add a pinch of salt, ½ c raisins and several drops of flavoring extract of choice: vanilla, rum, almond or lemon. (VARIATION: ¼–½ t cinnamon may be used in place of flavoring extracts.) Mix well, transfer dough to greased, flour-sprinkled babka pan and bake in preheated 350° oven about 1 hr. It is fully baked when a wooden pick comes out clean. Glaze or dust with confectioners' sugar as above.

SILESIAN BABKA *(babka śląska)*: Mash 1 oz fresh yeast with 1 T sugar and stir in 5 T very warm milk, then set aside to rise. Beat 2 egg yolks and 1 whole egg and cream with ⅓ c sugar. Add risen yeast mixture, 3½ c flour, ½ c warm milk, 2 T grated orange zest, 1 T grated lemon zest and ½ t salt. Combine ingredients well and knead until dough is smooth. Gradually work in ½ c melted butter and continue kneading until it is fully absorbed. Place dough in warm place until doubled in bulk. While it rises, melt 2 T butter in saucepan. Prepare crumb topping by combining 2½ T confectioners' sugar with ½ c flour and add melted butter and 2 pinches of cinnamon. Stir to combine ingredients and set aside. Place risen dough into well-greased and floured Bundt pan. Brush top with half a beaten egg and coarsely grate crumb topping over top. Bake in preheated 350° oven about 1 hr, or until wooden skewer comes out clean.

SAND BABKA *(babka piaskowa)*: Combine ¾ c flour, ¾ c potato starch and 4 t baking powder and sift together. Cream 1 c plus 2 T butter, gradually adding 4 raw egg yolks, grated rind and juice of 1 lemon and mix well. Gently fold in 4 stiffly beaten egg whites. Transfer to greased, flour-dusted babka pan and bake in 350° oven 1 hr or so. When cool dust with confectioners' sugar or ice.

CHEESECAKE *(sernik)*: Sift 1½ c flour onto board and cut in 1 stick cold butter. Beat 4 eggs with 4 T confectioners' sugar and add to flour mixture. Sprinkle with 2 T milk and 2 t baking powder, quickly work ingredients into a dough and chill in fridge 30 min. Meanwhile grind or process 1½ lb white cheese, and blend together with 2 cold, well-mashed potatoes. Cream ¾ c butter with 1 c confectioners' sugar and 1 t vanilla sugar. Continue mixing and gradually add 5 egg yolks and cheese mixture. When fully blended, sprinkle with 3 T potato starch, add 1 c plumped raisins and 2 T finely chopped candied orange rind. Mix ingredients and fold in 3 stiffly beaten eggs whites. Roll out ⅔ of the dough ¼″ thick to fit lightly greased round pan. Top with cheese filling and smooth top. Roll remaining dough into pencil-thick strands and arrange latticework on top of cheese. Brush top with beaten egg and bake in preheated 350° oven about 50 min.

JELLIED CHEESECAKE, UNBAKED *(sernik z galaretką bez pieczenia)*: Grind or process 1⅓ lb farmer cheese and mix with ⅔ c whipping cream. Beat 3 egg yolks with ¾ c sugar and ⅔ c soft butter until smooth and fluffy, gradually adding cheese and cream mixture. Beat until smooth. Stir in ½ c rinsed raisins and ½ finely chopped candied lemon and orange rinds. Grease bottom and sides of springform pan generously. Cover bottom of pan with vanilla wafers or Lorna Doone biscuits—just as they are or crushed. Pour cheese mixture over them and refrigerate 2 hr. Decorate top of cheesecake with drained canned peach slices and cherries and drench with 1 c cool but still ungelled orange-flavor gelatin dessert prepared according to directions on pkg. Refrigerate at least 4 hr before serving or until well set.

ALMOND MAZURKA *(mazurek migdałowy)*: Cream 1¾ c butter with ⅔ confectioners' sugar until fluffy. Gradually stir in 2⅓ c flour, 4 cold, ground hard-cooked egg yolks (use the chopped whites in any salad), 1 c finely chopped, blanched almonds, 1 beaten raw egg and ⅛ t salt. By hand, work ingredients into a dough and chill in refrigerator 30 min. On lightly floured board roll out into a rectangle no more than ¾″ high. Use flat of knife to even out the sides. Transfer to lightly greased cookie sheet and bake in preheated 375° oven 40–45 min or until a nice golden hue is obtained. When cooled slightly, glaze top and sides with homemade or store-bought chocolate or vanilla icing. Decorate top with almond slices.

FRUIT MAZURKA *(mazurek owocowy)*: Into 2 c flour, sifted onto breadboard, cut ¾ c cold butter or margarine. Sprinkle with ½ c confectioners' sugar and 1 T vanilla sugar. Blend with pastry-blender to a groat-like consistency. Add ⅓ c Egg Beaters (or Better'n Eggs or similar product) and quickly combine ingredients into a dough. If necessary, add 2–3 T water to bind dough. Roll dough into a ball, wrap with aluminium foil and refrigerate 30 min. Place dough on board, cut off and set aside ¼ of the dough and roll the larger piece into a ¼″-thick rectangle. Place dough in baking pan. Use reserved ¼ of dough to form finger-thick rolls between palms of hands and use them to make a rim along the edges of dough in pan. Make sure the rim is solid and uniform on all 4 sides because it has to hold in the filling. Press filling down lightly so it adheres to dough rectangle. Bake in preheated 375° oven about 20 min or until golden. Allow to cool in pan. Set on serving plate and spread area within rim with cherry, raspberry or apricot jam. If you have a pastry tube, try writing *Alleluja* with white icing on the jam-covered surface.

CRUMB-TOP FRUIT MAZURKA *(mazurek owocowy z kruszonką)*: Cut ½ lb butter into 3 c flour, add in 4 egg yolks and 1 scant c confectioners' sugar. Quickly work ingredients into a smooth dough, wrap in foil and refrigerate several hr. Divide dough into 2 parts. Roll out one half and fit it into square or rectangular baking pan. Spread with *powidła* or other thick jam. Coarsely grate the remaining dough over jam, evenly covering the entire surface. Bake in preheated 400° oven about 20 min or until nice and golden. When cool, cut into squares.

MAZURKA CAKE, WAFER-TYPE, EASY *(mazurek na waflu, łatwy)*: Buy 4 plain, large, square or rectangular wafers from a pastry-supply, gourmet, specialty or European import shop. Place 1 wafer on cutting board, spread thinly with apricot or cherry jam, cover with another wafer, press down gently and spread with canned chocolate or white frosting, cover with another wafer, spread it with jam and cover with a 4th wafer. Cover with clean dishtowel, weight down with something heavy and refrigerate. Just before serving spread top and sides with frosting and sprinkle top generously with ground walnuts. Cut into squares and serve. NOTE: You can also make this mazurka using large sheets of *opłatek*. Decorate as desired (see Mazurka Decorating, page 121).

HAZELNUT MAZURKA, EASY *(mazurek orzechowy łatwy)*: Mix 1½ c uncooked rolled oats with ½ c ground hazelnuts (filberts) and brown in hot, dry frying pan, stirring constantly. When cool, stir in 4 T sour cream. Separately, beat 3 raw egg yolks with 1 c confectioners' sugar until white and combine with oat-nut mixture. Add 1 level t baking powder, several drops almond extract and a pinch of salt. Mix well. Beat 3 egg whites to a stiff froth and gently fold into mixture. Transfer mixture to greased square or rectangle baking pan of a size that allows the batter to attain a height of ¾″. Smooth top and even out sides. Bake in preheated 375° oven about 20 min or until golden.

After cake has cooled, glaze with icing, made by combining ⅔ c confectioners' sugar, 2 T cocoa, juice of 1 lemon and 1 T boiling water. Decorate top with hazelnut halves. (OPTIONAL: For a cake-bottom mazurka, line greased pan snugly with Lorna Doone cookies, crushing 2 or 3 and sprinkling crumbs over surface of cookie base.) Transfer mazurka mixture to cookie base, even out top and sides, and trim away cookies that protrude beyond the sides of your mazurka square or rectangle. Bake as above.

MAZURKA DECORATING *(dekorowanie mazurków)*: It is traditional to decorate the top of this typical Polish Easter cake with seasonal motifs. Usually decorations or inscriptions in dark icing are applied to a light-colored surface and vice-versa so they stand out. The most common inscription is *Alleluja.* Depending on the decorator's artistic flair, an Easter Lamb with cross-emblazoned banner as well as Easter eggs and pussy willows may be drawn free-hand. On a white or other light-colored iced surface draw 3 or 4 slightly curving brown lines (pussy-willow twigs). Almond slices make excellent pussy-willow buds, applied at intervals along ¾ the length of the twigs.

EASTER CHEESE DESSERT, TRADITIONAL *(pascha, tradycyjna)*: Sieve 2¼ lb full-cream (not low-fat!) farmer cheese. Separately cream 5 egg yolks with 1¼ c sugar, stir in 1 c light cream. Stirring constantly, heat mixture nearly to boiling point, but do not boil. Remove from flame, stir in the cheese, ½ c butter, ¾ c plumped raisins, ½ c chopped blanched almonds, 1 t grated orange zest and 1 t vanilla. Mix well and place mixture on cheesecloth. Tie cheese mixture in cheesecloth into a ball and hang it up to drip dry, twisting ball to extract moisture. When no more moisture can be extracted, place cheesecloth-covered cheese under something heavy in fridge and chill overnight.

EASTER CHEESE DESSERT, EASY *(pascha, łatwiejsza)*: Soak 1 heaping T raisins in a jigger of cognac or brandy. Grind 1¼ lb farmer cheese or dry cottage cheese twice or whirl it to a powder in food processor. In saucepan beat 5 raw egg yolks with 1½ c confectioners' sugar until white and fluffy, gradually adding ½ c light cream. Place saucepan on low flame and heat mixture, mixing constantly, but do not boil. Set aside to cool. Combine cheese with yolk mixture, add the drained raisins and about ½ c chopped blanched almonds and/or walnuts, 1–2 T finely chopped candied orange rind and 1 t vanilla extract. Mix ingredients well and place in sieve lined with 2 layers of cheesecloth. Cover with plate and weight down with 1-qt jar filled with water. Refrigerate overnight. Next day, turn out onto serving plate. Decorate top with whole almonds, walnut meats, raisins and strips of candied orange rind. (OPTIONAL: Top may first be decorated with grated chocolate.)

SUGGESTED POLISH EASTER MENUS

The following menus include easy recipes any beginner can try as well as foods better suited to experienced cooks. These suggestions will enable you to hold the simplest Easter meal for two or three, have the whole gang over for *Święcone* or plan a *Święconka* at your parish or club. Both country-style and more upscale gourmet selections are provided. NOTE: Many of the items listed (including roast meats, pâté, *ćwikła* and baked goods) are readily available at Polish delis and markets.

Small, Simple Święcone

I.

White Easter soup with egg *(biały barszcz z jajkiem)*
Hard-cooked eggs in horseradish sauce *(jaja na twardo z sosem chrzanowym)*
Polish rye bread, butter *(chleb, masło)*
Polish ham, sliced cold *(polska szynka)*
Beet and horseradish salad *(ćwikła z chrzanem)*
Mixed vegetable salad *(sałatka jarzynowa)*
Jellied cheesecake *(sernik z galaretką)*

II.

Hard-cooked eggs in Easter sauce *(jaja na twardo z sosem do święconego)*
Roast pork loin, cold sliced *(schab pieczony)*
Polish rye bread, butter *(chleb, masło)*
Accompaniments (dodatki)—*ćwikła,* pickled mushrooms, horseradish, spiced plums
Green-pea salad *(sałatka z zielonego groszku)*
Hot fresh sausage, baked *(pieczona biała kiełbasa)*
Hazelnut mazurka *(mazurek orzechowy)*

Family/Country-style Święcone

Easter ryemeal soup with egg *(żurek wielkanocny z jajkiem)*
Mashed potatoes garnished with fatback nuggets *(kartofle ze skwarkami)*–eaten on the side with the soup
Hard-cooked eggs *(jaja na twardo)*—plain, whole, shelled (with salt and pepper, horseradish, *ćwikła* or sour-cream sauce provided on the side)
Polish rye bread, butter *(chleb, masło)*
Bean salad *(sałatka z fasoli)*

Cooked bacon, cold sliced *(boczek gotowany)*
Cold sliced meats *(zimne mięsa)*—ham, picnic ham *(baleron),* roast pork, roast veal, boiled beef tongue, headcheese *(salceson)*
Jellied pig's feet *(zimne nogi)*—provide vinegar in cruet
Accompaniments *(dodatki)*—*ćwikła,* horseradish, pickled mushrooms, spiced plums
Hot fresh kiełbasa, baked *(biała kiełbasa pieczona)*
Easter babka *(babka wielkanocna)*
Crumb-top fruit mazurka *(mazurek owocowy z kruszonką*
Cheesecake *(sernik)*

Gourmet Święcone

Clear beet soup with hot pasty *(barszcz czerwony czysty z pasztecikiem)*
Herring in horseradish mayonnaise *(śledzie w majonezie chrzanowym)*
Smoked salmon garnished with dill *(łosoś wędzony z koperkiem)*
Assorted bread and rolls *(pieczywo mieszane)*
Hard-cooked eggs in caper sauce *(jaja na twardo w sosie kaparowym)*
Hard-cooked eggs with caviar *(jaja na twardo z kawiorem)*
Deviled eggs stuffed with mushrooms *(jaja nadziewane pieczarkami)*
Deviled eggs stuffed with sausage *(jaja nadziewane kiełbasą)*
Accompaniments *(dodatki)*—gherkins, olives, beet and horseradish salad, pickled mushrooms, spiced pears, spiced cherries
Cold meat platter *(półmisek zimnych mięs)*—ham, smoked pork loin (Canadian bacon), sliced turkey, beef tenderloin, pâté, veal tongues in aspic
Leek and cheese salad *(sałatka z porów z serem)*
Pork-loin stuffed with prunes *(schab nadziewany śliwkami)*—serve cold or hot
Easter cheese dessert *(pascha)*
Almond mazurka *(mazurek migdałowy)*
Saffron babka *(babka z szafranem)*

TRADITIONAL POLISH SOUPS

A big bowl (1½ to 2 c) of soup has long been the traditional first course of Poles' daily dinner. Some of the heartier varieties can be meals in themself. At festive dinners, soup is served as the second course, following the cold starters. A daintier clear *barszcz,* bouillon or clear mushroom soup is right at home at the fanciest gourmet banquet. Most soups are served hot, but Polish cuisine also has some interesting cold soups known as *chłodniki* (literally "coolers"). Savory soups predominate, but there are also a number of sweet varieties, especially fruit soups served mainly in summer. Look for other typically Polish soups among the Wigilia, Lent, Easter and Old Polish Cookery suggestions.

CHICKEN SOUP *(rosół z kury)*: This is the typical soup served at Sunday dinner, weddings and other family occasions. A fryer/broiler can be used, but for that rich, old-time flavor a mature stewing chicken is preferable. Wash 1 cut-up 3-lb chicken, place in pot, add 1 T salt and 2½–3 qt water, bring to gentle boil and cook 90 min or until meat is fairly tender. (Cook only 45 min if a fryer is being used). Skim off scum until no more forms. To broth add 1 portion soup greens (see page 30) and 1 halved onion (impaled on fork and charred over flame), 1 whole tomato, 6 peppercorns, 2–3 grains allspice and 1 bay leaf. Cook until vegetables are tender. Strain and discard all spices. Vegetables may be used in some other dish, but the carrots may be diced and served in the soup. Serve over homemade or store-bought egg noodles, egg-drop dumplings or poured-batter noodles, cooked diced potatoes, cooked rice or barley. NOTE: If weight-watching and calorie-counting, refrigerate broth overnight and discard congealed fat (or freeze it in ¼ c batches for future roux-making) before reheating. Garnish with a little finely chopped parsley and/or dill before serving. NOTE: The boiled chicken may be removed from bone and served in the soup, used for the main course (in a sauce, for example) or used for ground dishes (pâté, *paszteciki, pierogi*, etc.)

BEEF BROTH *(rosół wołowy)*: Wash 1½ lb bone-in beef and drench with 8 c cold water. Bring to boil very gently, skimming off scum. Add 2 t salt and cook 2 to 2½ hr. Add 1 portion soup greens (see page 30) with or without a slice of savoy cabbage, 1 halved onion (charred over flame revealing blackened concentric rings), 6 peppercorns, 2–3 grains allspice and 1 small bay leaf. Cook another 30 min or until vegetables are tender. Strain, refrigerate to remove congealed fat and serve as above.

ROYAL (BEEF AND CHICKEN) BROTH *(rosół królewski)*: Proceed as in above recipe using 1 lb bone-in beef. When it has cooked 90 min, add 1 lb chicken and continue cooking about 30 min. Add 1 portion soup greens (see page 30) and peppercorns, onion, allspice and bay leaf as above. Serve as above. VARIATION: After straining broth and setting aside vegetables for other use, add 3–4 oz finely chopped chicken livers, bring to boil and switch off heat. Garnish with chopped dill and serve over noodles of choice.

POURED-BATTER NOODLES *(lane kluski)*: Fork-blend 2 small eggs, 6 T flour and 2 pinches of salt until mixture is smooth. Stir in 1 T hot chicken broth or as much as needed to get a nice pourable batter and beat with fork until smooth. Pour batter in a thin stream into a pot of rapidly boiling water and cook about 2 min. Remove with slotted spoon and serve in broth. NOTE: These noodles can be cooked in the hot broth but that makes it turn cloudy.

BEEF BOUILLON *(bulion wołowy)*: Wash 3 lb bone-in beef, place in pot with 8 c cold water and slowly bring to boil. Reduce heat, skim scum from surface until no more forms. Add 1 dry bolete mushroom, 1 t salt and cook on low 1 hr. Halve 2 onions and scorch over gas flame, directly on coil of electric range or in dry frying pan until blackened rings form on surface of onion. Add to pot together with 1 portion soup greens (see page 30), 1 sm bay leaf, 6 peppercorns and 2 grains allspice. Simmer another 2 hr or until meat falls away from bone. (Save meat for *paszteciki* below and soup vegetables for salad or other dish.) Refrigerate room-temp stock. To serve, remove congealed fat from surface and heat to boiling. Season with 1 t Maggi, salt and pepper to taste. The juice of ½ lemon will perk up the flavor. Serve in bouillon cups or teacups with *paszteciki*.

MUSHROOM SOUP, CLEAR *(czysta zupa grzybowa)*: This typical Wigilia soup can also served in a cup like bouillon or beet soup on other occasions. The mushrooms with which it was cooked can be used to make the *paszteciki* filling. NOTE: For non-Wigilia use, it may be made with meat stock. See Wigilia section for the recipe, page 41.

TOMATO SOUP, CLEAR *(zupa pomidorowa, czysta)*: A convenient way to prepare this soup is to combine 4 c tomato juice (out of a can or carton) with 2 c meat stock. Bring to boil and season to taste a pinch of sugar and a little lemon juice. Garnish with fresh chopped dill. Serve in bouillon cups with *paszteciki* or pastry fingers.

MEAT AND MUSHROOM-FILLED PASTRIES *(paszteciki z mięsem i grzybami)*: In 3 T fat sauté 6 oz fresh sliced mushrooms with 2 coarsely chopped sm onions until browned. Grind mushrooms and onions with ½ lb cooked beef, chicken and/or pork. Add 1 sm egg, 2–3 T bread crumbs and season with Maggi, pepper, a pinch of marjoram. Mix well. Break open two 8-oz pkg refrigerator crescent-roll dough and spread dough sheets on lightly floured board. Dip fingers in flour and press down on manufacturer's perforations to obliterate them. Cut each sheet lengthwise into 2 equal strips, run filling down center of strips and fold dough over it. Pinch to seal edges. Cut dough at angle into 2″ pieces and bake on baking sheet seam-side down according to directions on pkg. Serve hot with beef bouillon (above), beet soup (below) and other clear soups. NOTE: *Paszteciki* may be filled with just meat or just mushrooms rather than a mixture of the two. HINT: If you want to make your own *paszteciki* dough from scratch (and for a large crowd that is certainly the more economical way to go!), see *Polish Heritage Cookery.*

CLEAR BEET SOUP *(czysty barszcz czerwony)*: Scrub 1 lb small beets and cook in water to cover or bake in med-hot oven 60 min or until fork-tender. When cool enough to handle, dice and place in pot together with 4 c meat stock, 1 c beet-sour, ½ oz rehydrated and cooked dried mushrooms and their liquid and 1 c apple juice. Bring to boil and switch off heat. Cover and let stand 30 min. Add 1–2 cloves crushed garlic, 1 jg dry red wine and season to taste with a little sugar and lemon juice, salt, pepper and marjoram. Heat nearly to boiling, strain and serve in twin-handled barszcz cups or large teacups. Hot *paszteciki* or pastry fingers are the traditional accompaniment. HINT: The leftover beets (cooked or canned) may be added to a mixed-vegetable salad.

CLEAR BEET SOUP, EASY *(czysty barszcz czerwony łatwy)*: Combine in pot 3 c beet juice from plain canned or pickled beets with 1½ c apple juice and 2 c meat stock. Bring to boil and add 1 jg dry red wine, 1–2 cloves crushed garlic and (optional) ½ mushroom bouillon cube dissolved in ½ c boiling water. Season to taste with salt, pepper and a pinch of marjoram and a bit of sugar if desired. Serve hot in teacups as the soup course with *paszteciki* (see page 193) on the side.

BEET SOUP/BARSZCZ, CREAMED *(barszcz czerwony zabielany)*: Prepare soup as for clear beet soup (above), but add the beets and mushrooms, diced or sliced. Fork-blend 1 heaping T flour with 1 c sour cream until smooth and use to cream soup. This soup may be served over quartered hard-cooked eggs. (OPTIONAL: Garnish with a little chopped dill.)

UKRAINIAN BARSZCZ *(barszcz ukraiński)*: In pot combine 8 c water and ¾–1 lb pork bones. (HINT: The bones cut away from pork chops to make Polish-style breaded pork cutlets are ideal for this purpose!) Add 1 bay leaf, 6 peppercorns, 2 grains allspice and 1 t salt. Bring to boil, reduce heat and simmer about 1 hr, skimming scum from surface. Add 2 peeled, diced, raw beets and 1 portion diced soup greens (see page 30), including an extra onion and simmer until tender. Remove any meat from bones, dice and add to soup (discard bones). Add a slice of savoy cabbage and 2 c diced potatoes and cook until tender. Add 1–2 c cooked (or canned, drained) pea-beans or lima beans, stir in 2 T tomato paste, 1 c beet-sour and 1–2 cloves crushed garlic and bring to boil. Cream with ½ sour cream fork-blended with a heaping T flour. Season with a little salt and sugar. NOTE: This hearty soup can be a meal in itself when served with rye bread.

BABY BEET-GREEN SOUP *(botwinka)*: Wash extremely well under running water 1 bunch baby beets (which should be no larger than small radishes) together with their greens (tops). Trim away any damaged or blemished sections. Chop quite fine and cook in a small amount of lightly salted water containing juice of ½ small lemon, until tender. Add to 6 c strained meat stock (veal stock is excellent!). Add about 1 c beet-sour and bring to boil. Remove from heat. Cream with ½ c sour cream and a heaping T flour. Simmer several min. Season to taste with salt, pepper, a pinch or two of sugar and a squeeze of lemon. Add ½ c or so juice from canned beets or 2 or more T beet concentrate to improve color. NOTE: In the absence of beet-sour, beet concentrate (several T) or 1 c canned beet juice plus several pinches citric acid may be used instead.

VEGETABLE-BARLEY SOUP, POLISH-STYLE *(krupnik polski)*: Soak 4 dried mushrooms in 1 c warm water several hr. Wash ½ lb or so meaty beef bones and place in soup pot containing 7 c water. Add the mushrooms and liquid and cook 60–80 min, skimming off scum. Add 1 portion soup greens (see page 30) and (optional) 5 peppercorns, 2 grains allspice and 1 bay leaf and cook until vegetables are tender. Strain soup. In separate saucepan cook ½ c pearl barley in 1 c strained stock. Dice vegetables, mushrooms and any meat attached to bones and return to soup together with the cooked barley and 2 peeled, diced potatoes. Cook until potatoes are tender. Salt to taste and garnish with 1 t chopped parsley. This hearty and satisfying soup has long been a cold-weather favorite.

SAUERKRAUT SOUP *(kapuśniak)*: Prepare stock by cooking ½–¾ lb meaty pork bones in 8 c water 1 hr, skimming off scum. Add 1 t salt, 2 carrots, 1 stalk celery, 1 onion, 1 bay leaf and 5 peppercorns and cook until meat comes away from bone. Drain 1 qt sauerkraut (reserving juice), rinse in cold water, drain, pressing out moisture, chop and add to strained stock. Cook on med heat, uncovered, 30 min. Dice meat from bones, and add to pot, then reduce heat and cook, covered, until sauerkraut is very tender. In skillet fry up 4 slices diced bacon with 1 chopped onion, stir in 3 T flour and simmer until browned, stirring constantly. Dilute with several T soup and stir into a smooth paste. Add to pot, stir and simmer several more min. If soup is not as tart as you like, add some reserved sauerkraut liquid. Salt and pepper to taste. One t sugar and ½ t caraway seeds may be added.

DUCK or GOOSE SOUP *(czernina/czarnina z kaczki lub gęsi)*: Place the cleaned giblets (make sure to cut open the gizzard and remove any semi-digested grain lodged therein!), neck, wings and rump of 1 duck or goose and (optional) ¾ lb pork ribs in pot containing 7 c water and cook 1 hr, skimming off scum. Add 1 portion soup greens (see page 30), 1 bay leaf, 2 cloves, 2 grains allspice and several peppercorns and cook until meat and vegetables are tender. Strain. Remove any meat attached to bones, dice giblets and return to stock. Add ½ c or more pitted prunes, ½ c diced dried apples and (optional) ⅓ c raisins and cook until fruit is tender. Remove from flame. Fork-blend blood of duck or goose (mixed with several T vinegar) with 1 heaping T flour and stir into soup. Simmer briefly. Adjust to taste with a little salt, sugar, vinegar. Serve over egg-noodle squares (*łazanki*) or other egg noodles, potato dumplings or diced cooked potatoes.

SPLIT-PEA SOUP *(grochówka)*: In soup pot combine 8 c water, 2 c yellow split peas, 1 portion soup greens (see page 30) and 1 extra onion, diced, ½–¾ lb diced smoked *kiełbasa* and/or ham, 1 bay leaf, and 8 peppercorns. Cook, covered, on low heat 2 hr, or until peas completely disintegrate. Add 1 c peeled, diced potatoes and cook until tender. Make a roux by frying up 4 slices diced bacon with 1 chopped onion and browning 2 T flour in the drippings. Stir into soup. Add 2 cloves crushed garlic, 1 heaping t marjoram and salt and pepper to taste. Simmer a few more min, then switch off heat and let stand for flavors to blend at least 15 min before serving.

DILL-PICKLE SOUP *(zupa ogórkowa)*: Peel ½ lb brined dill pickles (*ogórki kiszone*), grate coarsely and simmer in 1 T butter for 5 min or until tender. Add to 6 c meat or vegetable stock together with 1 c dill-pickle brine and bring to boil. Cream soup with ½ c sour cream fork-blended with 1 heaping T flour. Simmer briefly, salt and pepper to taste and garnish with a little chopped fresh dill. VARIATION: 2 c peeled, diced potatoes may be cooked in soup until tender. NOTE: Bottled dill-pickle purée is available at Polish markets and delis.

TOMATO SOUP *(zupa pomidorowa)*: Wash, hull and quarter 1¼ lb fresh tomatoes and simmer, covered, on low heat with several T stock and 2 T butter 15–20 min. Sieve into 6 c meat or vegetable stock and season to taste with salt, pepper and a little sugar. Cream with ½ c sour cream or 1 c milk fork-blended with 1 heaping T flour. Simmer briefly and serve over noodles or rice. VARIATION: When fresh vine-ripened tomatoes are out of season, simply stir 4–5 T tomato paste directly into hot stock and proceed as above. Canned tomato juice cooked with an equal amt of stock is also very good. NOTE: Poles are divided over whether noodles or rice are the best accompaniment to *zupa pomidorowa*, but noodle fanciers seem to have the edge!

PURÉED CHAMPIGNON MUSHROOM SOUP *(krem z pieczarek)*: Wash and dice 12 oz fresh, cultivated mushrooms and cook in 6 c meat or vegetable stock 30 min. Strain stock, process mushrooms and return to stock, add 2 T butter and 1 heaping T flour dissolved in ½ c half and half or 1 c milk. Simmer gently below boiling point for 5 min. Salt and pepper, garnish with chopped dill and/or parsley and serve with butter-fried croutons.

SPRING VEGETABLE SOUP *(zupa wiosenna)*: This soup makes use of the season's first baby vegetables. To 5–6 c hot meat stock add a total of 3 c diced vegetables in any proportion, including scallions, baby carrots, small kohlrabi, cauliflower florets, celery and peeled new potatoes. Cook until vegetables are tender but not overcooked (15–20 min). Thicken with 2 heaping T flour dissolved in ½–¾ c half & half or 1½ c milk and simmer several min longer. Salt and pepper to taste and garnish with finely chopped fresh dill, and a little chopped parsley (optional). You can make a similar soup any time of year, using mature fresh or frozen vegetables.

CAULIFLOWER SOUP *(zupa kalafiorowa)*: This is a typical summer soup. Break up 1 cauliflower (1 to 1¼ lb) into small florets, scald, drain and add to 6–7 c hot vegetable stock. Cook, uncovered, 10–15 min. Dissolve 1 heaping T flour in 1 c milk, add to pot and bring to boil. Add 1 T butter, salt and pepper to taste and garnish with fresh chopped dill. Serve over poured-batter noodles (see page 124) or croutons (see below).

CROUTONS *(grzanki)*: Allow roughly 1 slice white bread (preferably Italian, Vienna, kaiser rolls or anything else firmer than that mushy American white bread!) and 1 t butter per serving. Cut bread into ½″ squares and brown in melted butter in skillet to a nice crunchy golden brown at least on 2 sides, taking care not to burn croutons. VARIATION: Rye-bread croutons have extra zest and don't go soggy as quickly as those made with white bread.

CREAM OF SORREL SOUP *(zupa szczawiowa)*: Wash a handful of fresh sorrel (about ⅓ lb) very well in plenty of cold running water to remove all sand. Trim off and discard stems. Chop and simmer in 2 T butter in saucepan about 5 min. Dissolve 2 T flour in 1 c meat stock or bouillon, add to sorrel and simmer several min longer. Add to 5 c meat or vegetable stock and bring to boil. Remove from heat. Fork-blend ¾ c sour cream, gradually adding 1 c soup 1 T at a time. Gradually stir into soup and simmer several min. Serve over halved hard-cooked eggs, allowing 1 egg per serving. NOTE: In southern Poland, this soup is usually served with rice. HINT: Bottled sorrel is available at Polish markets and delis.

COLD BEET-GREEN SOUP *(chłodnik na botwince)*: Trim, wash well, drain and chop fine 1 bunch baby beets (including greens). Place in pot, cover with water, add 1 T lemon juice, ½ t salt, bring to boil, reduce heat and cook about 10 min. Set aside to cool. Peel and slice or dice 1 cucumber, chop

4 scallions (tops and bottoms), and slice very thin or coarsely grate 6–10 radishes. Combine with cold, cooked beets and 5 c cold soured milk (buttermilk or *kefir*). Add 2–3 T finely chopped fresh dill and refrigerate, covered, until well chilled. Serve over sliced hard-cooked eggs, allowing 1 egg per serving.

CHILLED LITHUANIAN BARSZCZ *(chłodnik litewski)*: Peel 1 cucumber, cut in half lengthwise, then slice thin into bowl or tureen. (OPTIONAL: Seed portion may be scooped out and discarded if desired.) Add 1 bunch scallions chopped, 6–8 coarsely grated radishes, 2 peeled, coarsely grated brined dill pickles and 1 c of the pickle brine plus 2–3 T finely chopped fresh dill. Drench with 6–8 c cold buttermilk or smooth-whisked sour milk (*zsiadłe mleko*; see below). Mix well, add 1 c beet-sour or several T beet concentrate. Salt and pepper to taste and add 1 t sugar. Refrigerate until well chilled. Serve cold over sliced hard-cooked eggs (1 egg per serving). VARIATION: One c cold roast meat (esp. veal) or ham may be added for a refreshing and nutritious meal in a bowl.

SOUR MILK *(zsiadłe mleko)*: Most American store-sold milk has been chemically or heat-treated to prevent curdling. Simply pouring it into a glass or crockery bowl and leaving it out in a warm place will eventually cause it to clabber, but it may become unpalatably bitter. To get around this problem, pour 1–2 qt whole or 2% milk into a glass or crockery bowl, reserving 1 c. With whisk beat the reserved milk with ½–1 c dairy sour cream or 1 c cultured buttermilk. Let stand in very warm place (80° is good!) until clabbered. Refrigerate until ready to use. Before serving, whisk until smooth. NOTE: Store-bought buttermilk or *kefir* can substitute for sour milk in most dishes. *Zsiadłe mleko* is also now commercially available at better Polish delis in America.

COLD CUCUMBER SOUP *(chłodnik ogórkowy)*: Peel 2 cucumbers, cut in half lengthwise, then slice thin into bowl or tureen. (OPTIONAL: Seed portion may be scooped out and discarded if desired.) Add 2 peeled, coarsely grated brined dill pickles and 1 c of the pickle brine plus 2–3 T finely chopped fresh dill. Drench with 6–8 c cold buttermilk or smooth-whisked sour milk (*zsiadłe mleko*). Salt and pepper to taste. Cover and let stand in fridge several hr for flavors to blend. Serve over sliced hard-cooked eggs in bowls.

COLD FRUIT SOUP *(zupa owocowa/chłodnik owocowy)*: Start with about 3 c of any of the following single fruits or any combination thereof: small strawberries; blueberries; sour cherries (pitted or unpitted); peeled and sliced apples and/or pears; or halved, pitted plums. Place fruit in pot, add 5–6 c water, bring to boil, reduce heat and simmer 8–10 min or until fruit is fully cooked. Dissolve 1–2 T potato starch (or cornstarch) in ½ c water or milk and stir into hot soup. Sweeten to taste (with sugar or sweetener). (OPTIONAL: Season with a pinch of cinnamon, ground cloves or ground nutmeg.) Simmer 2–3 min. Serve over cooked egg noodles or fried croutons. A dollop of sour cream (or low-fat yogurt) may be added to each bowl. NOTE: This and other fruit soups may be served hot, warm, at room temp or chilled.

COLD RHUBARB SOUP *(chłodnik rabarbarowy)*: Wash, trim and dice 1 lb young rhubarb and place in pot. Add 5–6 c water, bring to boil, reduce heat and simmer several min or until rhubarb is tender. Remove pot from flame. Dissolve 1–2 T potato starch (or cornstarch) in ½ c water or milk and stir into hot soup. Add a heaping T strawberry or cherry jam or jelly to improve the soup's color, then sweeten to taste (with sugar or sweetener). Simmer 2–3 min. Serve over cooked egg noodles or croutons. A dollop of sour cream (or low-fat yogurt) may be added to each bowl.

FAMILY/COUNTRY-STYLE/REGIONAL FAVORITES

The following dishes are better suited to family dinners and other informal gatherings than many of those listed in the Polish Holiday/Banquet/Dinner-Party Favorites. It is precisely such hearty dishes of peasant origin that many Polish Americans think of whenever "Polish food" is mentioned. However, it is not always possible to make a fine-line distinction between upscale banquet fare and more basic dishes contained in this section. For instance, roast chicken with dill and liver stuffing, sometimes referred to as "polonaise" *(po polsku)*, has been included among the banquet entrées, although it is a popular family Sunday dinner favorite. This section contains a number of one-pot dishes, which are easy to serve at club suppers, picnics, festivals and as take-outs. A few foods associated with different regions of Poland have also been included. Many other dishes of regional origin have gone nationwide and are found throughout this book. Look for those all-time family favorites—*pierogi* and *gołąbki*—in special sections all their own.

Many of these stick-to-the-ribs dishes were prepared whenever Poland's countryfolk celebrated the Christmas and Easter holidays, weddings, harvest fests and other special occasions. That is when a hog would be butchered, a slew of chickens would be killed and, in well-to-do families, even a fattened calf might be sacrificed. The results were plenty of meat, fatback and variety (organ) meats for sausages and other pork-butcher products including head-cheese (*salceson*) and *kaszanka*. For the adventurous, a recipe for the latter (known in English as buckwheat sausage, blood sausage or blood pudding) has been provided below. There were also soup bones for hearty autumn and winter potages. Although most of the entries in this section are hot dishes, we start with some of the cold foods typical in the peasant cottage of yesteryear. Most of the non-clear soups listed in Traditional Polish Soups are also part of Poland's rural heritage.

COLD COUNTRY-STYLE MEATS *(zimne mięsa)*: The country folk of Old Poland loved their meat every bit as much as the well-to-do classes. Maybe even more, because most of the time they couldn't afford it and adhered more strictly to the year's many fast days. But rather than choice hams, loins, roasts, veal breast, turkey and pâté, their cold-meat platter was likely to contain less pricey treats such as *kiszka kaszana* (buckwheat sausage), *salceson biały* (headcheese), *salceson czarny* (blood sausage), *salceson ozorowy* (tongue sausage), cold sliced cooked bacon (see index) and ordinary varieties of smoked *kiełbasa*: *swojska* (home-style), *chłopska* (peasant) and *wiejska* (country). Many of these old favorites continue to have numerous devotees today—both in Poland and across Polonia. Jellied pigs' feet (see page 114) or *zimne nogi* are a good example.

HARD-COOKED EGGS IN SOUR CREAM *(jajka na twardo w śmietanie)*: Hard-cooked eggs have long been another good basic rural staple. As a cold appetizer or supper they are often drenched with sour cream sauce: fork-blend 1 c sour cream with 1 T white vinegar, ¼ t salt and (optional) 1 heaping t horseradish. (OPTIONAL: Sweeten to taste with a little sugar if desired.)

WHITE CHEESE AND GARDEN GREENS *(twarożek z zieleniną)*: This dish is a frequent guest on the Polish breakfast table and can also be served for a light supper. With fork mash 1 lb farmer cheese (white cheese) with several T sour cream to form a thick spread. Add 1 heaping T finely chopped fresh chives and 2–3 chopped scallions (tops and bottoms). Several coarsely grated radishes and a roughly 2″ length of peeled cucumber may be added. Mix well, season with salt, pepper, paprika and (optional) a pinch of caraway seeds. Serve with kaiser rolls, rye bread or French bread and butter. VARIATION: Process a container of creamed cottage cheese briefly to obliterate those little globs and proceed to season and garnish as above.

LARD SPREAD, HOMEMADE *(smalec domowy do chleba)*: This old country-style, cold-weather energy-booster began making a comeback among highly urbanized Poles towards the end of the 20th century. At present, it is kind of a retro thing—sophisticated, educated Poles often enjoy this old treat not only during cold-weather activities, but also at house-party buffets. The recommended accompaniment is vodka. Dice 2¼ lb white pork fatback (*słonina*) and render in frying pan until pale golden. Add 1 T salt (if your fatback is the unsalted kind), 1 finely diced onion, 1 cooking apple (peeled, cored and diced) and 2–3 cloves finely chopped garlic. Simmer until fatback nuggets turn a deep golden. Remove from heat, add 1 t marjoram and ⅛ t freshly ground pepper. Stir. When cooled to room temperature, transfer to jar or crockery container and refrigerate. Use as a spread on rye bread. It will keep in the fridge up to 2 weeks. NOTE: Hot lemon tea (plain or spiked) is an absolute "must" to wash down this hearty treat. It's a great snack to take along to outdoor activities such as sleigh rides and campfires.

BACON, BAKED (*boczek pieczony/gotowany*): Cooked slab bacon is not only a popular cold cut in the Polish countryside but is often featured at big-city Easter breakfasts and nameday parties. To bake, place a 1-lb piece of fresh (unsmoked) slab bacon in pot, scald with boiling water to cover, and cook 20 min. Place on rack in baking pan. Season with salt and pepper, caraway, marjoram and (optional) 1–2 cloves crushed garlic or a little garlic powder. Bake in 375° oven 30–40 min or until fork-tender. When cooled to room temp, refrigerate and slice when cold. Serve as a cold cut alone or with other cold roast meats. Rye bread, mustard, horseradish and/or *ćwikła* are typical accompaniments. NOTE: May also be served as a hot dish and is esp. good cooked with sauerkraut.

COUNTRY-STYLE RELISHES (*dodatki wiejskie*): Cold dishes were often accompanied by crunchy vegetables, pickles and the like. Brined dill pickles might have been laid out whole, rather than cut into spears, and in season there were whole radishes, sliced cucumber and tomatoes. Pickled mushrooms were common to the peasant cottage and the lord's table alike, in fact the poor commoner was closer to these edible fungi in the surrounding forests.

POTATOES AND SOUR MILK (*kartofle z zsiadłym mlekiem*): This old peasant favorite was especially enjoyed in hot weather, and farmwives would bring this dish to their husbands working in the fields. Peel and cook potatoes in lightly salted water and drain well when fork-tender. Dot with butter or spoon *skwarki* (see page 17) and their drippings over them. Garnish with chopped dill if desired. Serve with a bowl (about 1½ c) cold sour milk, buttermilk or *kefir* (a kind of liquid yogurt).

PORK RIBS AND SAUERKRAUT (*żeberka zapiekane w kapuście*): Rinse in plenty of cold water 2 qt sauerkraut, drain, squeeze out moisture, place in pot and scald with boiling water to cover. Cook on med-high heat 45 min. Cut 4 lb pork spare ribs into 2- or 3-rib portions. Sprinkle with salt and pepper, dredge in flour and sauté in hot fat (lard, bacon drippings, oil) on both sides till slightly browned. Transfer sauerkraut to baking pan, interspersing it with the ribs and 1 c pitted prunes (optional). Add a bay leaf, sprinkle sauerkraut with ½ t caraway seeds and bake in 325° oven 2–2½ hr or until meat is very tender. Serve with boiled potatoes.

PORK RIBS AND SAUERKRAUT ANOTHER WAY *(żeberka w kapuście inaczej)*: Preheat oven to 350°. Drain 1 qt sauerkraut and rinse in large pan of cold water, swishing it around with your hand. Drain well, chop coarsely, place in pot, scald with boiling water to cover, bring to boil and reduce heat. Add 1 mushroom bouillon cube and cook, uncovered, 20 min, then cover and continue simmering several min. Divide 2½ lb spare ribs or pork loin-back ribs into 2-rib portions. Rinse, pat dry and place bone-side down on rack in uncovered baking pan. Bake about 1 hr. Transfer sauerkraut to roaster and into it mix 1 diced peeled apple. Add ribs, covering them with sauerkraut and sprinkle with 2–3 T rib pan drippings. In bowl mix 1 heaping T *powidła* with 2 level T tomato paste and ¼ t Kitchen Bouquet and stir into sauerkraut. Cover and bake another 60 min at 350°. Season with a little pepper, marjoram and garlic powder, stir lightly and let stand in oven another 20 min for flavors to blend. Serve with boiled or mashed potatoes and a grated salad containing horseradish.

PORK RIBS AND ONIONS *(żeberka z cebulą)*: Cut 4 lb lean pork spareribs into 2-rib pieces, salt, pepper, dust with flour and brown in hot fat on both sides. Transfer to Dutch oven roaster, sprinkle with 1 T caraway seeds, add 1 c water and cook 1 hr, covered, on med-low flame or in 350° oven. Slice 4 onions and brown in leftover rib-browning fat. Cover ribs with onions and cook another 45 min or until ribs are very tender.

BOILED PORK HOCKS *(golonka)*: Allow 1 hock per serving. If hocks have any traces of bristle, singe it off over flame and wash well. Place hocks in pot, drench with boiling water to cover by 3″. Add 2 t salt and bring to boil. Skim away scum until no more forms. Cover and cook on med-low heat 90 min. For 3 lb hocks add 2 carrots 2 quartered onions, 1 stalk celery and 1 bay leaf and cook until meat is fork-tender. Serve with rye bread or boiled potatoes and horseradish or Polish-style mustard. Braised cabbage, stewed sauerkraut and pea purée are also traditional accompaniments, and beer is a "must" to wash it down!

PORK HOCKS AND SAUERKRAUT *(golonka zapiekana w kapuście)*: Wash and rinse 4 pork hocks (allowing 1 per person). Place in pot and scald with boiling water to cover. Add 1 t salt, bring to gentle boil and skim off scum until no more forms. Add 1 portion diced soup vegetables (see page 30; carrot, celery, parsley root, onion), 5 peppercorns, 2 whole cloves garlic and 1 bay leaf, reduce heat and cook, covered, 90 min. Separately, cook 1 qt drained, rinsed sauerkraut in 3 c boiling water 1 hr. Transfer half the sauerkraut, drained, to roasting pan or large casserole, place the hocks on top of it, smother them with remaining sauerkraut, add 2 c hock stock and bake 1 hr, covered, in 325° oven. Thicken with several t flour if desired.

BRAISED BABY CABBAGE AND SAUSAGE *(młoda kapusta duszona z kiełbasą)*: Remove the skin from 1 lb smoked *kiełbasa*. Dice *kiełbasa* or cut into thin half-slices. Place in pot, add boiling water to cover and simmer, covered, 30 min. Wash well 1 head baby cabbage at the loose-leaf stage (not yet formed into a compact head). Trim away base and any wilted or damaged leaves. Chop cabbage coarsely and add to sausage pot. Mix well and simmer until tender. In saucepan lightly brown 2 T flour in 2 T bacon or fatback drippings and stir into cabbage. Simmer, covered, another 5 min. Season with salt and pepper and sour to taste with lemon juice (1–2 t). Serve with bread or boiled, dilled new potatoes (see page 154) for a complete summer meal. This is a nice summer Polish fest treat.

CARROTS, MAZURIAN-STYLE *(marchew po mazursku)*: Wash and scrape 2¼ lb carrots, cut into rounds, place in pot, add 1 t sugar and 1 c milk mixed with ½ c boiling water. Cook about 10 min (carrots should be only partially cooked), add 3 fair-sized peeled potatoes, diced, sprinkle with salt and cook until potatoes and carrots are done. Mash well and serve drenched with fried fatback nuggets. NOTE: This item has not been included among the vegetables, because it was once eaten with bread as a typical supper dish of the Mazurian peasantry. It can, of course, be served as a cooked vegetable to accompany main dishes.

CHICKEN STEW, POLISH-STYLE *(potrawka z kury)*: This is a good way to use up the boiled chicken from chicken soup. In skillet melt 2–3 T congealed fat from chicken soup and in it simmer 4–8 oz sliced fresh mushrooms and 1 minced onion until fully cooked. Add 1 heaping T flour dissolved in 2 c chicken stock and ½ c milk and simmer, stirring to get a nice, smooth sauce. Remove cooked chicken from bone, dice (2–3 cups) and add to sauce together with diced cooked carrot and (optional) celeriac. Simmer, covered, on low heat 5 min. Season with salt, pepper, paprika and juice of ½ lemon. Garnish with chopped parsley and serve over rice, noodles or mashed potatoes.

BOILED BEEF WITH HORSERADISH *(sztuka mięsa z chrzanem)*: Wash, dry and place in pot 2–3 lb beef shank, rump, chuck or short ribs, scald with 8 c boiling water and cook 75–80 min, skimming off scum until no more forms. Add 1 portion soup greens (see page 30), spices (peppercorns, bay leaf, several grains allspice) and 2 t salt and cook another hr or until meat is fork-tender. In 1½ c slightly cooled stock dissolve 3 slightly heaped T flour, add ⅛ t salt and 1 heaping T (or more to taste) prepared noncreamed horse-radish. Bring to boil in saucepan and simmer briefly. Season with a little lemon juice and sugar to get a balanced sweet, sour and tangy taste. Remove from heat and allow to cool slightly. Stir in ½ c sour cream or non-fat yogurt. Heat but do not boil. Pour over beef on platter and serve with boiled or mashed potatoes and sauerkraut salad. NOTE: The strained, degreased stock makes a good beef broth.

BRAISED RABBIT *(królik duszony)*: Rinse and pat dry dressed, quartered (preferably young) rabbit. Place in bowl, cover with buttermilk or whey and refrigerate overnight. Next day, discard buttermilk, wipe rabbit, salt and pepper, sprinkle with flour and brown on all sides in hot fat (lard, butter or fat-back drippings) in Dutch oven or heavy skillet with tight-fitting lid. Add 1 c meat stock or water and simmer on stovetop or bake in 350° oven until tender (about 1 hr). HINT: Rabbit is very good cooked with onions, mixed vegetables (onions, carrots, turnips, potatoes) or apples (peeled, cored, halves). Season with marjoram and/or ground juniper.

GROUND PORK CUTLETS, FRIED *(mielone kotlety)*: Soak 2 stale bread rolls (about ¼ lb) in water or milk until soggy. Fry 2 sliced onions in a little fat until golden. Run drained, soaked bread and onions through meat grinder or process briefly. Combine with 2¼ lb ground pork, add 2 eggs, mix well by hand to blend ingredients and salt and pepper to taste. Form 12–16 meatballs depending on size desired. Fry in hot fat as is or, if you prefer crustier cutlets, first dredge in flour, a 50/50 flour and bread-crumb mixture or bread crumbs alone. They may also be breaded: dipped in flour, egg wash and bread crumbs. Fry to a nice golden brown on both sides, flattening them somewhat with spatula. (NOTE: Polish ground cutlets are oval-shaped—a cross between a flattened meatball and a thick patty.) Reduce heat, cover and simmer on low another 10 min or so until fully cooked. The pan drippings may be used to garnish the potatoes or groats with which the cutlets are served. VARIATION: May also be made with ground pork and beef, pork and veal or pork-veal-beef mixture. NOTE: Although minced cutlets (large meat-balls) are not considered elegant and would be out of place at a fancy banquet or dinner-party, they are a favorite standby of many Poles. Since they are less messy than meatballs in gravy, they are ideal for outdoor fests and picnics, family-style community suppers and the like. They can be slipped into a bun to form a "Polish burger" or handheld and eaten cold with a slice of rye bread and a crunchy dill pickle on the side. (See Polish Fest/Picnic/Community Supper Foods, page 202.)

BAKED CHICKEN, POLISH-AMERICAN WEDDING–STYLE *(kurczaki na polonijne wesele)*: Many Polish Americans associate chicken prepared in this manner with old-style Polonian weddings, festivals and community suppers. Season cut-up chicken with salt, pepper and paprika, rub all over with oil, place in pan and bake in 450° oven 15 min, turning once. Baste with water or stock, reduce heat to 350° and bake 60–80 min or until done, basting every 15 min and turning when bottom has browned. Allow about ¾ lb chicken (uncooked weight) per serving. Use drippings as gravy base. Serve with mashed potatoes and sliced cucumbers with sour cream.

CITY CHICKEN, POLISH-AMERICAN WEDDING–STYLE *(fałszywe kurze udka)*: Although not of Polish origin, this tasty dish has been so commonly featured at Polish-American weddings in the Detroit area that it has been included here by popular request. Use just cubed veal or alternating cubes of pork and veal. Impale cubed meat on wooden skewers, salt and pepper, dip in flour, egg wash and bread crumbs and brown on all sides in hot fat. Transfer to rack in roasting pan, add about 1″ water and bake, covered, in 350° oven about 1 hr or until tender. Also see mock chicken legs (below).

MOCK CHICKEN LEGS, POLISH-AMERICAN WEDDING–STYLE *(fałszywe udka inaczej)*: Prepare meat as in meatloaf recipe (below). Tear off meatball-sized pieces of meat mixture and impale on wooden skewers. Mold into the shape of chicken drumsticks, rounded at the top and tapering off towards the bottom, leaving about 1″ of the skewer protruding. (NOTE: If meat mixture is too soft and does not hold its shape well, work in several t potato starch, mix well and repeat process.) Bread and brown slowly in fat on all sides. Transfer to baking pan and bake in 350° oven 60 min.

MEATLOAF *(klops)*: In a large bowl, mix ¾ c plain dry bread crumbs and ¾ c milk or water. Mix in 1½ lb ground pork, veal or pork-veal-beef mixture, add 1–2 grated onions and 2 eggs. Mix well by hand until thoroughly blended. Season to taste with salt, pepper, a pinch of marjoram and (optional) 1 crushed clove garlic or a dash of garlic powder. Mix well, shape into a loaf and place at the center of a cake pan greased with oil. (Polish meatloaf is not normally made in a loaf pan!) Add 1 c water to pan and bake about 1 hr in preheated 350° oven. Use pan drippings as gravy base if desired.

MEATLOAF, EGGLESS *(klops bez jaj)*: Proceed as above but substitute 1 med peeled, grated raw potato for the eggs.

MEATLOAF, KRÓLEWIEC–STYLE *(klops królewiecki)*: This is a regional variation of the above 2 recipes. Proceed exactly as for either meatloaf above, but to your meat mixture add 3–4 finely chopped anchovy fillets (out of a can). Mix mixture well by hand to blend. You won't taste the anchovies as such, but they will give your meatloaf an interesting flavor twist many people enjoy.

DIETETIC MEATBALLS *(klopsiki dietetyczne)*: Prepare meat mixture as in meatloaf or eggless meatloaf (above). Bring to boil 4 c water to which 1–2 mushroom bouillon cubes have been added. Take small pieces of meat mixture and between floured hands roll into walnut-sized balls. Drop into boiling mushroom bouillon and cook 10 min or until fully cooked (check one for doneness). If they fall apart in the bouillon, work 1 t cornstarch and/or some additional bread crumbs into meat mixture. Remove cooked meatballs with slotted spoon and serve. If you want a nice, light gravy to go with them, pour off 1 c of the liquid in which they cooked, add ¼ c cold milk and stir in 1 heaping T flour. Pour it into the pot, mix well and season to taste with salt and pepper if needed, and a sprinkle of vinegar if desired. Add the meatballs to the sauce and simmer gently several min.

POLISH PORK STEW *(gulasz wieprzowy)*: Rinse and pat dry 1½ lb cubed stewing pork. Shake meat in flour-filled plastic bag to coat evenly. In heavy skillet, brown meat on all sides in 3 T hot fat. Remove meat from skillet with slotted spoon and lightly brown 3 sliced onions in the same drippings. Return meat to skillet, add 2–3 sliced carrots, 1 small diced turnip (optional), 1 bay leaf and ½ c beer. Reduce heat and simmer, covered, on low heat 45–60 min or until meat is tender, stirring occasionally. Add a little water if stew begins to sizzle. Drench with ½ c sour cream fork-blended with 1 T flour and simmer briefly. Dilute with meat stock or water if too thick. Season with salt and pepper, ¼ t paprika, ¼ t marjoram, ¼ t crushed caraway seeds and 1 clove crushed garlic. Stir ingredients and simmer briefly. Garnish with chopped parsley if desired. Serve with poured-batter dumplings or groats (buckwheat, barley, millet) of choice.

NOODLES AND CHEESE *(kluski z serem)*: This simple dish is a favorite with many, including the Strybel family. It can be made with homemade or store-bought egg noodles. Simply cook the noodles in boiling salted water until tender, drain well, return to pot and stir in crumbled white (farmer) cheese (½–1 c crumbled cheese per 3–4 c cooked noodles. Turn out onto platter and top with fried fatback nuggets and as much of the drippings as you like. (OPTIONAL: Add a dollop of sour cream to each portion.)

SILESIAN LIVER AND GROAT SAUSAGE *(krupnioki śląskie)*: In large pot combine 2¼ lb singed and rinsed pork rind and pork head meat (jowls, snout, tongue, ears, etc.), ½ lb pork jowls, ½ lb lean pork and 1½ lb pork lungs. Add water to cover by 2″ and 1 T salt and cook on low until tender (several hr). Dice ½ lb white salt pork and fry until crunchy. Remove golden nuggets from drippings with slotted spoon and grind with 1 large quartered onion and ½ lb raw pork liver. When meat is tender, strain. If necessary add enough water to stock to make 6–7 c. In it, cook 4 c buckwheat groats. After liquid is absorbed, cover pot and place groats in 350° oven for 1 hr. Remove any bone and gristle from cooked head meat and lungs and grind. Combine with ground liver mixture, cooked groats and 3–4 c fresh pork blood. Mix ingredients well and season with salt, pepper, a little marjoram and 2 pinches ground allspice. Stuff hog casings (like for *kiełbasa*) with mixture, twisting into links every 10″ or 12″. With strong thread or twine tie each twist in 2 places then cut into individual links. Plunge *krupnioki* into boiling water and cook at a gentle boil 25 min. After cooling, they may be served cold or fried in hot fat—either sliced or removed from casing like hash. Rye bread and a cold stein of beer are perfect accompaniments. Serve at St. Barbara's Day functions. NOTE: If you are unable to prepare or purchase genuine *krupnioki*, store-bought *kiszka* is the next best thing.

SILESIAN LIVER AND BREAD SAUSAGE *(żymloki śląskie)*: In large pot combine 1½ lb singed and rinsed pork head meat, 1⅓ lb pork jowls, ½ lb boneless veal, 1½ lb veal or pork lungs and ⅓ lb pork rind. Add water to cover by 2″ and 1 T salt and cook on low until tender (several hr). When meat is tender, set aside. Grind 1½ lb pork liver and set aside. Strain cooked meat, discarding any bone or gristle. Mix meat with ground liver and grind together. Soak about 5 c bread crumbs in enough of the strained stock to get a soft consistency. Combine with ground meat and 2–3 c lb fresh pork blood. Mix ingredients well. Season with salt and pepper (generously), a pinch or 2 ground allspice and grated nutmeg and about 1 t marjoram and mix again. Stuff mixture into hog casings and cook in boiling water like *krupnioki* above.

BUCKWHEAT SAUSAGE/KISZKA, HOMEMADE *(kaszanka domowa)*: Bring 6 c water to boil and add 2¼ lb pork fatback cut into 6 pieces. Cook 5 min, remove fatback and add 2¼ lb buckwheat groats to water and cook 30 min. Remove from heat, cover and set aside. In separate (5-qt pot) place pork heart, pork kidneys (cut up and presoaked in several changes of water), pork lungs and pancreas and drench with cold water to cover. Bring to boil and cook 45 min. Add pork liver and cook another 10 min. Remove meat from pot and cool, reserving stock. Coarsely grind organ meats, combine with diced fatback, add groats, 4 c pork blood (mixed with a T salt to prevent coagulation), stir in organ-meat stock and season mixture with salt, pepper and marjoram. Fill pork casings with mixture loosely, twisting into 12″–15″ links and tying both ends with string before separating. Bake on greased baking sheet in 400° oven 25 min on each side.

BUCKWHEAT SAUSAGE, FRIED WITH ONIONS *(kaszanka z cebulą)*: Heat 3 T lard in skillet. Cut 2 lb Polish buckwheat sausage (store-bought or homemade) into 1″ slices and fry. Reduce heat so grains of buckwheat do not explode. Slice 2 onions thin and fry separately or in the same skillet, as preferred. When *kiszka* browns on one side, turn slices over, scatter the partially fried onion slices all over the *kiszka*, cover and simmer several min longer until the other side gets nicely browned. Serve with rye bread and dill pickles.

BUCKWHEAT GROATS AND CHEESE *(kasza gryczana z twarogiem)*: Cook 2 c buckwheat groats as directed (see Cooked Vegetables and Main-Dish Accompaniments, page 155). Dice ⅓–½ lb salt pork (fatback) and fry to a nice golden brown, stirring frequently. Transfer hot *kasza* to serving platter, top with 2 c crumbled farmer cheese and garnish with salt-pork nuggets and as much of the drippings as you like. (See next recipe.)

FARMER'S FARE/PEASANT'S DELIGHT *(chłopskie jedzenie)*: Prepare buckwheat groats and cheese as in preceding recipe but stir in 1–2 c hot mashed potatoes. Salt and pepper and season with several pinches ground mint. Serve with a bowl of cold sour milk or buttermilk on the side.

BUCKWHEAT PIE, LUBLIN-STYLE *(lubelski pieróg gryczany)*: Mash 1 cake yeast with 1 t sugar, stir in about 5 T flour and ½ c warm milk, mix and set in warm place to rise. Then, add 1 beaten egg yolk and ½ beaten whole egg, 1 slightly heaped c flour and ¼ t salt. Mix well with wooden spoon, then work by hand, adding several T water if dough is too thick to handle. Knead until air blisters appear. Gradually add 2 T melted butter and continue to knead until fully absorbed. Sprinkle top of dough with a little flour, cover with cloth and keep in warm place until doubled in bulk. Work dough briefly on board and roll dough into a rectangle about ⅔″ thick. Spread filling (buckwheat-cheese mixture in farmer's fare recipe, above) over dough leaving 1″ margin round the edges. Carefully bring one longer end up over filling. Cover with other overlapping end and seal seam. Turn out onto greased, floured baking sheet seam-side down and tuck ends under. Let rise until doubled in bulk. Brush with ½ beaten egg and bake in preheated 400° oven about 1 hr. This can be a light meal in itself with hot milk on the side. NOTE: The same dough is used in *kulebiak* and *paszteciki.*

POTATO PIE *(baba kartoflana)*: Grate 2¼ lb peeled potatoes into sieve placed over container to catch the drippings. When drippings have settled, pour off clear liquid and add remaining white sediment (potato starch) to grated potatoes. Dice ¾–1 lb slab bacon or thick-sliced bacon and fry into golden brown nuggets. To grated potatoes add bacon nuggets and some of the drippings (in old peasant cookery every last drop of drippings was used!), 3 eggs, 1–2 grated onions, 2–3 cloves crushed garlic, salt and pepper and mix well. Grease baking dish with bacon drippings, add potato mixture no more than 2 to 2½″ high and bake in preheated 375° oven 1 hr or until done. Serve hot with sour cream and hot tea. VARIATION: Instead of fried bacon, cooked diced pork (roast, hocks, ribs) may be used. NOTE: This robust dish is not for those with digestive problems!

POTATO PANCAKES *(placki kartoflane)*: Grate 2¼ lb peeled potatoes as in preceding recipe. To grated potatoes, add 1–2 grated onions, about 2 T flour, 2 eggs and salt and pepper. Mix well and spoon batter into hot fat. With spatula flatten pancakes slightly, since thin ones cook better. Fry to a nice crispy, golden brown on both sides and drain on absorbent paper. Serve immediately with just sour cream, just sugar or both sour cream and sugar. Some people like them just plain, perhaps with only a pinch of salt for flavoring. They can also be drenched with a gravy, esp. mushroom sauce.

CRÊPES/THIN PANCAKES *(naleśniki)*: In bowl combine 1 scant c milk with 2 beaten eggs and ⅛ t salt and whisk until smooth. Gradually add 1¼ c flour, sifted, whisking constantly until lump-free and air blisters appear on surface. Whisk in about 1 c water—or just enough to have a thin, pourable batter. The traditional way is to grease a small, hot frying pan with a 1″ square of pork fatback impaled on fork, pour in a little batter, tilt frying pan to coat entire surface and fry on high heat. Flip crêpe over and cook briefly on other side. Stack fried *naleśniki* on inverted plate. Regrease pan before adding more batter. HINT: Those who often prepare *naleśniki* might do well to invest in a special nonstick crêpe pan. NOTE: *Naleśniki* can be spread with any of the fillings given for *pierogi* (see page 145). See *Polish Heritage Cookery* for illustrations showing the different ways of rolling and folding *naleśniki*. Your crêpes may be served in any of the following ways:

- ✦ Hot from the pan, spread, rolled or folded and served
- ✦ Fried to a nice golden or golden brown in a little butter
- ✦ Dotted with butter in baking dish and baked in preheated 375° oven 30–45 min
- ✦ As croquettes *(krokiety)*, breaded and fried in fat to a golden brown
- ✦ Plain or topped with sour cream (all except the meat-filled variety) or dusted with confectioners' sugar (only the sweet variety)

CHEESE PANCAKES *(racuchy serowe)*: Grind or process to a powder 1 lb farmer cheese. Stir in 2 eggs and gradually add 1½ c flour, stirring the whole time. When mixture is smooth, stir in 2 c soured milk (buttermilk or *kefir*) and 2–3 T sugar. Beat well with whisk or handheld mixer at least 5 min.

Spoon into hot lard, butter or oil and fry to a nice golden brown on both sides. Drain well on absorbent paper. Dust with confectioners' sugar or serve with fruit syrup or preserves of choice. NOTE: This old rural recipe did not call for any leavening agent, but if you prefer a fluffier pancake you may add ½ t baking soda and ½ t baking powder.

GOŁĄBKI (CABBAGE ROLLS)— AN ALL-TIME FAVORITE

Stuffed cabbage rolls known in Polish as *gołąbki* (literally "little pigeons") rank among Polonia's favorite dishes and have numerous devotees among non-Polonians as well. We have therefore given them a corner all their own, although they also fit nicely into other sections of this book. They are the main attraction at *gołąbki* festivals, *gołąbki* suppers or *gołąbki* nights and share the stage with other Polish favorites at festivals, picnics or other food-related events. Cabbage rolls stuffed with a meat and rice mixture are by far the most common, but other versions are also worth recommending.

GOŁĄBKI/CABBAGE ROLLS, PREPARATION *(przygotowywanie gołąbków)*: Core a 3-lb cabbage, place cored-side down in pot of hot water to cover and simmer to wilt leaves. Remove outer leaves as they wilt to rack or absorbent paper to drain. When cool enough to handle shave down the thick central vein of drained cabbage leaves or pound it with kitchen mallet to soften. Place an oblong scoop of filling at the base end of each leaf. Fold sides of leaf over filling and roll up away from filling. After the *gołąbki* have been rolled, line the bottom of a roasting pan with half the leftover undersized, damaged or otherwise unused cabbage leaves. Place the cabbage rolls snugly in roaster no more than 2 layers. Drench with sauce or stock (about 2–3 c) of choice (for varieties, see recipes below) and cover with remaining unneeded cabbage leaves. Surrounding the *gołąbki* with extra leaves will prevent them from scorching. Bake, covered, in preheated 350° oven 1 hr. Reduce heat to 325° and cook another hr. Switch off heat and leave in oven another 20 min or so for flavors to blend.

CABBAGE ROLLS, MEAT AND RICE-FILLED *(gołąbki z mięsem i ryżem)*: Prepare filling by combining 1 lb raw ground meat (pork, pork and beef, pork-veal-beef combination, or ground dark-meat turkey) with 4–6 c undercooked rice, 1–3 chopped butter-fried onions and 1 egg. Mix ingredients well and salt and pepper to taste. Drench cabbage rolls in roasting pan with either of the following sauces. NOTE: Prepare extra sauce on the side for your gravy boat, for those who like to drench their *gołąbki* and accompanying mashed potatoes with sauce.

Tomato Sauce: Prepare one of the following:

- ✦ 3 c tomato juice (plain or containing several dashes Tabasco or ¼ c spicy-style ketchup)
- ✦ 3 c purėed tomatoes or stewed tomatoes
- ✦ 3 c stock (meat or vegetable) mixed with several T tomato paste
- ✦ 2 c canned tomato soup mixed with ½ c ketchup (regular or spicy) and ½ c water

Sour-Cream Sauce: Drench uncooked *gołąbki* with 3 c homemade stock or store-bought beef or poultry bouillon (cubes, granules); when cabbage rolls are cooked, pour off any remaining pan liquid that has not been absorbed, stir in 1 c sour cream and enough stock to make 3 c sauce; ½ a mushroom bouillon cube will greatly improve its taste; drench cabbage rolls with sauce and bake another 15–20 min.

Sauceless, Pork-Nugget-Garnished: Drench *gołąbki* with 2½ c homemade stock or store-bought beef or poultry bouillon (made with cubes or granules); transfer cooked cabbage rolls to platter and drench with ¼ lb golden brown fatback nuggets (*skwarki*) and their drippings.

CABBAGE ROLLS, MEAT AND GROAT-FILLED *(gołąbki z mięsem i kaszą)*: Proceed as above (meat and rice-filled rolls), but substitute cooked barley, buckwheat groats, Kraków groats (fine buckwheat) or millet for the rice.

CABBAGE ROLLS, COOKED-MEAT AND RICE/GROAT-TYPE *(gołąbki z pieczenią i ryżem/kaszą)*: Proceed as in either of the preceding two recipes but substitute cooked ground meat (roasts, chops, dark-meat turkey, chicken, etc.) and/or ground, skinned smoked *kiełbasa* for all or some of the raw ground meat.

CABBAGE ROLLS, MEAT-FILLED *(gołąbki nadziewane mięsem)*: This will remind many of meatballs wrapped in cabbage leaves, because that's exactly what they are. Break up 2 stale bread rolls into bowl and drench with milk to cover. When soggy, grind and combine with 1 lb raw ground meat (as in meat and rice-filled *gołąbki* above). Add 2 chopped butter-fried onions, 1 egg and any leftover milk from the rolls. Mix well and salt and pepper to taste. If mixture is too soft, mix in a small amount bread crumbs.

<u>CABBAGE ROLLS IN MUSHROOM SAUCE</u> *(gołąbki w sosie grzybowym)*: Prepare cabbage rolls as in any of the recipes above. Add a mushroom bouillon cube to the water that rice or groats are cooked in. While *gołąbki* bake, wash and slice or dice 12–16 oz fresh mushrooms (portobello are esp. good). Stew them in 2–3 T butter with 1 finely chopped onion until cooked (about 15 min). Add 1 mushroom bouillon cube dissolved in 2 c hot water, mixed with 1 c sour cream fork-blended with 1 heaping T flour. Simmer 10 min. When cabbage rolls are cooked, add any remaining pan liquid to mushroom sauce. Salt and pepper to taste. Ladle mushroom sauce over *gołąbki* and garnish with chopped dill and/or parsley (optional). 1 oz cooked chopped dried bolete mushrooms will make these gourmet *gołąbki* even more exquisite.

<u>CABBAGE ROLLS, MUSHROOM AND RICE-FILLED</u> *(gołąbki z grzybami i ryżem)*: In 3 T butter, margarine or oil sauté 8–12 oz fresh (preferably portobello) mushrooms (washed and chopped fine) with 2 med chopped onions. Combine with 3–3½ c preferably slightly undercooked rice, cooked with ½ mushroom bouillon cube. Add 1 raw egg and mix to blend ingredients. Salt and pepper to taste and (optional) garnish with 1 T chopped fresh parsley. Fill pre-wilted cabbage leaves as usual, drench with 3 c vegetable stock (in which ½ mushroom bouillon cube has been dissolved) and bake in preheated 350° oven at least 2 hr. Serve drenched with mushroom sauce (see above recipe) or sour-cream sauce (see page 143).

<u>CABBAGE ROLLS, MUSHROOM AND GROAT-FILLED</u> *(gołąbki z kaszą i grzybami)*: Prepare cabbage leaves as for basic *gołąbki.* Chop and fry 8–16 oz fresh mushrooms and 2 onions in 3–4 T butter until tender and combine with 4 c slightly undercooked groats (buckwheat, barley, millet) or rice. Stir in 1–2 eggs, salt and pepper generously and add a heaping T fresh, finely chopped dill and/or parsley. In roaster drench with 2 mushroom bouillon cubes dissolved in 4 c hot water.

<u>CABBAGE ROLLS, GROAT AND POTATO-FILLED</u> *(gołąbki z kaszą i kartoflami)*: Peel, cook and mash well ¾ lb potatoes and set aside. Grate 2¼ lb peeled, raw potatoes, pouring off liquid. In 4 T oil fry 3 chopped onions until lightly browned. Combine mashed and grated potatoes, add fried onion and add ¼ c uncooked Kraków kasha (fine-milled buckwheat groats). Mix ingredients well and salt and pepper rather generously to taste. Use mixture to fill prescalded cabbage leaves, roll up and place snugly in baking pan. Scald with boiling salted water or vegetable stock to cover, bring to boil and cook, uncovered, 15 min. Cover, transfer to 350° oven and bake 2 hr. After switching off heat, leave in oven until cooled to room temp. Refrigerate until needed. To serve, brown on all sides in hot oil.

CABBAGE ROLLS, BREADED AND FRIED *(gołąbki smażone panierowane)*: A tasty, change-of-pace way of preparing *gołąbki* (esp. when the extra calories are no problem!) is to bread and fry cooked cabbage rolls. This works best with smaller *gołąbki* (made with smaller cabbage leaves). *Gołąbki* for breading should be dry (not swimming in sauce!). Dredge cold cabbage rolls in flour, egg wash and bread crumbs and fry in fairly deep (1″) hot fat to a nice golden brown on all sides. Drain on absorbent paper before serving.

PIEROGI—ANOTHER POLISH SHOWCASE DISH

Next to *kiełbasa* and *gołąbki, pierogi* rank among the best-known Polish foods. Variously known in English as filled dumplings, dough pockets or even "Polish ravioli," they are right at home at family dinners, parish suppers, Polish festivals, Lenten take-aways and many other occasions. There are several ways of preparing the dough and numerous fillings. The basic *pierogi* are followed by other filled and unfilled dumplings known by such names as *kołduny*, *pyzy*, *knedle* and *kluski*.

PIEROGI/FILLED DUMPLINGS, BASIC RECIPE *(pierogi)*: Set a large pot of lightly salted water on high heat. Sift 2¼–2½ c flour onto board. Sprinkle with ½ t salt. Deposit 1 small egg at center and use knife to mix outlying flour into egg. Gradually add about ½ c fairly hot water in a thin stream and work mixture by hand into a dough. (OPTIONAL: Adding 1–2 T salad oil will produce a more elastic dough.) Knead well until dough is smooth and elastic and no longer sticks to hand. On lightly floured board, roll out ⅓ of the dough thin, about 1/16″, leaving the remainder under a warm inverted bowl so it doesn't dry out. With drinking glass or biscuit cutter cut dough-sheet into rounds. Place a spoonful of filling just off center of each dough round, cover filling with other half of the dough circle and pinch edges together to seal. If dough is on the dry side, brush edges lightly with water or lightly beaten egg white and pinch together with floured fingers to ensure a good seal. Drop small batches of *pierogi* into boiling water so they can float freely without crowding. When boiling resumes, reduce heat to gentle boil and cook 5–10 min, testing one for doneness. (Exact cooking time varies depending on size of *pierogi*, thickness of dough and type of filling used.) Remove with slotted spoon and serve at once. Or allow them to cool, and reheat by frying in butter. NOTE: Some *pierogi* dough variations follow.

Pierogi Dough, Sour-Cream-Based *(ciasto pierogowe na śmietanie)*: These proportions are easy to remember; 2 c flour, 1 c sour cream, 1 small egg and ½ t salt. Work ingredients together to form a smooth dough. Roll out and proceed as with the basic recipe above. This recipe produces an extremely nice and soft dough shell for your *pierogi.* It is the favorite *pierogi* dough of the author's mother, Angeline Kupczyńska-Strybel.

Pierogi Dough, Eggless *(ciasto pierogowe bez jaj)*: Sift 2 c flour onto board. Add ¾–1 c hot water in thin stream, mixing with knife. Sprinkle with ½ t salt. Work well by hand, kneading until dough is smooth and small air blisters appear when it is cut open. Roll out no more than ⅓ of the dough at a time, keeping the remainder in a warm inverted bowl so it doesn't dry out.

MEAT-FILLED PIEROGI *(pierogi z mięsem)*: These *pierogi* are favored by city-dwellers, while the meatless variety are more typical of the countryside. Soak a crumbled-up stale bread roll in water. Dice 1″ square pork fatback and brown lightly with 2 finely chopped onions. Grind ¾ lb cooked (boiled or roast) beef together with the onions and squeezed-out roll. Mix well and salt and pepper to taste. Add 2 T bouillon if very dry. NOTE: An economical way of preparing these for a community event is to have club members donate frozen cooked meats from their home freezers.

LIGHTS-FILLED PIEROGI *(pierogi z płuckami/dudami)*: This is an economical way of preparing meat *pierogi* that many say are tastier than the all-beef variety. Soak stale bread roll in water. Cook ¾ lb veal lights (lungs) with 1 portion soup greens (see page 30), bay leaf and 8 peppercorns in 8 c water 1 hr. Brown ¼ lb diced bacon with 2 finely chopped onions. Grind the cooked lights, bacon and onions and roll. Add 1 egg and mix well. Salt and pepper to taste. NOTE: Part lights and part beef are another possibility. Suggestion: Save the lights stock for *żur.*

CHEESE AND POTATO PIEROGI *(pierogi z serem i kartoflami/ "ruskie")*: Cook 1 lb peeled potatoes in boiling salted water until tender, drain, mash and set aside to cool. To potatoes add ½ lb farmer cheese or dry cottage cheese, mashed in with potato-masher or processed to a ground-like consistency in processor. Sauté 2 med finely chopped onions in 2 T oil until tender and lightly browned. Mix ingredients well and season with salt and pepper and (optional) a pinch of ground dried mint leaves. NOTE: In Poland these are known as *"ruskie"* (Ruthenian) *pierogi*, but in the former Polish city of Lwów (now Lviv in Ukraine), they are widely referred to as *"polskie pierogi"*.

CHEESE-FILLED PIEROGI *(pierogi z serem)*: Combine ¾ lb farmer cheese or dry cottage cheese, pulverized to a powder in food processor, ¼ t salt,

½ t sugar and 1 raw egg yolk into a smooth filling. VARIATION: Those that prefer sweet cheese pierogi may add 2–3 T sugar and (optional) ¼ t vanilla extract. ¼–⅓ c plumped raisins and/or ¼ t grated lemon zest may also be added.

POTATO AND ONION-FILLED PIEROGI *(pierogi z kartoflami)*: Cook 6–7 med potatoes until tender, drain well, steaming off moisture, and mash thoroughly or put through ricer. Dice 3–4 slices bacon and brown with 2 finely diced onions. (NOTE: For meatless *pierogi*, fry the onions in 2–3 T butter or oil.) Add fried mixture to potatoes, stir in 1 egg and (optional) 1 T bread crumbs. Salt and pepper to taste. (OPTIONAL: To improve color, to mixture add 1 T chopped chives, parsley or dill or a combination thereof.)

SAUERKRAUT AND MUSHROOM-FILLED PIEROGI *(pierogi z kapustą i grzybami)*: Rehydrate, cook and chop 1 oz dried mushrooms. Drain, rinse and redrain 3 c sauerkraut and cook in water to cover containing 1 mushroom bouillon cube, covered, 30 min. Uncover and allow liquid to steam away. Transfer to colander and when cool enough to handle, chop. Return sauerkraut to pot, add cooked mushrooms and liquid and 1 chopped, butter-browned onion and simmer, covered about 20. Drain in colander pressing out all moisture. Salt and pepper to taste. These *pierogi* are often served on Wigilia.

CABBAGE-FILLED PIEROGI *(pierogi ze słodką kapustą)*: Core and shred 1¾ lb cabbage, place in pot, cover with water and 1 T salt and cook 30 min from the time it comes to a boil. Drain in colander and press out moisture. When cool enough to handle, chop. Brown 1 chopped onion in 3 T butter or oil or with 1 heaping T diced fatback or bacon. Combine with cabbage and simmer 15 min, stirring to allow moisture to evaporate. Drain and press out moisture. Add 1 T bread crumbs and salt and pepper to taste. (OPTIONAL: Add 1 T chopped dill.) VARIATION: Browning 8 oz or so chopped fresh mushrooms (or 1 oz cooked dried mushrooms) with the onion will greatly enhance these *pierogi*, which will then be called *pierogi ze słodką kapustą i grzybami.*

MUSHROOM-FILLED PIEROGI *(pierogi z grzybami)*: Soak 1 slice crumbled-up stale French or Vienna bread or a small roll in ½ c milk. Wash and slice 1 lb fresh mushrooms, place in skillet with 1 med–lg chopped onion and 3 T butter and fry, uncovered, on low heat, stirring frequently, until moisture evaporates. Grind or process mushrooms, onions and soaked bread, add ¼ c bread crumbs and mix well. Salt and pepper to taste and (optional) garnish with 1 T chopped fresh parsley. (NOTE: Portobello mushrooms are best.)

GROAT AND CHEESE-FILLED PIEROGI *(pierogi z kaszą gryczaną i serem)*: Combine 2 c cooked buckwheat groats with 1 c mashed farmer cheese and 2 chopped onions sautéed in 3 T butter, margarine or oil. Mix well to get a uniform consistency. Stir in 1 small egg and salt and pepper to taste. (OPTIONAL: Season with a pinch or two of ground dried mint leaves.)

LENTIL-FILLED PIEROGI *(pierogi z soczewicą)*: Swish around 1 c dried lentils in a pot of cold water so impurities float up. Pour off water and rinse in sieve. Transfer to cooking pot, add 2½ c water and cook until tender (35–40 min). Fry 2 finely chopped onions in 2 T butter until soft and golden. To drained, cooked lentils add the onions, 2 cooked potatoes, mashed well, and (optional) 1 ground hard-cooked egg. Season with salt, pepper and marjoram and use to fill pierogi-dough rounds. Serve the cooked *pierogi* drizzled with melted butter. This is a speciality of the Podlasie region (northeastern Poland).

BLUEBERRY-FILLED PIEROGI *(pierogi z jagodami)*: Remove any leaves or stems from about 1 lb fresh blueberries, rinse and drain well in colander or sieve. Some cooks sprinkle these with 2–3 T sugar, but that makes berries release more liquid. It's better to sprinkle the cooked *pierogi* with granulated or confectioners' sugar to taste. (OPTIONAL: The berries may be seasoned with a sprinkle of cinnamon.) Sprinkling them with 1 t potato starch should firm up the filling and make it less runny.

FRUIT-FILLED PIEROGI *(pierogi z innymi owocami)*: *Pierogi* can be filled with other fruit, in particular strawberries (wild or cultivated), raspberries, pitted cherries and diced apples. The same sugaring principle applies—it is better not to add any sugar to the filling and let individual eaters sweeten portions on their plates. NOTE: Strawberry *pierogi* can be made by wrapping 1 large, hulled, washed and drained strawberry in each dough round.

PRUNE-FILLED PIEROGI *(pierogi ze śliwkami)*: These are a kind of dessert *pierogi* suitable for Wigilia. In water to cover, soak for several hr as many pitted prunes as you plan to make *pierogi*. Add 1 T sugar and cook on low heat, stirring frequently. Prunes should be tender but still in 1 piece (not disintegrated). Add 1–2 t lemon juice and simmer briefly. When cooled to room temp, use each prune to fill 1 dough round which should be just big enough to enfold it. Serve these hot *pierogi* with sour cream, unbeaten whipping cream or (for weight-watchers) plain low-fat yogurt.

PIEROGI TOPPINGS *(okrasa do pierogów)*: The toppings used to garnish cooked *pierogi* depend on their fillings:

Savory Meatless Pierogi: melted butter (Butter Buds or equivalent); butter-browned bread crumbs; sour cream or plain low-fat or no-fat yogurt; fried pork fatback nuggets and drippings.

Meat-Filled Pierogi: fried pork fatback nuggets and drippings; chopped onions browned in butter, margarine, oil or fatback/bacon drippings; mushroom gravy (like that suggested for cabbage rolls in mushroom sauce, above).

Fruit-Filled and Other Sweet Pierogi: melted butter (Butter Buds or equivalent); butter-browned bread crumbs; confectioners' sugar; granulated sugar; sour cream; heavy sweet cream.

LITHUANIAN MEAT DUMPLINGS *(kołduny litewskie)*: Combine ¾ lb ground beef tenderloin or ground lamb with ⅓ lb ground beef suet. (Or, use just fatty hamburger.) Simmer 1 grated onion in 1 T butter and add to meat mixture together with 3–4 T cold meat stock. Work well by hand to combine ingredients. Season with salt, pepper, marjoram and a pinch ground allspice. Prepare dough like for *pierogi,* roll out thin, cut into 1¾″ circles, fill dough rounds with spoonfuls of filling and seal well. Cook in boiling beef stock or water. When they float up, cook 2 min longer. Remove with slotted spoon and serve with melted butter or drenched with sauce (mushroom, sorrel, etc.) Another way is to serve them in bowls full of hot broth or clear beet soup.

PIEROGI, SMALL BAKED *(pierożki pieczone)*: Combine 1 scant c flour with ¼ t salt and sift. Cut in ½ c cold butter and 1½ T cold water and quickly work into a dough. Roll into a ball, wrap in foil and refrigerate 30 min. Roll dough out thin, cut into 2″–2½″ circles, fill with filling of choice and seal. Bake in 350° oven about 30 min.

PIEROGI, SMALL FRIED *(pierożki smażone)*: Prepare *pierogi* as in preceding recipe but fry in ½″ hot lard or oil to a nice golden brown on both sides. Drain on absorbent paper before serving. These can be a meal in themselves or a soup accompaniment.

PIEROGI, LAZY *(leniwe pierogi)*: In bowl beat 3 T soft butter, adding 3 egg yolks, 1 at a time and beating the whole time. Add 1 lb mashed or ground farmer cheese. Fold in 3 stiffly beaten egg whites, alternating with 1 c flour. Mix gently and salt lightly. Turn out onto lightly floured board and roll into 1″ thick strands. Flatten with knife blade and cut at an angle into ⅔″ dumplings. Cook in boiling lightly salted water. When they float up, check for doneness and cook a little longer if required. Remove with slotted spoon and drain in colander. Serve with melted butter, butter-browned bread crumbs, confectioners' sugar or sugar and sour cream.

POTATO DUMPLINGS *(kluski kartoflane/pyzy)*: First of all, put a 3–4 qt pot of water containing 1 T salt on stove to boil. When water is fairly hot, wash, peel, and dice or slice 3–4 medium-sized potatoes. Place in blender or food processor together with 1 egg and whirl until grated. Transfer mixture to mixing bowl. Add 3 c cold leftover mashed potatoes, 6 T flour, 1 T cornstarch and 1 t salt. Mix ingredients by hand until uniform. Tear off pieces of the dough, between floured palms roll into walnut-sized balls and drop into boiling water. When boiling resumes, cook about 5 min. Check one for doneness. Remove with slotted spoon and serve immediately. These are traditionally topped with salt-pork or bacon cracklings and their drippings. Also serve with gravy dishes instead of potatoes.

POTATO DUMPLINGS, FILLED LARGE *(cepieliny/kartacze)*: These large spindle or dirigible-shaped dumplings (*cepieliny* is the polonized version of the pre-WWII German Zeppelin) hail from the Polish-Lithuanian borderlands and are most popular in the northeastern Podlasie (Białystok) region. Combine 3–4 c coarsely ground cooked beef and/or pork with 1 lg chopped onion simmered in a little fat and 1 egg, mix well and season with salt, pepper and (generously) marjoram. Cook 4 med peeled potatoes in water, drain and mash. Grate 4 med raw peeled potatoes (by hand or in processor) and let drip in sieve, collecting liquid. When liquid settles, pour off clear liquid and add white sediment (starch) to grated potatoes. Combine both potato mixtures, add 1 egg and several T flour and salt and pepper. Mix well to blend. Dough should be easy to shape and not too mushy. If it is, sprinkle in a little potato starch. Tear off fair-sized pieces of dough, flatten into a 4″–5″ pancake. Place a generous portion of filling at center of each circle, roll up, pinch edges together and form into spindle-shaped dumplings. Cook in boiling, lightly salted water 20–25 min or until fully cooked. Remove with slotted spoon and serve immediately with browned bacon or fatback nuggets and onions. WARNING: Not for delicate eaters!

COOKED VEGETABLES AND MAIN-DISH ACCOMPANIMENTS

The following cooked vegetables, potatoes and grains are usually side dishes accompanying the main course. But many of them can be meals in themselves.

BEETS, COOKED POLISH-STYLE *(buraczki)*: Dice or grate coarsely 1½ lb cooked (boiled or baked, and peeled) beets. Lightly brown 1 heaping T diced fatback, add 2–3 T flour and brown slightly, stirring constantly. Remove from heat, stir in several T water and cook, stirring until bubbly. Pour over beets, add 2 peeled, coarsely grated cooking apples, mix well and simmer several min. Season to taste with salt, pepper, sugar and lemon juice or dill-pickle brine. Simmer briefly and let stand a bit for flavors to blend. A typical accompaniment to beef, game and ground-meat dishes. NOTE: When man-power is at a premium, drained canned beets are a real time-saver used in this and other recipes calling for cooked beets. The leftover liquid makes a good base for *barszcz.*

BEETS, CREAMED *(buraczki ze śmietaną)*: Dice or grate coarsely 1½ lb cooked (boiled or baked, and peeled) beets. Season with salt, pepper and sugar and add 2 T flour dissolved in ¼ c stock. Bring to boil. Stir in ½ c sour cream and season to taste with a little vinegar. Heat briefly but do not boil.

SPINACH, POLISH-STYLE *(szpinak po polsku)*: Trim and wash well 2¼ lb fresh spinach, place in pot, scald with boiling water to cover and cook 5 min from the time boiling resumes. Drain and chop or process spinach. In saucepan make a roux from 3 T butter and 2 T flour, add 2 cloves crushed garlic and simmer briefly without browning. Add the spinach, 2 eggs fork-blended with ½ c sour cream and simmer several min. Season with salt and pepper and a little lemon juice. Good with veal dishes and boiled beef.

CAULIFLOWER POLONAISE *(kalafior po polsku)*: Remove any green leaves from base of cauliflower and trim off core. Place cauliflower cored-side down in a pot tall enough so the cauliflower is at least 3″ from the top rim. Add cold water coming ⅔ of the way up the cauliflower and 1 t salt, bring to boil, reduce heat and cook, covered, at a gentle rolling boil 20–30 min or until fork-tender. Meanwhile, in saucepan heat 3–4 T butter until it bubbles, stir in 2–3 T bread crumbs and simmer, stirring frequently, until nicely browned. Remove cooked cauliflower from pot, drain well, place on serving platter and spoon the browned bread-crumb topping over it. This can be an accompaniment to roast chicken or other meats or a nice vegetarian meal in itself with some sliced tomatoes and dilled, buttered new potatoes on the side (see page 154).

VEGETABLES POLONAISE *(jarzyny po polsku)*: Other vegetables may be prepared the same way as cauliflower Polonaise, including wax and string beans, brussels sprouts, asparagus, carrots, peas, peas and carrots, cabbage, etc. Simply cook vegetable in lightly salted water until tender, drain well and garnish with browned buttered bread-crumb topping. (OPTIONAL: Instead of plain water, vegetables may be cooked in stock or simply add a bouillon cube to the pot.) NOTE: Adding a little sugar (1 t or so per 2 c water) will improve the taste of many vegetables.

VEGETABLES, OLD POLISH–STYLE *(jarzyny po staropolsku)*: Before the advent of the now-classic Polonaise topping (above), the most common way of serving most cooked vegetables was to boil them until tender, drain and garnish with *skwarki.* This is a particularly good way to serve boiled vegetables of the turnip family (turnips, rutabagas, kohlrabi) as well as potatoes and root vegetables (carrots, parsnips, celeriac). Cook 2 lb of any of the above vegetables, peeled and cubed or thickly sliced, in lightly salted boiling containing 2 t sugar for 20–25 min or until fork-tender. Old rutabaga may require longer cooking. Drain well and spoon golden brown pork cracklings and their drippings over the vegetables. Together with peas and pork cracklings (see Old Polish Cookery, page 187), these could enhance the atmosphere of any Old Polish theme banquet or party.

BRAISED CABBAGE *(kapusta duszona)*: Shred 1 large head of cabbage, place in pot, scald with boiling water to cover, bring to boil and cook, uncovered, 10 min. Drain. To cabbage add 2- 3 c degreased meat or smoked-meat stock and 2 peeled, diced cooking apples and cook on med-low until cabbage is tender (30–45 min). In 2–3 T fatback or bacon drippings, brown 2–3 T flour, stirring in a little cabbage stock to get a thick paste. Stir roux into cabbage and simmer, covered, 10 min longer. Season with salt and pepper, caraway seeds (optional) and juice of ½ lemon. A sprinkling of chopped dill is also good. Let stand several min for flavors to blend. VARIATION: Instead of the apples, use 2 skinned, diced fresh tomatoes, or 1 apple plus 1 tomato. Serve with roast pork, breaded pork cutlets and other pork dishes.

STEWED SAUERKRAUT *(kapusta kiszona duszona)*: Rinse 2 qt sauerkraut under running water. Rinse it lightly if you like your sauerkraut on the tart side and well if you prefer a milder version. (OPTIONAL: Chop coarsely.) Place in pot, scald with 3 c boiling water, bring to boil and cook, uncovered, 15 min. Add 1 bay leaf, cover and cook on med-low 30 min. Add 1 mushroom bouillon cube and ½–1 t caraway seeds (optional). Dice and fry ¼ lb fatback. When pale golden add a chopped onion and simmer until browned. Stir in 1 heaping T flour, brown lightly and add to sauerkraut. (OPTIONAL: Add 1–2 t sugar. [Polish-American cooks sometimes use brown sugar.]) Cook another 30 min. The ideal accompaniment for pork dishes as well as fried fish.

SAUERKRAUT AND PEAS WITH PORK CRACKLINGS *(kapusta z grochem ze skwarkami)*: This is another Old Polish favorite that differs from the popular Wigilia dish through the addition of fatback. It could be a cold-weather meal all in itself, with some boiled potatoes on the side, or an accompaniment for meat dishes. Cook 1 c yellow split peas in 2½ c water until tender. Or, soak whole dried yellow peas overnight in water and cook the next day until tender. Prepare sauerkraut with ½ oz rehydrated dried boletes. Add drained, cooked peas. Fry 2–4 oz diced pork fatback until golden, add 2 chopped onions and simmer to a nice golden brown, stirring frequently. Stir in 2 T flour and brown lightly. Add several T sauerkraut liquid from pot, simmer briefly, stir mixture into sauerkraut and cook, covered, on low heat at least another 30 min, stirring occasionally. NOTE: This dish can also be made with chickpeas or beans (navy, lima, Great Northern, pea-beans)—either soaked overnight and cooked until tender, or canned and well drained. Season to taste with about 1 t sugar, salt and pepper and several pinches of ground caraway.

RED CABBAGE WITH WINE, BRAISED *(czerwona/modra kapusta duszona z winem)*: Discard outer leaves from med head of red cabbage, cut in half and slice thin with knife. (Shredding with grater produces too fine a cut.) Place in pot, add 1–1½ c cold water and bring to boil. Stir, reduce heat and simmer, covered, about 20 min. Meanwhile, fry ⅛ lb diced salt pork, adding 2 chopped onions when nuggets are golden and fry to golden brown. Stir in 1 slightly heaped T flour and fry into a golden roux. Remove from heat and stir in ¼ c vinegar. To cabbage add 1 large peeled, coarsely grated apple, a jigger dry red wine and the vinegar-roux mixture and stir well. Add 1 T sugar, salt and pepper, and simmer, covered, 10 min or so. Serve with pork, duck, goose or game.

PURÉED PEAS *(purée z grochu)*: Rinse well 1 lb whole, hulled, yellow dried peas and soak overnight in preboiled water cooled to room temp. Next day, cook in same water until tender. Drain, salt to taste and sieve, grind or purée in processor. On serving platter garnish with ¼ lb diced fatback browned with 1–2 chopped onions. Once a standard fixture on the Old Polish table, this time-honored dish remains a favorite accompaniment for boiled pork hocks or pork roast. VARIATION: Drained, canned chickpeas may be used when there isn't time to soak and cook dried peas.

BOILED POTATOES *(kartofle/ziemniaki gotowane/z wody)*: Peel and rinse 2¼ lb potatoes. Cut larger ones in half so that all pieces are of roughly equal size. Transfer to pot, add 1–2 t salt and water to cover and cook until done (20–30 min). Drain well, return to pot, shake pot over heat until all moisture steams away. Turn out onto serving dish if the main course includes gravy. If not, dot hot potatoes with butter or garnish with fatback nuggets and a little of their drippings. A sprinkling of fresh chopped dill always perks up the flavor and appearance of boiled potatoes.

POTATOES COOKED IN JACKETS *(kartofle/ziemniaki w mundurkach)*: Scrub well but do not peel 2¼ lb small, roundish potatoes of roughly equal size. Place in pot, add 1–2 t salt, scald with boiling water to cover and cook until done. These may be eaten with the skins (like American-style baked potatoes), with a little salt and butter. They may also be peeled under cold running water (the skins will slip off easily!) and served whole, mashed, fried or in salads. NOTE: Many potato lovers insist that only potatoes cooked in jackets provide full potato flavor.

MASHED POTATOES, PLAIN *(kartofle/ziemniaki tłuczone)*: Cook 2¼ lb potatoes peeled or in jackets (as above). After steaming off moisture (and peeling the ones in jackets under cold running water), mash well or run through ricer. IMPORTANT: Add no milk or butter! Contrary to general American practice, Poles differentiate between mashed potatoes and puréed potatoes that contain milk and butter. When mashed potatoes are drenched with rich gravies or fatty toppings (pork cracklings, bacon nuggets, pan drippings, etc), it makes no sense from a dietary standpoint to additionally increase their fat content with butter and milk.

PURÉED/WHIPPED POTATOES *(kartofle/ziemniaki purée)*: Cook 2¼ lb potatoes peeled or in jackets as above. After steaming away moisture and peeling the ones in jackets, mash well and run through ricer. Dot with 2 T butter and mash again, gradually adding 6–8 T milk. Traditionally puréed potatoes are served with festive holiday dishes such as roast turkey and other fowl. A sprinkling of chopped dill and/or parsley will improve their flavor and appearance.

DILLED NEW POTATOES *(młode kartofelki z koperkiem)*: This is probably the Poles' favorite form of potatoes, and most look forward to summer when *młode kartofelki* become plentiful. If you can get young, walnut-sized new potatoes, instead of peeling them use nylon scrubber to scrub away the thin skins under cold running water. Place 2½ lb scrubbed new potatoes in pot, cover with boiling water, add 1 t salt and cook on med heat about 30 min or until fork-tender. Drain. Dot with butter (about 1 T) and garnish with finely chopped fresh dill. Toss gently to evenly coat potatoes with melting butter and dill. NOTE: Apart from being part of main courses such as roast chicken or breaded pork cutlets, dilled new potatoes make a nice summer lunch or light supper served with a bowl of cold buttermilk or sour milk (eaten with a spoon like soup) on the side.

POTATO BALLS, FRIED *(kuleczki kartoflane)*: This gourmet rendition of the potato is usually served on special occasions with roast turkey and other festive roasts. Cook 2½ lb potatoes in skins in boiling water until soft. Peel under cold running water and push through ricer or sieve. Add 3 eggs and season with salt, pepper, a pinch of grated nutmeg and 1 t sugar. Mix well to blend ingredients. Between palms of hands roll snowball-fashion into cherry-sized balls, roll in flour and fry in hot butter to a nice golden brown on all sides. Drain on absorbent paper. (OPTIONAL: Add a T or so chopped dill and/or parsley to mixture before frying.)

BUCKWHEAT GROATS *(kasza gryczana)*: Slosh 2 c buckwheat groats around by hand in pot full of cold water to remove impurities and pour off. Transfer to sieve, rinse under cold running water, drain and press out moisture. In pot combine 3 c water, 1 t salt and 2 T fat (butter, lard, fatback or bacon drippings or oil [for fast-days]) and bring to boil. Add groats in thin stream so boiling doesn't stop. Stir with wooden spoon. Cover and cook on low until all water is absorbed. Stir with wooden spoon, cover and transfer to preheated 350° oven for 1 hr. Serve with beef, meatballs, game dishes, mushroom sauce or fried fatback nuggets. NOTE: For extra-fluffy *kasza*, after water has been absorbed, wrap covered pot in old newspaper or a dishtowel, bath towel or blanket and smother with a featherbed or pillows. In 3–5 hr, the groats will be ready to serve—hot and fluffy with each kernel separated.

KRAKÓW (FINE-MILLED) BUCKWHEAT GROATS *(kasza krakowska)*: Mix 1–2 c Kraków buckwheat groats with a small egg or with just the egg white to coat as evenly as possible. Spread out on baking sheet and dry out in warm 325° oven, stirring and flattening with spoon, about 60 min. Into pot pour 1½ times as much water as there is *kasza*, add 2 T fat and ½ t salt and bring to boil. Gradually add the *kasza*, stir and cook, covered, on low until water is absorbed. Transfer, covered, to preheated 350° oven for 25–30 min. Serve as you would ordinary buckwheat groats. As a meat accompaniment it is especially good garnished with chopped fresh dill. It is also used in poultry stuffing.

BARLEY GROATS *(kasza jęczmienna)*: Slosh 2 c pearl barley around by hand in pot of cold water to remove impurities and pour off water. Rinse sieve under cold running water, drain and press out moisture. In pot combine 4 c water, 1 t salt and 2 T fat (butter, lard, fatback or bacon drippings, oil [for fast-days]) and bring to boil. Add barley in thin stream so boiling doesn't stop. Give it several stirs with wooden spoon, cover and cook on low until all water is absorbed. Stir with wooden spoon, cover and transfer to 350° oven for 1 hr. Serve with sauces, meat dishes, and in gravy and stews.

BARLEY, WHOLE-GRAIN *(pęczak)*: See Old Polish Cookery, page 185.

MILLET GROATS *(kasza jaglana)*: See Old Polish Cookery, page 185.

DROPPED DUMPLINGS *(kluski kładzione)*: Bring a large pot of lightly salted water to boil. Break 1 egg into bowl, add 1 c flour, sifted, ¼ t salt and just enough water to form a thick batter. Beat with spoon until air blisters appear. Scoop up portions of batter in the shape of small, elongated dumplings and drop into boiling water. Dip spoon into boiling water between additions. When all dumplings are in pot, give it a stir, cover and cook 3–4 min.

Remove with slotted spoon and drain in colander or sieve. These dumplings are mainly served (like potatoes or pasta) as an accompaniment to stews and other gravy-type meat dishes or in soups.

POTATO DUMPLINGS/"LITTLE HOOVES" *(kopytka)*: Peel and cook 2¼ lb potatoes (6–7 med) in lightly salted water until soft, drain well, steam off moisture and mash well. Transfer to floured board to cool. Add about 2 c flour, 1 egg and ½ t salt and quickly work ingredients into a dough. Between hands form into finger-thick strands and cut at an angle into 1″–2″ pieces. Drop into boiling salted water, cover and when boiling resumes, cook 2–3 min. Remove with slotted spoon. *Kopytka* are a good accompaniment for stews and gravy-type dishes and can be a vegetarian dish in themselves, garnished with butter-browned bread crumbs. HINT: A good time to prepare *kopytka* is when you have leftover mashed potatoes on hand. TIP: Instant mashed potatoes may be used in this recipe.

POLISH VEGETARIAN DISHES

Both in Poland and America, vegetarian lifestyles are growing in popularity among the younger generation for both health and humanitarian reasons. And many people, who are not vegetarians, are cutting down on animal fat and cholesterol to stay trim and fit, and have come to enjoy the taste of meatless foods. At the same time, one hears complaints that Polish food is mainly about heavy and fattening meat dishes. Actually, nothing could be further from the truth. While most Poles have traditionally preferred meat to other foods, the fact that there were once nearly 200 fast days a year, and that many people couldn't afford meat even when it was permissible, has led to a variety of vegetarian substitutes. Many of them fit in nicely with today's vegetarian set who should be able to find something to their liking and not feel left out at Polonian suppers, festivals and picnics. Since such people should also be attracted to the Polish cultural legacy (not turned away or turned off!), perhaps at fests and functions meatless dishes should be grouped together (on the menu or at one section of the food concession) as "vegetarian delights" (*przysmaki wegetariańskie*) or "vegetarian corner" (*kącik jarosza*).

Two traditional Polish showcase foods—*pierogi* and *gołąbki*—offer numerous meatless versions (see pages 142 and 145), which many nonvegetarians prefer to the meat-filled varieties. This book also contains a variety of meatless pasta dishes, *naleśniki* and other pancakes, mushroom and grain dishes. (For meatless breaded cutlets containing beans, groats, cabbage, cheese, potatoes, mushrooms, etc., see *Polish Heritage Cookery*). And, of course, there is that vegetable-lover's delight, *bukiet z jarzyn* (cooked vegetable bouquet), which might group together on a single dinner plate: cauliflower Polonaise, buttered carrots, wax beans, dilled new potatoes with sliced vine-ripened tomatoes on the side. With the exception of scalded lettuce, all the salads presented below are 100% meatless. So there are plenty of vegetarian selections to choose from.

TYPICALLY POLISH SALADS

CUCUMBERS AND SOUR CREAM *(mizeria)*: Peel 2 nice-sized cucumbers and slice into thin rounds. Sprinkle with salt and let stand 30 min. Pour off liquid. Sprinkle with freshly ground pepper, 2–3 pinches sugar and 1 T lemon juice or vinegar. Lace with ½–⅔ c fork-blended sour cream (or plain yogurt for weight-watchers). (OPTIONAL: Garnish with chopped dill.)

CUCUMBERS AND VINAIGRETTE *(mizeria z winegretem)*: Slice, salt and drain cucumbers as above. Toss with 1–2 sm onions sliced thin and broken up into rings. Dress with vinaigrette (see below) to taste.

VINAIGRETTE *(winegret)*: Even the Polish spelling cannot disguise this obviously French import, which has had many devotees in Poland for ages. It is especially recommended to accompany either bland-tasting main courses or those in creamy sauces, when the classic sour-cream dressing would provide too much richness. To prepare slightly more than ½ c vinaigrette dressing, combine ⅓ c cider or white wine vinegar with salt and pepper to taste, 1–2 cloves crushed garlic (or ¼ t garlic powder) and (optional) ¼ t Provençal seasoning (or Italian seasoning). Mix well and stir in ¼ c extra-virgin olive oil or other salad oil of choice. VARIATION: Lemon juice may be used in place of all or some of the vinegar. NOTE: French and Italian gourmets might shudder at the thought, but Polish cooks sometimes add a pinch or 2 sugar to their vinaigrette.

LETTUCE SALAD, POLISH-STYLE *(zielona sałata po polsku)*: For a genuine Polish-style salad, select Boston or Bibb lettuce (rather than iceberg, leaf, romaine or other varieties). Twist off and discard the core that holds the leaves together. Separate the leaves and wash well, dry and place in shallow serving dish. (Polish-style lettuce salad is not ordinarily served in deep salad bowls.) If the leaves are quite long, tear each into 2 or 3 pieces. To dress 2 sm to med heads lettuce, fork-blend ⅔–¾ c sour cream with juice of ½ lemon, ¼ t salt and ½–1 t sugar and pour over lettuce. VARIATIONS: 1) after dressing the lettuce decorate the top with 2 sliced hard-cooked eggs; 2) scatter 8–10 thinly sliced radishes over the lettuce before or after dressing with sour-cream sauce; 3) scatter 4–5 chopped scallions over lettuce before or after dressing; 4) garnish the basic recipe or variants 1–3 with chopped chives.

LETTUCE AND VINAIGRETTE *(zielona sałata z winegretem)*: Dress any of the versions of lettuce salad described in the preceding entry with vinaigrette (instead of sour cream) to taste.

SCALDED LETTUCE SALAD *(sałata parzona)*: Core, wash and dry 3–4 small heads of Boston lettuce. Break up leaves into salad bowl. In skillet fry ⅛ lb diced pork fatback into golden brown nuggets, stir in 1 t sugar, ¼ t salt (if using unsalted fatback) and about 4 T cider vinegar. Immediately drench lettuce with hot, sizzling mixture and toss to coat leaves evenly. Serve with roasts or boiled meat. With bread on the side this can be a light lunch or supper.

TOMATO SALAD *(sałatka z pomidorów)*: Wash and slice 2–3 firm tomatoes and arrange on large serving dish in a single layer. Chop 1 med onion fine. Salt and pepper tomatoes and sprinkle with a little lemon juice. Sprinkle a little chopped onion at center of each tomato slice. VARIATION: Slice, arrange and season tomato slices as above. Slice 2 small onions wafer thin and arrange on top of tomato slices. Sprinkle salad with chopped chives or scallions. NOTE: This salad is very good dressed with vinaigrette. It can also be dressed with liquefied sour cream, but it should be added just prior to serving—otherwise the salad will become "soupy."

CUCUMBER AND TOMATO SALAD *(sałatka z ogórków i pomidorów)*: Assemble several tomatoes and onions and a cucumber or two of roughly equal circumference. Peel and slice the onions and cucumbers and slice the tomatoes. On a lettuce-lined serving platter arrange even rows of overlapping, alternating cucumber, tomato and onion slices. Fork-blend 1 c sour cream (or plain low-fat yogurt) with juice of ½ lemon and salt, pepper and a pinch of sugar to taste. Pour dressing down the center of each row, garnish with some chopped chives and (optional) 2 chopped hard-cooked eggs and dust with paprika. Serve at once, as long standing can make this salad "soupy".

SPRING-ONION SALAD *(surówka ze szczypioru)*: Wash well, drain and chop 4 bunches of green spring onions. Sprinkle with salt and pepper and drench with sour-cream sauce as in lettuce salad, Polish-style (see page 157); 2–3 diced hard-cooked eggs may be added.

RADISH SALAD *(surówka z rzodkiewek)*: Trim if necessary, wash, dry and slice thin (with knife or on slicer blade of handheld grater) 2–3 bunches radishes. Place in serving dish and toss with ½ c finely chopped fresh dill. Salt, sprinkle with 1–2 t sugar and drench with ½ c fork-blended sour cream.

RADISH, CUCUMBER, GREEN-ONION SALAD *(surówka w rzodkiewek, ogórka i szczypioru)*: Trim, wash, dry and slice 2 bunches radishes. Peel and slice thin 1 cucumber. Chop 4–5 scallions. Toss ingredients together and dress with sour-cream sauce as in lettuce salad, Polish-style (see page 157). (OPTIONAL: Garnish with 2–3 sliced hard-cooked eggs dusted with paprika.)

CARROT, APPLE AND HORSERADISH SALAD: *(surówka z marchwi, jabłek i chrzanu)*: Combine 4 washed, peeled finely grated carrots with 2–3 peeled, cored, coarsely grated apples. Sprinkle with lemon juice, toss and stir in 1–2 heaping T prepared horseradish. Season to taste with salt (sparingly), sugar and lemon juice. (OPTIONAL: Mix in 1 heaping T sour cream and/or mayonnaise.) This is a typical grated salad served in the colder months when fresh greens are less plentiful.

CELERIAC AND APPLE SALAD: *(surówka z selerów i jabłek)*: Peel and grate 1 med celeriac and sprinkle with lemon juice. (NOTE: Celeriac may be finely or coarsely grated as preferred.) Combine with 3 peeled, cored, finely diced or coarsely grated cooking apples and toss. Season to taste with salt, pepper, a little sugar and a little more lemon juice as required. Lace with ⅔–¾ c mayonnaise. Garnish with chopped parsley or chives.

CELERIAC AND PEAR SALAD *(surówka z selerów i gruszek)*: Peel and grate 1 med celeriac and sprinkle with lemon jucice. (NOTE: Celeriac may be grated finely or coarsely as preferred.) Combine with 3 firm, peeled, cored, finely diced pears and toss. Season to taste with salt, pepper, a little sugar and a little more lemon juice as required. Lace with fork-blended mixture of ⅓ c sour cream and ⅓ c mayonnaise.

LEEK SALAD *(sałatka z porów)*: Remove and discard (or freeze and use for soups) green tops from 3 leeks. Cut leeks in half lengthwise and wash well under running water to remove any imbedded grit. Cut each half in half lengthwise which should give you 12 leek sticks. Place them on cutting board side by side and dice fairly fine. Place in bowl. Add 2 peeled cooking apples, diced fine, sprinkle with lemon juice and toss ingredients. Season with salt, pepper and a little sugar and lace with mayonnaise. VARIATION: For a heartier supper salad, add ¾ c or so diced yellow cheese.

CABBAGE SALAD/COLESLAW *(surówka z białej kapusty)*: Shred or grate 1 sm head cabbage, sprinkle with salt and let stand at room temp 30 min. Pour off any liquid and squeeze dry. Sprinkle with lemon juice, season with a little sugar and pepper and lace with fork-blended mixture of ⅓ c sour cream and ⅓ c mayonnaise. Good with pork dishes, esp. those not containing gravies.

COLESLAW WITH VINAIGRETTE *(surówka z białej kapusty z winegretem)*: Shred or grate and salt cabbage as above. Dress with several T vinaigrette to taste. If vinaigrette is the unsweetened kind, add a little sugar to taste. (See lettuce and vinaigrette, page 158.)

COLESLAW WITH CRANBERRIES *(surówka z białej kapusty i żurawin)*: Shred or grate and salt cabbage as above. Process ⅓–½ c raw cranberries and mix with ½ c sour cream. Stir into cabbage and season with a little sugar as desired. Serve with poultry.

RED CABBAGE AND APPLE SALAD *(surówka z czerwonej kapusty i jabłek)*: Trim and shred 1 sm red cabbage. Scald with boiling water to cover and let stand several min. Drain well. Toss with 1–2 peeled, coarsely grated apples and 1 grated onion. Dress with vinaigrette and sweeten to taste with a little sugar. (OPTIONAL: About ⅓ c plumped raisins may be added.) VARIATION: Lace with a heaping T or so mayonnaise.

SAUERKRAUT SALAD *(surówka z kwaszonej kapusty)*: Drain and rinse 2 c sauerkraut, press out moisture and chop. Place in salad bowl and tear apart so it doesn't stick together. Add 1 chopped onion, 1 finely grated carrot and 1 finely diced, peeled apple. Season with pepper and sugar, drizzle with salad oil and toss. Garnish with chopped chives for a nicer presentation. (OPTIONAL: Salad may also be seasoned with caraway.) Excellent with fried fish. NOTE: Sauerkraut salad is often prepared with just grated carrots and/or chopped onions.

DILL PICKLE SALAD *(sałatka z kiszonych/konserwowych ogórków)*: Slice 4–5 large dill pickles (brined, vinegar type or some of each) into thin rounds. Toss with 2–3 sm onions, sliced and broken up into rings, and 1 peeled diced apple (optional). Add 1–2 cloves crushed garlic, toss and dress with salad oil. Good with bland-tasting foods such as boiled meat.

POLISH SALAD BOUQUET *(bukiet polskich surówek)*: Some Polish restaurants offer a combination plate comprising a sampling of 3 or 4 typical salads. A nice color contrast is provided by, for instance, small adjacent mounds of grated carrot salad, red cabbage salad and pale green cucumbers in cream, arranged on a bed of green lettuce. In addition to individual combination portions, this same concept may be carried over to serving platters, providing guests with an opportunity to sample different kinds of salads or help themselves to the ones they like best.

POLISH FESTIVE BREAKFAST

Polonian organizations often sponsor club breakfasts for members and guests, parishes hold communion breakfasts and many Polish-American families come together at least once a week for a big Sunday breakfast. For whatever reason, this has become the least ethnically authentic meal. Everyone has heard of kiełbasa dinners, gołąbki fests and pierogi suppers, but all too often the first meal of the day in much of Polonia runs along the lines of the Anglo-mainstream breakfast: crunchy-munchy–style cold cereals, toast and jam, pancakes and syrup, doughnuts and other sweet cakes. When eggs appear, even they are usually served in a most un-Polish way. This section has therefore been provided for the benefit of those who occasionally hold community or festive family breakfasts without realizing how culturally diluted they have become. Here are but a few typically Polish breakfasts. See *Polish Heritage Cookery* for recipes not listed in this book.

FESTIVE COMPANY BREAKFAST *(uroczyste śniadanie dla gości)*: To a considerable extent, festive Polish-style breakfasts held in honor of special guests are similar to the Old Polish breakfasts (below) as well as the traditional Easter breakfast *(święcone)* in that they tend to feature heartier foods such as cold meat and fish do not shun a "nip" of *coś mocniejszego* (something stronger). Eggs are no stranger to the festive Polish breakfast table, but these are often served in ways (stuffed in shells, in a glass, scrambled with *kiełbasa*, hard-cooked in sauces, etc.) not widely known in America. Some examples follow.

I.

- ✦ **Hot bouillon**: served in teacups or bouillon cups
- ✦ **Assorted cold-meat platter**: roast pork loin, roast beef, roast veal, ham, smoked pork loin etc.
- ✦ **Condiments**: horseradish, *ćwikła*, mayonnaise-based sauces, marinated mushrooms, pickled pumpkin, spiced cherries, etc.
- ✦ **Mixed baked goods**: rye, dark-rye, whole-wheat and white (French, Italian, Vienna) bread and rolls (kaiser, crescents, etc.), unsalted butter
- ✦ **Hot stuffed eggs** (in shells)
- ✦ **Hot lemon tea**
- ✦ **Fresh in-season fruit**: strawberries, plums, cherries, apples, pears, oranges (in winter)
- ✦ **Finale**: coffee cake *(placek)*, espresso-strength coffee, spot of brandy (optional)

II.

- **Cold fish platter**: black caviar, smoked salmon, smoked eel, fish in aspic, sprats, sardines (lemon wedges)
- **Chilled champagne** (French), or dry sparkling wine of choice (optional)
- **Mixed baked goods**: rye, dark-rye, whole-wheat and white (French, Italian, Vienna) bread and rolls (kaiser, crescents, etc.), unsalted butter
- **Mushroom omelet,** garnished with chopped chives
- **Lemon tea or coffee** (white or black)

III.

- **Pâté**: (pork, goose, turkey or mixed), tartar sauce, pickled mushrooms, radishes, scallions
- **Mixed baked goods**: rye, dark-rye, whole-wheat and white (French, Italian, Vienna) bread and rolls (kaiser, crescents, etc.), unsalted butter
- **Eggs in a glass**: cook room-temp eggs in boiling water 2½–3 min; quickly scoop out contents of 2 cooked eggs with spoon into prescalded juice glass, add a pat of butter and serve; provide salt and pepper for guests to custom-season their portions
- **Egg breads**: *babka, chałka*, *drożdżówki,* honey, *powidła*, jam
- **Hot tea** with fruit preserves (on the side)

HEARTY COUNTRY-STYLE BREAKFAST *(pożywne wiejskie śniadanie)*: *Żur* (ryemeal soup) was once a breakfast staple in the Polish countryside, and hot milk soups, sausage and eggs were also common. Perhaps some of the following suggestions could be incorporated into Polonia's breakfast scene.

I.

- **Sour ryemeal soup**, boiled or mashed potatoes, garnished with fried fatback nuggets, on the side
- **Fried kiszka** (with or without fried onions)
- **Accompaniments**: light and dark rye bread and butter, mustard, dill pickles
- **Hot raspberry tea**

II.

- **Hot milk soup**: allow about 1 c hot milk and ½ c cooked millet or barley per serving; a pat of butter may be added to each serving; may be eaten salty or sweet
- **White cheese,** laced with sour cream and chopped scallions and/or chive
- **Rye bread** (light or dark), butter
- **Scrambled eggs, peasant-style** *(chłopska jajecznica)*: dice and fry up 4–5 slices thick-sliced bacon with 1 chopped onion and 2 c cooked diced

potatoes; add 8 beaten eggs and, when partially set, swirl around briefly until cooked but still moist

III.

- **Fried *kiełbasa***: ordinary smoked *kiełbasa (zwyczajna)* cut into ½" rounds and browned on both sides in lard, bacon drippings or other fat
- **Accompaniments**: rye bread, butter, horseradish, mustard, dill pickles
- **Buckwheat pie** *(pieróg),* fried in butter (or cooked buckwheat groats garnished with golden brown fatback nuggets)
- **Hot milk** (in winter) or **cold buttermilk** (in summer)

IV.

- **Cold meats**: headcheese, cooked slab bacon (sliced), cold *kiszka*
- **Accompaniments**: rye bread, butter, mustard, horseradish, brined dill pickles
- **Boiled potatoes,** garnished with fried fatback (salt-pork) or bacon nuggets
- **Hot mint tea**

OLD POLISH BREAKFAST *(śniadanie staropolskie)*: In the olden days, almost any hearty food could be served for the day's first meal, however beer soup was considered a typical breakfast food. Here are some of the dishes served in the manor houses of Old Poland.

I.

- **Beer soup,** with cubed white cheese and croutons
- **Cold meat platter**: roast turkey, goose, beef, pork, veal, venison
- **Assorted baked goods**: rye, dark-rye, whole-wheat and white (French, Italian, Vienna) bread and rolls (kaiser, crescents, etc.), unsalted butter
- **Condiments**: *ćwikła*, assorted pickled fruits, vegetables and mushrooms
- **Spirits**: hot honey-spice cordial *(krupnik)*
- **Steak roll-ups** in mushroom sauce, buckwheat groats
- **Cakes**: knot cake (*sękacz*) and wheel cake (*kołacz*)
- **Old Polish coffee**: double strength (1 T or coffee measure per 3 oz water) whitened with hot coffee cream

II.

- **Wild-game pâté** (made with venison, boar or hare and fatty pork)
- **Condiments**: tart gherkins (*korniszony*), caper sauce
- **Assorted baked goods**: rye, dark-rye, whole-wheat and white (French, Italian, Vienna) bread and rolls (kaiser, crescents, etc.), unsalted butter
- **Hard-cooked eggs** (hot) in horseradish sauce

- ✦ **Hot meat dish**: pork or wild-boar roasts (seasoned with juniper) and cooked with apples or mushrooms
- ✦ **Starchy complement**: cooked millet groats
- ✦ **Wine**: mead or Hungarian Tokay
- ✦ **Fruit**: bowls of fresh in-season fruit (cherries, plums, blackberries, blueberries, apples, pears, etc.) or dried fruit (raisins, prunes, dried cherries, dates, figs, etc.) set out at intervals on the breakfast table

III.

- ✦ **Hot vegetable-barley soup** with mushrooms (*krupnik*)
- ✦ **Cold smoked goose breasts** *(półgęski)*
- ✦ **Condiments**: spiced fruits, pickled mushrooms
- ✦ **Hunter's bigos,** with breadstuffs on the side (below)
- ✦ **Assorted baked goods**: rye, dark-rye, whole-wheat and white (French, Italian, Vienna) bread and rolls (kaiser, crescents, etc.), unsalted butter
- ✦ **Hot juniper beer**

POLISH CONTINENTAL BREAKFAST *(polskie śniadanie „kontynentalne")*: the concept of a "continental breakfast" was adapted by Polish hotels to accommodate the preconceptions of visiting Americans and other foreigners. Unlike the coffee and raised roll (Danish) that term connotes in America, Polish continental breakfasts are generally heartier and could include the following:

- ✦ **Juice**: often a choice of apple, blackcurrant, cherry, orange, grapefruit, tomato
- ✦ **Assorted baked goods**: rye, dark-rye, whole-wheat and white (French, Italian, Vienna) bread and rolls (kaiser, crescents, etc.)
- ✦ **Spreads**: unsalted butter, honey, jam, *powidła,* preserves
- ✦ **Cheese**: often small portions (triangles) of foil-wrapped processed cheese in various flavors
- ✦ **Cold meat**: ham, pâté, etc.
- ✦ **Cakes**: raised fruit-filled cakes, teacakes, *placek*
- ✦ **Beverages**: coffee, tea, cocoa, milk

TODAY'S POLISH FAMILY BREAKFAST *(śniadanie współczesnej polskiej rodziny)*: The typical breakfasts eaten in Poland today combine features of the different breakfast styles presented above. Most often, today's Poles make themselves *kanapki* (open-face sandwiches) from cheese and/or cold cuts set out on the breakfast table and wash them down with hot tea or white coffee, occasionally (esp. among young children) with hot milk or cocoa. Here are a few typical breakfasts you are likely to encounter when visiting relatives in today's Poland.

I.

- **Assorted, yellow sliced cheese** (e.g., Podlaski, Morski, Gouda, Edam, Tylżycki (Tilsiter(, Mazurski, Salami)
- **Baked goods**: rye bread, whole-wheat and kaiser rolls, French bread, butter
- **White coffee** (real or substitute/*ersatz*)
- **Fruit**: in-season variety

II.

- **Hot porridge** (oatmeal, cream of wheat, milk soup)
- **Boiled knackwurst** *(serdelki)* or franks *(parówki),* mustard, dill pickles, radishes
- **Baked goods**: rye bread, whole-wheat and kaiser rolls
- **Lemon tea**

III.

- **White cheese and chives**, laced with sour cream, salted and pepper (grated, radishes, scallions and cucumbers may also be added)
- **Baked goods**: rye bread, whole-wheat and kaiser rolls, French bread, butter
- **Fried or scrambled eggs,** fried in fatback or bacon nuggets or in sliced *kiełbasa*
- **White coffee** (real or *ersatz*)

IV.

- **Ready-made canned pâté**
- **Accompaniments**: horseradish sauce, sliced tomatoes, dill pickles
- **Baked goods**: rye bread, whole-wheat and kaiser rolls, French bread, butter
- **Spreads**: jam, preserves, honey
- **Lemon tea**

V.

- **Assorted canapés**: containing cheese, cold cuts, egg spread, fish spread, etc.
- **Fruit-filled raised pastries**
- **In-season fruit**
- **Tea or coffee**

POLISH-AMERICAN BREAKFAST BUFFET *(polonijny bufet śniadaniowy)*: Having studied the different Polish breakfast options presented above, we are now ready to prepare a Polish-style company breakfast at home or for club members, parishioners or invited guests in various community settings. In case your guests include those who think such substantial dishes are not suitable for breakfast, feel free to call it a "Polish brunch." Due to the great variety of interesting dishes available, this could be a good fund-raiser for Polish-American organizations and parishes. Such a buffet might include the following:

- **Polish breakfast soups**: hot milk and rice (or other grain)—Old Polish beer soup with cheese and croutons
- **Polish cheese medley**: platter or assorted cheeses—white, yellow, *oscypek, bryndza*
- **Hard-cooked eggs in sauces**: horseradish, mustard, green, Easter, caper, etc.
- **Polish canapé spreads**: egg, cheese and chives, soft pâté
- **Baked goods**: assorted breads and rolls (rye, whole wheat, white), unsalted butter
- **Roast meat platter**: sliced cold pork loin, beef tongue, roast beef, turkey
- **Smoked meat platter**: ham, smoked pork loin (Canadian bacon), assorted sliced Polish sausages and lunch meats
- **Condiments**: pickled mushrooms, vegetables and fruits, *ćwikła*, mustard, horseradish, bilberry sauce
- **Hot meats**: steak roll-ups (choice of several fillings), buckwheat groats
- **Hot eggs**: scrambled with *kiełbasa*, fried (sunny-side up) with *skwarki* (fatback nuggets) salt-pork nuggets, hot stuffed in shells, eggs in a glass, soft boiled
- **Cakes, egg breads**: raised fruit-filled cakes, babka, poppy seed roll, *placek, chałka, pączki*
- **Cold beverages**: juices (blackcurrant, apple, cherry, orange, grapefruit), bottled mineral water
- **Hot beverages**: coffee (black, white, *ersatz*), lemon tea, hot chocolate, hot milk
- **Spirits**: *krupnik* (hot honey-spice cordial), cognac/winiak, mead, mulled wine (circumstances permitting)

POLISH CAKES AND DESSERT DISHES

There are fewer recipes under the above heading than in other sections of this book not because Poles do not appreciate or are unfamiliar with cakes and dessert dishes, but because most of the traditional Polish favorites have already been presented among the Christmas, Mardi Gras and Easter selections. The following are therefore only a few additions needed to fill in the missing pieces.

POLISH APPLE CAKE *(szarlotka)*: This cake is as popular with the Polish people as apple pie is with Americans! Combine 2¾ c flour with 1 c confectioners' sugar, 4 egg yolks and ¼ t salt and blend ingredients into a uniform dough. Do not knead! Roll into ball, wrap in foil and refrigerate at least 30 min. Meanwhile, in pot combine 1 lb tart cooking apples, peeled and sliced, with ½ c sugar and simmer on low heat until apples are tender. To cooked apples add 1¼ lb peeled, diced or sliced uncooked apples. Season with several pinches cinnamon, nutmeg or ground cloves or a combination of any 2 or all 3 (1 pinch of each). Divide chilled dough in half. Roll one half out thin into a rectangle or square to fit your baking pan. Pierce all over with fork and bake in preheated 400° oven 10–15 min. Sprinkle surface of baked dough with 3–4 T crushed vanilla wafers and spread apple filling evenly over surface. Season with 1 t vanilla sugar. Roll out remaining dough half and cover apples. Reduce heat to 350° and bake 45–60 min. VARIATIONS: Several T raisins and or 1 T diced candied orange rind may be added to apple mixture. Slice cake into squares after it has cooled. HINT: If the apple filling seems too tart, dust cake with confectioners' sugar. Each portion may be topped with a dollop of real whipped cream just before serving.

POLISH PLUM CAKE *(placek ze śliwkami)*: Beat ½ c butter and 1 c sugar until smooth (about 2 min). Continue beating, adding 2 eggs, one at a time. Mix 2 c flour with 2 t baking powder and ¼ t salt and sift into bowl. Gradually stir in the butter-sugar-egg mixture, ½ t vanilla extract and ¾ c milk, beating the whole time until smooth. Transfer dough to greased square or rectangular baking pan. Top dough with ripe Italian plum halves (*węgierki*) cut-side up and sprinkle with a pinch or 2 cinnamon (optional). Dot with about 2 T cold butter and bake in preheated 350° oven 40–45 min, or until inserted wooden pick comes out clean.

PLAIN YEAST LOAF/COFFEE CAKE *(placek)*: Mash 1 cake yeast with 1 T sugar, add ¾ c warm milk and stir in 1 scant c flour. Mix, cover and set in warm place to rise about 1 hr. To yeast mixture add 4 yolks, beaten until lemony, with 1 c sugar, 2 c flour ⅛ t salt and 1 t grated lemon zest. Work ingredients into a dough, knead well and work in ⅔ c melted butter. Set aside in warm place to double in bulk. Transfer to greased, flour-sprinkled baking pan(s) and let rise again. Bake about 45 min in 375° oven.

CRUMB-TOP YEAST LOAF/COFFEE CAKE *(placek z kruszonką)*: Prepare cake as in preceding recipe. While dough is rising, combine ¾ c butter, ⅓ c sugar, ¾ c flour and 1 T vanilla sugar. Blend ingredients together with knife, roll into ball, wrap in foil and refrigerate. Just before popping *placek* into the oven, grate the refrigerated crumb-topping ball over top of loaf. Bake as above.

WHEEL-SHAPED WEDDING CAKE *(kołacz/korowaj)*: This was the traditional Polish wedding cake, and its name (*kołacz*—from the word for "wheel" = *koło*) suggest its round wheel shape. It was also served on other festive occasions. Prepare dough as for Easter *babka* (see page 117), but rather than a tube pan transfer it into a well-greased round springform pan no more than ½ full. Let rise in warm place until doubled in bulk. Meanwhile, grind or process 1½ lb farmer cheese. Beat 4 egg yolks with 1 c confectioners' sugar and 1 T vanilla sugar until smooth and creamy. Gradually mix in the ground cheese, 3 T potato starch, 4 T melted butter and ½–1 c rinsed, drained raisins. Mix ingredients, fold in 4 egg whites beaten to a froth and mix lightly. After dough rises, make an indentation at center with a dinner plate and fill indentation with cheese mixture. Smooth top, brush with beaten egg and bake in 375° oven about 50 min. NOTE: The wheel cake can also be made with poppy-seed filling (see Christmas cakes, page 59) or plums.

KNOT/LOG/BEGGAR'S CAKE *(sękacz/dziad)*: This cake, associated with Easter and other festive occasions, is still baked the original way (on a hand-cranked spit in front of an open flame) only in Poland's northeastern Podlasie (Białystok) region. Elsewhere, most Poles now buy it at their nearest pastry shop. If you want to try your hand at the traditional method, consult *Treasured Polish Recipes* or *Polish Heritage Cookery*. Easier baking-pan versions of this cake are presented in *Polish Cooking* and *Polish Heritage Cookery*.

DESSERT OMELET WITH FRUIT *(grzybek deserowy z owocami)*: With whisk, egg-beater or electric mixer beat 2 eggs with 1 level T flour, 1 T milk and a pinch of salt until foamy. In skillet heat 1 T butter, pour in egg mixture and tilt so it covers entire surface. Cook on med-high heat 30–40 seconds, picking up edges to let the egg liquid run to the bottom of skillet. When all the runny egg mixture is gone and bottom is nicely browned, flip over, cover and cook another 30–40 seconds. Slip onto plate and serve with fruit topping or syrup of choice (cherry, strawberry, raspberry). NOTE: As a main meal this is a single serving, but as a dessert dish it can be divided into 2 portions.

STRAWBERRY ICE CUP *(puchar lodowy z truskawkami)*: Hull, wash and drain 1 qt fresh, ripe strawberries. Halve or slice strawberries of roughly equal size and sprinkle with sugar (about 1 T sugar per 1 c berries). Let stand 30 min at room temp. Into parfait glasses place 1 scoop vanilla (or French vanilla) ice cream or frozen yogurt, a heaping T sugared strawberries, add another scoop ice cream, top with another spoonful of strawberries and, if the parfait glass permits, add another scoop ice cream and top with a little more strawberry mixture. Top with a dollop of real whipped cream and crown with 1 nice, whole, unblemished fresh (unsugared) strawberry. NOTE: This and similar light, refreshing desserts are a better finale to heavy banquet and dinner-party fare than rich cakes and pastries.

MIXED-BERRY ICE CUP *(puchar lodowy wieloowocowy)*: Into parfait glasses place 1 T washed, drained, fresh blueberries, top with 1 scoop vanilla (or French vanilla) ice cream or frozen yogurt, add 1 T washed, dried, fresh raspberries, follow up with another scoop of ice cream, and top with sliced, sugared strawberries (prepared as in preceding recipe). Top with a dollop of real whipped cream and crown with 1 whole, strawberry, raspberry or 3 blueberries.

PEARS IN CHOCOLATE *(gruszki w czekoladzie)*: This nice, light dessert (perfect after a heavy meal) is proof that gourmet treats need not be expensive, elaborate or difficult to prepare. On dessert plate pour a T chocolate sundae topping or other chocolate sauce of choice. On it place a well-drained canned pear half cored-side down. Pour 1 t chocolate sauce over it and top with a dollop of real whipped cream. Decorate cream topping with a whole, fresh berry (raspberry, strawberry, blackberry). That's all there is to it! (OPTIONAL: Chocolate topping may be enriched with rum or cognac [1 T per 1 c sauce]). VARIATION: Instead of chocolate sauce feel free to use other toppings such as raspberry syrup, vanilla sauce, etc.

STRAWBERRY KISIEL *(kisiel truskawkowy)*: This old-fashioned dessert remains popular in Poland and deserves to be promoted among Polonia. In pot combine 1 c water and about ½ c sugar and bring to boil. Remove from heat. Dissolve 3 T potato starch in ½ c cold water, stir into sugar water and bring to boil, stirring constantly. Add just under 1 lb hulled, washed, dried, crushed (processed) strawberries. Mix well. Portion out into dessert bowls pre-rinsed with cold water. Chill. Serve with cold milk, coffee cream, half & half or vanilla sauce (the latter can be easily whipped up by combining 1 c cold milk with just enough instant vanilla pudding mix to produce a nice, pourable sauce).

STRAWBERRIES AND SOUR CREAM *(truskawki ze śmietaną)*: This is a more earthy, down-home dessert, best suited to family gatherings or Polish fests, picnics or suppers. Hull, wash and drain fresh strawberries and either leave them whole (if they are small), halve or slice. Fill individual dessert dishes and provide sweetened sour cream (1 c sour cream fork-blended with a heaping T confectioners' sugar) for your guests, allowing ¼–⅓ c sweetened sour cream per serving. To make serving easier, use a ladle that size to dish out the topping.

SUGARED STRAWBERRIES, WHOLE *(truskawki z cukrem)*: This is an even simpler way to enjoy fresh strawberries. Place whole, hulled, washed strawberries in a bowl with a dish of granulated sugar next to it. Invite your guests to take the strawberries with their fingers, roll them in sugar and pop them into their mouth.

SUGARED TOMATOES *(pomidory z cukrem)*: This old treat has been forgotten by many, but it may be worth reviving. Sprinkle sliced tomatoes with sugar. Served in this manner, they taste something like red currants (*czerwone porzeczki*).

HONEYED CUCUMBERS *(ogórki z miodem)*: Peel cucumber and cut into spears. Drizzle with honey and serve. Many Polish Americans say this Old Polish treat tastes something like watermelon—only better!

FRESH FRUIT *(świeże owoce)*: Fresh fruit is often a much better follow-up to rich meals than cakes and other sweets. Especially recommended are in-season varieties. Wash, drain and make ripe strawberries, raspberries, cherries, plums, apples and pears available to your guests in bowls at different ends of the banquet or dinner table. In cold weather fresh fruits may be replaced by raisins, prunes (pitted) and other dried fruits as well as shelled nuts.

HOT BEVERAGES *(GORĄCE NAPOJE)*

These hot beverages are good as early-morning eye-openers or midday energizers and can help fend off the chill when the north wind is howling outside the window. They are the ideal warmer-upper to take in a thermos flask to a sleigh ride, skating party, ice fishing, a cold-weather hike through the woods, etc. Other hot beverages that also serve that purpose follow in the Hot Wine, Beer and Spirits section.

COFFEE *(KAWA)*

Some of the worst coffee in America is served at fast-food joints as well as Polish-American picnics, parish suppers and weddings. And to think that it was a Pole, Jan Kulczycki, fighting under the command of King Jan Sobieski in 1683, who got hold of the entire Turkish stockpile of coffee beans and set up one of Europe's first cafés in Vienna! And no poet has sung the praises of *kawa* (coffee) as eloquently as Poland's Adam Mickiewicz in his epic poem *Pan Tadeusz*. But, for whatever reason, we can thank not Polonia but our Italian fellow-Americans and companies such as Starbucks for introducing America to the darker, richer-tasting blends and such varieties as espresso, caffè latte and cappucino. But there is no reason in the world why the next Polonian testimonial banquet or this year's pączki party cannot be enhanced by a truly rich and flavorful cup of coffee rather than that tasteless swill that still passes for coffee in much of mainstream America. This is now easier than ever before because dark-roasted, fine-ground Polish-style coffee is becoming increasingly available in North America. NOTE: Never use what is known in America as "all-method grind" or "all-purpose grind" since it is too coarsely ground, does not release all the coffee's aroma and, as a result, is wasteful. You simply go through more coffee, hence it is heavily promoted by the U.S. coffee trade, which wants you to buy as much of their product as possible! For best results use espresso-grind or the finest of all Turkish-grind coffee as recommended for the individual brewing methods below:

Espresso-Pot Coffee *(kawa z ekspresu)*: The term "espresso-pot coffee," rather than "espresso coffee" has been deliberately chosen to indicate the brewing technique rather than the actual ground coffee. Black-roasted Italian espresso coffee is too dark and bitter for Polish tastes, hence I suggest you stick to the varieties listed in this book's Basic Ingredients and Procedures, page 23. To brew Polish-style café coffee you can use the classic, silvery stovetop pot or one of the high-tech electronic machines that automatically grind the coffee before custom-brewing each cup. Both the stovetop pot and electronic espresso machines make a superb cup of coffee. Use at least 1 standard measure (or heaping t) ground coffee per each 4 oz cup.

Coffee-Press Coffee *(kawa ze szklanego zaparzacza)*: This very simple, nonelectric contrivance consists of a glass beaker and a plunger-type device. All you do is prescald the container, add 1 coffee measure of espresso-grind coffee per 4 oz cup, drench with boiling water and let it steep a min or so, give it a stir (IMPORTANT: with a plastic or wooden spoon—a metal one may crack the beaker!), then gently depress the plunger all the way down. It makes an excellent cup of coffee.

Pot-Brewed Coffee *(kawa zaparzana w dzbanku)*: If you have an imported, hand-painted Polish porcelain coffee set in your china cabinet, here is how to use it. First measure the pot and see how many 4 oz cups it contains. Scald the pot with boiling water, pour it out, add 1 heaping t Turkish-grind coffee per each 4 oz cup and drench with rapidly boiling water. Cover with lid and let stand 2–3 min. If you have a tea cozy, use it to keep the pot hot. Stir vigorously and let stand another minute or so before pouring.

Turkish or Pot-Boiled Coffee *(kawa po turecku)*: In Turkish coffee pot, saucepan or other pot combine 1 heaping t Turkish-grind coffee per 4 oz cold water. Heat until boiling coffee rises and remove from heat. For stronger coffee, return to heat and let rise again. Serve immediately. May be poured into cups through a fine strainer for those who do not like so many dregs settling at the bottom of the cup. NOTE: In makeshift conditions (outdoor events, campsites, etc.) any large soup pot can be used to prepare coffee in this way for a larger group.

Automatic Drip Coffee Maker *(kawa filtrowana z zaparzacza)*: The Poles erroneously call this device an *"ekspres,"* although it bears no resemblance to a true espresso machine. Espresso or Turkish grind may be used in this method, which employs paper filters. Be sure to use 1 heaping t or 1 leveled coffee measure per each 4 oz of cold water. This method is acceptable on condition the brewed coffee is not allowed to stand too long on the heating plate. Make only enough for one round. If some want seconds, brew another round, as coffee soon becomes unpalatably heavy when kept on the heating plate for more than a few minutes.

Cup-Brewed Method *(kawa „po turecku", zaparzana w szklance lub filiżance)*: This is another Polish misnomer, hence the quotation marks round the *„po turecku"* (Turkish-style) in its name. Scald the cup or glass with boiling water and pour out. Add 1 heaping t or 1 level coffee measure Turkish-grind coffee to each cup and scald with 4 oz boiling water. Cover with saucer and let stand 1–2 min. Stir vigorously. When grounds settle, enjoy! For recent arrivals from Poland this widely used method may be a nostalgia trip, whereas many U.S.-born Polonians do not like the sight of dregs (grounds) at the bottom of the cup or glass.

WHITE COFFEE *(biała kawa)*: This is strictly a breakfast-style coffee. Prepare strong coffee according to any of the above methods. Fill cup or mug only ½ full and top up with hot milk. Sweeten to taste with sugar if desired.

COFFEE SUBSTITUTE *(kawa zbożowa)*: Poland's Inka brand is one of the best coffee substitutes available anywhere. Since it is made from roasted grain and contains no caffeine, it makes a nutritious hot breakfast drink that can be enjoyed by the entire family, including young children, who ordinarily do not drink coffee, and older people concerned about their high blood pressure. Use like instant coffee: place a heaping t of Inka (or American Postum) powder in cup and top up with hot water or milk and stir to blend. Sweeten with sugar if desired.

TEA *(HERBATA)*

TEA *(herbata)*: In addition to being a refreshing hot beverage, tea is a great warmer-upper highly recommended for outdoor activities during the colder months. It also settles an upset stomach—something that cannot be said about coffee. Choose the black tea that suits you best and one of the following brewing/serving methods.

Classic Polish Tea-Essence Method *(esencja z herbaty lisciastej)*: Depending on the strength desired, add several t of loose tea to prescalded teapot and top up with boiling water. Snugly set the china teapot into the opening of your stovetop hot-water kettle. Let the water in the kettle boil gently to warm the bottom of the teapot with steam so the tea can steep slowly to achieve peak strength. To serve, simply pour a little essence (the strong tea concentrate from the teapot) into a cup or glass and top up with boiling water. This makes it far easier to vary the desired strength than the now widespread cup-brewed teabag method (see below).

Pot-Brewing With Teabags *(esencja z herbaty w saszetkach)*: Those who prefer teabags to loose tea can proceed exactly the same way as in the preceding method. Simply place several teabags in a prescalded teapot and top up with boiling water. Allow to steep at least 15 min (over a steaming hot-water kettle or simply on a countertop). Pour the desired doses of essence into cups and top up with boiling water.

Samovar Method *(herbata z samowara)*: The samovar (literally "self-brewer"), a Russian invention that became a naturalized fixture on the Polish scene in the 19th century, is little more than an elegant version of the above tea-essence method. The samovar is a hot-water urn kept hot by either a charcoal fire or more recently an electric coil. The tea-essence pot is positioned at the top of the samovar and its bottom is warmed as it steeps just as in the preceding method. Individual portions of essence are poured from the tea-essence pot and the hot water for topping up comes from the samovar's spigot. HINT: Tea poured from a samovar is traditionally served in glasses fitted with special (often quite decorative and artistic) tea-glass holders that enable the hot glass to be held. NOTE: Even if it isn't being actually used, a shiny, classic samovar will add a touch of period elegance to your sideboard or buffet, just as candles are used at dinner parties for atmosphere, not lighting.

Cup-Brewing With Teabags *(herbata z indywidualnych saszetek)*: This method is not recommended when entertaining, since disposing of the drippy teabag is often a problem. Leaving it on the saucer wets the bottom of the cup and may cause drinkers to stain their clothes when they lift the cup. Some provide a special plate for diners to deposit their teabags, but on their way over they may drip and stain the tablecloth. Also, a plateful of used teabags is not an especially pleasant sight on the dinner table.

TEA WITH LEMON/LEMON TEA *(herbata z cytryną)*: Prepare tea according to any of the ways above and provide lemon slices on a separate plate with a small decorative two-pronged fork. The lemons may first be peeled and then sliced, with the rind (now often saturated with chemical preservatives) discarded. If the rind is left on, the lemon should be scalded, scrubbed and re-scalded before slicing.

RASPBERRY-FLAVORED TEA *(herbata z sokiem malinowym)*: Instead of the imitation-raspberry teas on the market these days, simply add 1–2 T pure (preferably Polish imported) raspberry syrup to each glass or cup of hot tea. For an added kick, add ½–1 jg vodka to each serving. Other fruit syrups (cherry, blueberry, currant, strawberry, etc.) may be used but lack the medicinal properties of raspberry syrup, which helps relieve colds.

RUM-FLAVORED TEA *(herbata z rumem)*: To each glass or cup of hot tea, sweetened to taste, add a little freshly-squeezed lemon juice and ½–1 jg rum. This may be prepared by the pitcher using about 3 jg rum per qt hot tea. NOTE: Vodka plus several drops of rum extract may be used if real rum is not available.

HOT WINE, BEER AND SPIRITS *(GRZANE TRUNKI, GRZAŃCE)*

Like rum-flavored tea (above), the following hot alcoholic drinks are usually associated with the colder months of the year. They are ideal for outdoor activities such as hayrides and sleighrides, skating and skiing parties, hunting trips, ice fishing and caroling parties. They are also good for indoor winter activities such as community Christmas suppers. Instead of a cash bar, provide pitchers of hot mulled beer on the tables for your guests to help themselves. Mulled wine might just hit the spot at a kolędy night.

MULLED BEER *(piwo grzane z korzeniani)*: In pot combine 1 qt beer, 3–4 T sugar, 1 bay leaf, 2 pinches each of cinnamon, ground cloves, ginger and (optional) a pinch of pepper. Heat to just below boiling, stirring to dissolve sugar and serve. Increase or decrease sugar and spices according to taste. NOTE: Instead of sugar, hot beer may be sweetened with fruit syrup or honey. It may contain only sugar or fruit syrup without the spices. The author recalls a tiny hole-in-the-wall beer, wine and sweet shop across from Warsaw's Polna

Street Market that displayed the following sign: *"Chcesz pożegnać się z troskami?–Wypij piwo z korzonkami!"* ("Want your cares to go away?—Hot, mulled beer will make your day!")

HOT JUNIPER BEER *(piwo jałowcowe grzane)*: This is a shortcut way of approximating this old Polish beverage. Combine 10–20 partially crushed (bruised) juniper berries *(jałowiec)* and 1 c water in saucepan. Bring to boil, reduce heat and simmer on low, covered, 10 min. Switch off heat and let stand until cooled to room temp. Strain, discarding crushed juniper, into bottle or jar. Add equal amt of 100-proof vodka, seal and store in fridge. To make hot juniper beer, heat 1 qt beer in pot, add a heaping T sugar and 1–2 jg of your juniper extract. If you don't have time to make your own juniper extract, simply add 2 jg store-bought gin. NOTE: Juniper beer can also be enjoyed cold—simply add 1 jg of juniper extract or 2 jg gin to 1 qt cold beer.

MULLED WINE *(wino grzane z korzeniami, grzaniec)*: In pot combine 1 qt dry red wine, 5–6 T sugar, a grating of nutmeg and a pinch or two of cinnamon and ground cloves and heat to boiling. Add 1–2 slices of lemon. You can also use a sweet red wine, in which case omit or decrease the amount of sugar.

MULLED WINE, CREAMY *(wino grzane z żółtkami)*: Beat 8 raw egg yolks with 8–10 T sugar until white and creamy. Gently heat 1 qt dry white wine containing 1 broken-up vanilla pod but do not boil. Pour hot wine into yolk mixture in thin stream, vigorously whisking. Pour into prescalded glasses and include a slice of lemon with each portion.

HONEY-SPICE LIQUEUR, OLD POLISH *(krupnik staropolski)*: The Vigil supper is too solemn an occasion for high-powered libation. Some families serve no alcoholic beverages whatsoever at this repast, others limit things to a glass of wine or a nip of a homemade cordial. One favorite is this delicious old honey liqueur which is served hot as a great cheer-enhancer and warmer-upper. In saucepan combine 1 c honey, 1″ piece of vanilla pod, 3 cloves, a small piece of cinnamon bark, 2 grains allspice, a small piece of ginger root, 1″ piece of lemon rind (with bitter white inner skin removed) and (optional) 6 peppercorns. Bring to gentle boil, stirring frequently and simmer until honey just begins to brown. Stir in 1 c boiling water, bring to boil, remove from heat and let stand, covered, 10 min. Stir in 1½–2 c 190-proof grain alcohol *(spirytus)*. WARNING: Be sure there is no flame anywhere nearby, because the alcohol vapors could catch fire! Only after the alcohol has been blended with the honey mixture can the saucepan be heated a bit.

HONEY-SPICE LIQUEUR, EASY *(krupnik staropolski łatwiejszy)*: In saucepan combine 1 c honey; 1 t vanilla extract; ⅛ t each of ground cloves, cinnamon and ginger root; a pinch of ground allspice; 2 pinches citric acid and (optional) 2 pinches ground pepper. Bring to gentle boil, stirring frequently and simmer until honey just begins to brown. Stir in ½ c boiling water, bring to boil, remove from heat and let stand, covered, 10 min. Stir in 3–4 c 100-proof vodka and let stand, covered, 10 min. Heat briefly, but do not boil. Strain through cheesecloth-lined funnel into decanter and serve hot in crystal liqueur glasses. NOTE: Using ground spices does not appreciably alter the flavor of *krupnik* but it will turn out cloudier than the preceding traditional version.

POLISH HANGOVER REMEDIES *(leczenie kaca)*: Polish remedies to deal with that "morning after" thirst are usually on the tart side and help to replace the natural minerals washed away by alcohol. The most common are the following:

- ✦ **Pickle-juice drink**: fill half a glass with brine-cured dill-pickle juice and top it up with ice-cold carbonated mineral water or club soda
- ✦ **Tart dairy drink**: cold whey, sour milk, buttermilk or *kefir* may also help
- ✦ **Lemon drink**: squeeze the juice of 1 lemon into a glass and fill it with ice-cold carbonated mineral water or club soda (OPTIONAL: 1 t honey may be added)
- ✦ **"Polish alka-seltzer"**: To a glass of cold carbonated mineral water (club soda) or even cold tap water add 1 t white vinegar and 1 t baking soda, stir quickly and drink down at once while still fizzy
- ✦ **Ryemeal soup**: Poles regard tart-tasting *żurek* as a traditional morning-after eye-opener/thirst-quencher in much the way that the French regard onion soup
- ✦ **Clear beet soup**: red *barszcz* is also used for this purpose; if using ready-to-eat/drink *barszczyk* (Hortex, Krakus) out of a carton, add the juice of ½–1 lemon to each glass and serve cold or hot

TRADITIONAL POLISH CONDIMENTS

This is but a small sampling of the various condiments (relishes, pickled vegetables, mushrooms and fruits as well as sauces) that traditionally accompany Polish foods, and those presented here are meant primarily for current use rather than long-term storage. For other condiment recipes, including those with longer shelf life, see *Polish Heritage Cookery* or simply pick up their imported or North American-made commercial versions at Polish markets, delis and import shops.

PREPARED HORSERADISH, HOMEMADE *(chrzan tarty z octem, domowy)*: In pot combine 1 c 6% distilled vinegar, ½ c water, 1 T sugar and 1 t salt, bring to boil and set aside to cool. Wash a horseradish root (about 4 oz), scrape and grate fine, preferably outdoors or in a well-ventilated place, since the fumes can be overpowering. The root can also be cut up into cubes and run through a meat grinder or grated in a food processor. (NOTE: The horseradish root will be easier to grate or process if it is soaked in cold water several hr or overnight). Scald the grated horseradish with boiling water to cover. When cooled to room temp, drain off water and stir in as much of the marinade as needed to get the consistency you want. Transfer to jar, seal and refrigerate. (OPTIONAL: A grated, tart cooking apple may be added for flavor to horseradish due to be used up shortly, but that will shorten its shelf life.) Use as you would store-bought prepared horseradish.

MAYONNAISE, HOMEMADE *(majonez domowy)*: For homemade mayonnaise to succeed, all ingredients must be at room temp, so take them out of the fridge at least 2 hr before preparing. In a bowl beat with whisk, egg-beater or electric mixer 1 large raw egg yolk, 1 t brown prepared mustard and ½ t salt, gradually adding 1 c salad oil in a thin stream. If using a whisk, beat in only one direction. Beat until mayonnaise becomes very thick. It may be thinned with a little cold meat stock, milk or water. Season with pepper (white pepper if you don't like the dark flecks of black pepper) and a little lemon juice (2 t–1 T) and confectioners' sugar (1–2 t) to taste. Use as is on hard-cooked eggs, with cold meats or hot or cold fish, or in any recipes calling for mayonnaise. NOTE: Should your mayonnaise curdle during preparation, try increasing the speed of your electric mixer. If that doesn't help, beat in 1 T hot water. If even that doesn't work, beat another raw room-temp egg yolk and gradually beat in the curdled mayonnaise. Suggestion: If you plan to make your own mayonnaise on a regular basis, pick up a mayonnaise-making device at a kitchen-equipment shop. NOTE: Look for different mayonnaise- and horseradish-based sauces in this book's Easter food section. NOTE: Those concerned about contracting salmonella from uncooked egg yolks should stick to store-bought mayonnaise. (Imported Polish brands are also available.)

TARTAR SAUCE, HOMEMADE *(sos tatarski domowy)*: Combine ⅔ c homemade (above) or store-bought mayonnaise with ¼ c sour cream, 2 T mustard and 1 T prepared horseradish. Add ¾ c finely chopped vegetables and greens: gherkins and/or dill pickles, scallions, chives, pickled mushrooms and capers. Fork-blend and season to taste with salt, pepper, lemon juice and confectioners' sugar. Use to garnish cold fish, pâté and other cold meats, hard-cooked eggs, etc. VARIATION: 2 ground or finely chopped hard-cooked eggs may be added.

MUSTARD *(musztarda)*: Except for picnics, outdoor fests and ordinary family meals, mustard should be presented not in the jar it came in but in an elegant mustard pot or condiment dish. For the varieties of Polish-style mustards see Basic Ingredients and Procedures, page 26. NOTE: If you want to try your hand at making your own, see *Polish Heritage Cookery*.

BEET AND HORSERADISH RELISH, TRADITIONAL *(ćwikla tradycyjna)*: In pot combine ⅔ c 6% distilled (white), cider or wine vinegar, ½ c water, 1 t salt, 2 T sugar, 1 t caraway, 2 grains allspice, 1 crumbled bay leaf and 8 peppercorns. Bring to boil, reduce heat, cover and simmer 10 min. Scrub 4 beets but do not peel. Bake in preheated 350° oven 90–120 min, or until a fork goes in easily. Plunge into cold water and, when cool enough to handle, peel. Grate coarsely, toss with 2–3 heaping T freshly grated or prepared horseradish. Pour strained, slightly cooled marinade over beet mixture, seal and refrigerate overnight. This is a traditional condiment served with cold meats and hot *kiełbasa* at Easter time and any time.

BEET AND HORSERADISH RELISH WITH APPLE *(ćwikla z jabłkiem)*: Scrub 4 beets but do not remove skin. Place in preheated 350° oven and bake 90–120 min or until a fork goes in easily. Plunge into cold water and, when cool enough to handle, peel. Grate coarsely, toss with 2–3 heaping T prepared horseradish and 1 c or more applesauce and pack into jar. In pot combine ⅔ cider vinegar, ⅔ c water, 1 t salt, 2 heaping T sugar, 1 t dill seed, 1 crumbled bay leaf and 8 partially crushed peppercorns. Bring to boil, reduce heat, cover and simmer 10 min. Pour strained, slightly cooled marinade over beet mixture, seal and refrigerate overnight.

BEET AND HORSERADISH RELISH, EASY *(ćwikła łatwa)*: Combine 2 c coarsely grated canned or diced, drained pickled beets with 2–3 T prepared horseradish and 1 c applesauce. Season with salt, pepper, ground caraway, sugar and vinegar to taste. Cover and chill overnight. Serve with ham, *kiełbasa* and other hot or cold meats. NOTE: Save the beet juice and use to make easy clear beet soup.

PICKLED MUSHROOMS *(grzybki marynowane)*: Choose 2 lb smallish fresh mushrooms of roughly equal size. Wash well and plunge into a large kettle of boiling salted water. Cover and cook 15 min. In separate pot combine 1½ c 6% distilled, cider- or wine vinegar, 1½ c or slightly more water (if a milder-flavored product is desired), ½ t salt, 1 t–2 T sugar, 1 crumbled bay leaf, 3 grains allspice, 10 peppercorns and (optional) 1 pod cayenne pepper. Bring to boil, reduce heat, cover and simmer 15 min. With slotted spoon transfer mushrooms to jars. Pour room-temp marinade over mushrooms to cover, seal and refrigerate overnight before serving. NOTE: Polish-style pickled mushrooms differ from those of other nations by virtue of not containing any oil in their marinades.

MUSHROOMS, PICKLED, EASY *(grzybki marynowane łatwe)*: Prepare marinade as in previous recipe but add 1 medium-sized coarsely chopped onion. Simmer marinade until onion is tender, then set aside to cool. Place 2 c drained canned button mushrooms in bowl (their liquid may be added to soups or gravies). Strain marinade, discarding onion and spices, and pour it over mushrooms. Let stand at least 2 hr before serving. NOTE: A wide variety of pickled mushrooms imported from Poland are available to those who prefer not to prepare their own.

SPICED PICKLED PLUMS *(śliwki w occie)*: Wash well and drain 2¼ lb firm Italian plums. With pin or sharp wooden pick puncture each plum in several places. Place plums in 1-pt or ½–pt jars. Prepare marinade by combining in pot 1¼ c distilled or cider vinegar, 1½ c water, 1–1½ c sugar, 10 cloves, 6 peppercorns, 4 grains allspice, a small piece of cinnamon bark and 1 bay leaf. Bring to boil, reduce heat and simmer, covered, 10 min. When slightly cooled, pour strained marinade over plums in jars to cover. Seal lids and let stand until cooled to room temp. Tighten lids if necessary, then rinse and wipe jars to remove any marinade. Store in fridge. An excellent relish with the cold meats of traditional Polish starter courses.

SPICED CHERRIES *(czereśnie w occie)*: Fill a quart jar with washed, well-drained black or white sweet cherries with stems intact. In saucepan combine 1 c water and ⅔ c cider vinegar. Add 10 cloves, 3 peppercorns, 2 grains allspice, 2 bay leaves, a small piece of cinnamon bark and ½ c sugar. Bring to boil, reduce heat, cover and simmer on low 15 min. Let marinade stand 10 min then pour it over cherries through sieve. Seal and store at room temp. Ready to use in 1–2 days. NOTE: The stems make this Old Polish condiment a decorative platter-trimmer and conversation piece, since they will be something new to most Polish Americans who are more used to olives and spiced peaches.

SPICED PEARS, CHERRIES or PLUMS, EASY *(gruszki, wiśnie lub śliwki w occie łatwe)*: When there is no time to prepare these typical Polish meat accompaniments from scratch using fresh fruit, canned fruit may be the next best thing. Combine ½ the syrup from your canned fruit with an equal amt cider vinegar. Add 2 crumbled bay leaves, 8 cloves, 8 peppercorns, 4 grains allspice and (optional) ½ t coriander. Bring to boil, reduce heat, cover and simmer gently 5 min. Set aside to cool. In separate bowls arrange drained canned pear halves, peach halves, whole purple plums or black cherries. Strain marinade, discarding spices, and pour it over canned fruit. Let stand at least 20 min before serving. Drain off marinade and serve spiced fruit as a relish with cold meats, aspic dishes, salads, etc.

PICKLED/MARINATED PUMPKIN *(dynia w occie/marynowana)*: The beautiful, bright golden-orange hue of pickled pumpkin cubes adds color to any relish tray. Cut 2¼ lb fresh, firm pumpkin (skinned and cleaned of pulpy seed portion) into ½″–¾″ cubes and parboil in lightly salted water 3 min. Drain and set aside. In saucepan, combine 1 c 6% vinegar, 2 c water, 1 c sugar, a piece of cinnamon bark and 6 cloves. Bring to boil and add the pumpkin. Simmer on low until pumpkin cubes become glossy. Remove from heat and let stand till cooled to room temp. Ready to use after draining or refrigerate until needed. Keeps up to a week. VARIATION: For a zingier relish, add several peppercorns, 1–2 grains allspice and a bay leaf to marinade.

BILBERRY SAUCE *(borówki do mięsa)*: The bilberry *(Vaccinum oxycoccus)*, a European favorite, is a small cranberry, whose different varieties are known in English as fenberries, cowberries, red huckleberries, mountain cranberries or wild cranberries. They are available at Polish markets and delis in America as a kind of jam, often prepared with pears or apples. Use straight from the jar as a sauce for roast turkey and game birds or "doctor" it up as shown below.

BILBERRY-HORSERADISH SAUCE *(borówki z chrzanem)*: Fork-blend 1 c bilberry jam or sauce (it may be variously labeled!) with 1 t or more prepared horseradish. If too sweet, stir in a little lemon juice.

BILBERRY/CRANBERRY-PEAR SAUCE *(borówki/żurawina z gruszką)*: If bilberries are not available, combine 2 c briefly processed whole-style canned cranberry sauce with 1 c drained canned pears, diced, and juice of ½ lemon. Mix well. Excellent with meats, hot or cold. NOTE: Bilberries and cranberries are close enough in taste to be interchangeable. Because of their tart and tangy taste, both are used primarily as sauce for roast fowl.

CRANBERRY-MUSTARD SAUCE *(sos żurawinowy z musztardą)*: Briefly process 2 c whole-style cranberry sauce so that small pieces are still visible. Combine with 1 T mustard and juice of ½ lemon. Serve with cold meats.

CRANBERRY-CURRANT SAUCE *(sos żurawinowo-porzeczkowy)*: Briefly process 2 c whole-style cranberry sauce so that small pieces are still visible. Combine with 1 c redcurrant jelly, juice of ½ lemon and 1 level or heaping t horseradish. Serve with cold meats or hot roast fowl.

TANGY PLUM SAUCE *(sos śliwkowy, pikantny)*: Process 1 c pitted spiced plums and some of their juice. Combine in saucepan with ½ c (preferably less sweet) *powidła*, ½ tomato purée, 1–2 cloves crushed garlic, 2 jg dry red wine and 2–3 T vinegar. Add a pinch of ground cloves or juniper, bring to boil and simmer on low, whisking until smooth. Season with salt and pepper to taste. Several dashes Tabasco will add zing to your sauce. Serve like steak sauce, as an accompaniment to hot or cold meat and sausage or use as a glaze for roast meats.

COUNTERTOP BRINED DILL PICKLES *(ogórki kiszone do bieżącego użytku)*: Wash well about 4 lb of 3″–4″ pickling cucumbers and allow to drip dry. In the bottom of a well-scrubbed, prescalded earthenware crock or gallon glass jar place 3 stalks of mature pickling dill, 3 to 4 1″-long slivers of horseradish root, half a horseradish leaf (optional), 5 cloves of garlic and 2–3 cherry-tree leaves (optional). In pot combine 6 c water (nonchlorinated well water is best!) with 3 T kosher salt, bring to boil and remove from heat. When it cools a bit, pour the warm brine over the cucumbers to cover. Place a scalded, inverted dinner plate or other dish over the cucumbers to keep them submerged and weight it down with a qt jar full of water. Keep on kitchen counter for 3 days, then move to cooler place. Ready in 10 days. When pickles are used up, strain the remaining brine and store in fridge tightly sealed. Use it to add tang to roasts, soups, stews and gravies.

OLD POLISH COOKERY

Most of what is known today as Polish cuisine was shaped during the 19th century. Naturally, it has evolved since then, but is essentially and recognizably the same. Old Polish cookery *(kuchnia staropolska)* is a term loosely applied to the foods and culinary styles from the Middle Ages to the end of the 18th century. At one time the Polish cuisine of the more prosperous classes was highly seasoned, since the copious use of exotic Oriental spices was regarded as a status symbol. Spices such as cinnamon, cardamom, nutmeg, cloves and ginger were commonly used to flavor meat dishes. *"Pieprzno i szafranno, mościa Waćpanno"* (peppery and saffrony, my fair maiden) was the order of the day to the kitchen staff of the duke's castle and the lowliest petty-gentry manor house alike. When trying to re-create many Old Polish dishes, the now widely available Chinese five-spice mixture or American pumpkin-pie seasoning are a good substitute for *przyprawa do pierników* (honey-spice–cake seasoning). One of the few remaining vestiges of that flavor trend is "gray sauce" (a gingerbready raisin gravy), now used today almost exclusively over boiled beef tongue and poached carp. "Black sauce" is even rarer, but it is sure to be enjoyed by all czernina-lovers.

Saffron was widely used to impart a beautiful golden hue and subtle flavor to various dishes and cakes. Various groats, especially millet, and cooked dried yellow peas, were dietary mainstays on nearly every table before potatoes became common during the 19th century. Game dishes, washed down with mead and beer, were widely served.

There was, of course, no exact start-up or cut-off date for Old Polish cuisine. Among the upper crust, it began giving way to French influence early on, while in remote rural areas it continued well on into the 19th century. The gentry lifestyles extolled by Mickiewicz in *Pan Tadeusz* were those of 1811–12, but the *bigos* he described was the old-style, layered variety rarely encountered anymore. Perhaps it is among the dishes worth reviving at Old Polish theme parties, dinner-dances or banquets. Dancers in old *szlachta* finery would help set the proper mood for such a feast. Or what about holding a *Kościuszko*, Pułaski Day or Third of May banquet featuring the foods familiar to the people of those times? REMEMBER: If you decide to follow the above suggestion, do *not* serve potatoes with the meal. They hadn't been "discovered" yet!

BEET SOUP WITH MARROW-BONE *(barszcz z rurą)*: In soup pot drench 1 lb beef marrow bones with some meat attached and 1 lb lean pork with 8–10 c water. Cook 1 hr, skimming off scum. Meanwhile in oven, bake 4 scrubbed but unpeeled beets until tender (about 1 hr). To soup pot add 2 carrots, 2 leeks and 1 onion studded with several cloves and cook until meat and vegetables are tender. Peel slightly cooled beets (or peel the hot beets under cold running water), cut into quarters, slice thin and add to strained stock. Add about 2 c beet-sour (m/l to taste) and bring to boil. Dice the meat and soup vegetables and add to soup together with the marrow. Or, grind the meat and vegetables, add an egg and enough bread crumbs to get a firm filling, salt and pepper to taste and use mixture to fill *uszka* (tiny ear-shaped dumplings—see page 40). Serve the cooked *uszka* in the soup.

OLD POLISH BROTH *(rosół staropolski)*: In pot containing 8–10 c water combine 1½ lb bone-in beef or veal and (optional) 1 dressed pigeon. (A partridge, 2 quail or other small game birds may be used instead.) Cook 1½ hr, add 2 carrots, 2 parsley roots, 2 onions, 2 cloves garlic and ½ t salt and cook another hr or until meat is tender. Salt and pepper to taste. Strain. Dice meat and return to soup. Garnish with chopped dill and several pinches ground rosemary. Serve with grated egg barley (see page 43).

ROYAL (BEEF AND CHICKEN) BROTH *(rosół królewski)*: Drench 1½ lb bone-in beef with 10 c cold water. Bring to boil very gently, skimming off scum. Add 2 t salt and cook 90 min. Add ¾ lb stewing chicken and continue cooking about 30 min, skimming off any scum. Add 1 portion soup greens (see page 30) including a slice of savoy cabbage, 1 halved onion (charred over flame until blackened concentric rings appear), 6 peppercorns, 2–3 grains allspice and 1 small bay leaf. Cook until meat and vegetables are very tender. (NOTE: In Old Poland fat was considered a delicious "energy food" so a good broth was one with a ¼″ layer of fat floating on the surface. To adjust this soup to today's palates, strain and refrigerate overnight. When read to serve, remove all but 3–4 T congealed fat before reheating.) Add 3–4 oz finely chopped chicken livers (with veins and membranes removed), bring to boil and switch off heat. Garnish with chopped dill and serve over cooked buckwheat groats or cooked barley. VARIATION: Instead of chicken livers, to strained, reheated broth add 3 oz fresh, small, thinly sliced mushrooms and cook about 15 min. After switching off heat, let stand covered 10 min. HINT: Use the cooked meat and vegetables to prepare the meat and fruit gruel (below).

MEAT AND FRUIT GRUEL *(brejka z mięsem i owocami)*: Dice the cooked meat and soup vegetables from any of the preceding recipes and combine with twice that amount of cooked barley, rice or millet (see page 185). Add ½–1 c diced, pre-soaked mixed dried fruit (including raisins and pitted prunes) and 2 c meat stock and simmer 20 min. Add 1 c dark beer and cook another 15 min. Season with salt, pepper and several pinches honey-spice–cake seasoning or Chinese five-spice mixture. Sweeten with a little honey if desired. Serve in soup bowls and eat with spoon. NOTE: In Old Poland this mixture would be cooked down into a mushy gruel.

BIGOS, OLD POLISH *(bigos staropolski)*: Bigos and similar dishes were once known as *miszkulancja* in Polish (from the Italian *mescolanza* "mixture or hotch-potch"). Old Polish *bigos* differed from today's version because of a preponderance of spit-roasted wild game, and the dish was cooked in layers rather than everything being uniformly chopped up. Rehydrate and cook 3 oz dried mushrooms in 3 c water, slice mushrooms into strips and return to stock. Rinse 2½–3 qt sauerkraut, drain well and combine in pot with 1 small head shredded cabbage. Scald with boiling water and cook, uncovered, 30 min. Drain. Intersperse sauerkraut with ½ lb thick-sliced bacon cut into 1″ pieces. Drench with 3 c strained ham, *kiełbasa* or other smoked-meat stock and cook over med heat, stirring occasionally about 45 min, or until most of the liquid evaporates. In saucepan, simmer 1 c chopped onion in 2 T lard or bacon drippings until golden. In a Dutch oven, arrange:

- ✦ a layer of sauerkraut-cabbage-bacon mixture, add ½ lb smoked Polish sausage cut into thin rounds and the onions;
- ✦ another layer of sauerkraut mixture and top with 1–2 lb diced, preferably rotisserie-cooked or oven-roasted, boneless game (venison, wild boar,

hare, pheasant, etc.); if unavailable use beef or dark-meat fowl (duck, goose, dark-meat turkey, guinea hen);

- ✦ a third layer of sauerkraut mixture and top with ½ lb presoaked, mixed, pitted, dried fruit (prunes, cherries, pears, apples) diced;
- ✦ a fourth layer of sauerkraut mixture, topped with ½ lb hunter's sausage *(kiełbasa myśliwska),* cut into thin rounds, and the mushrooms and their liquid;
- ✦ a final layer of sauerkraut mixture; drench it with 1 c mead (or ¾ c dry white wine and 3 T honey) and season with 1 t ground cubebs (*Piper cubeba*—a spice), 1 t ground cumin and ¼ t ground cinnamon.

Cook on low, stirring with wooden spoon to prevent scorching, until most of the liquid has cooked out. Cover and bake in 300° oven 3 hr, stirring occasionally. Switch off heat and keep in oven until cooled to room temp. Refrigerate overnight. Prior to serving season with salt and pepper to taste and simmer on low another hr or so.

GRAY SAUCE, OLD POLISH *(szary sos)*: Prepare a roux from 2 T flour and 3 T butter. Remove from heat and stir in 3 c stock. Add ¼–⅓ c crushed or ground stale *piernik* (Polish honey-spice cake, domestic gingerbread or spice cake) and simmer several min. (NOTE: If spice-cake crumbs are unavailable, use plain bread crumbs, 1 t honey and a pinch of cinnamon, cloves and nutmeg.) Add ½ c red wine or mead. Season to taste with salt, pepper, Polish honey-spice–cake seasoning, lemon juice and sugar to achieve just the right sweet, sour and winey flavor with pronounced spicy overtones. Darken with several drops caramel or Kitchen Bouquet. Add ⅓–½ c raisins and ⅓ c chopped or slivered, blanched almonds. Simmer briefly. Dilute with a little stock if required. After switching off heat, cover and let stand 10 min for flavors to blend. VARIATION: Use chopped dried mixed fruit instead of just raisins. A T or so *powidła* may also be added. NOTE: Usually served today with boiled beef tongue or poached carp, this sauce can be used to impart an Old Polish flavor to any meat. If the caterer of your 3rd of May or Pułaski Day banquet can offer only "regular" roast beef, pork, veal, turkey or chicken, supply your own gray sauce to ladle over the meat before it comes to table.

BLACK SAUCE, OLD POLISH *(czarny sos)*: This differs from gray sauce mainly because it contains some blood. Use anywhere from ½–1 c blood (from duck, goose, pig, rabbit) to which a little vinegar has been added. Prepare a roux from 2 T flour and 3 T butter. Remove from heat, stir in 3 c stock and 1 heaping T *powidła* and simmer briefly, whisking until smooth. (NOTE: Some crushed or ground stale *piernik* may be added as in preceding recipe.) Remove sauce from heat. Add the sieved blood and whisk to blend. Season with salt and pepper and about 1 t ginger, ½ t ground cloves and ¼ t cinnamon and a little cider vinegar or wine vinegar to taste. Simmer briefly, whisking frequently. Add any sliced cooked fowl (duck, goose, turkey, chicken) or rabbit and simmer in sauce on very low heat. Switch off heat and let stand, covered, for at least 15-20 min for flavors to blend. VARIATION: Raisins and/or chopped pitted prunes may also be used in this sauce.

MILLET GROATS *(kasza jaglana na sypko)*: Rinse 1 c millet groats *(kasza jaglana)* by swishing around in a pot of cold water. Drain well. Place in saucepan, add 3 c water, bring to boil and cook 1–2 min. Drain in sieve to remove the millet's bitter edge and rinse well under cold running water. Drain well, return to saucepan, add 1½ c cold water or, better yet, milk (or half milk/half water) and ½ t salt and bring to boil. Cover saucepan, reduce heat and cook on low heat until liquid is absorbed (2–3 min). Switch off heat and let stand covered about 5 min. Fluff up with fork before serving. Good with savory toppings (gravies, pan drippings, fried fatback or bacon nuggets, fried onions, etc.) as well as sweet ones (fruit preserves, plum butter, jam, syrup, canned fruit-pie filling, etc.) as a dessert dish.

BARLEY, WHOLE-GRAIN *(pęczak)*: Rinse in a pot of cold water 2 c whole-grain barley, pour off water and drain well in sieve. In pot combine 6 c water, 1 t salt, 3 T fat, bring to boil and gradually add washed whole barley. Stir, bring to boil, reduce heat and simmer covered on low until all water is absorbed. Stir again and transfer, covered, to preheated 350° oven for 1 hr. Serve with gravy-type dishes or garnished with fried fatback or bacon nuggets. Ideal for gatherings with a peasant or Old Polish theme.

SAFFRON RICE *(ryż z szafranem/ryż szafranny)*: Whereas cooked millet (also barley and buckwheat) were daily staples on the Old Polish table, for more festive occasions saffron-flavored rice, which exuded an aura of elegance and sophistication, was the preferred choice. Dissolve 1 or 2 pinches of saffron in 1 T vodka. Rinse 1 c rice in sieve under cold running water, drain and press out excess moisture. Transfer to saucepan, add 2 c water, ½ t salt and the saffron mixture and bring to boil. Cover, reduce heat and cook on very low heat about 18–20 min or until tender. Switch off heat and let stand 5 min before serving. NOTE: This easy-to-prepare dish can add an Old Polish accent to any Polonian banquet. Team it up with meat in gray sauce, creamed cucumbers and beets and horseradish (*ćwikła*) and you'll have come up with a typical Old Polish banquet menu. Throwing in a dish of cooked, whole yellow peas topped with golden brown pork nuggets (see page 187) can only enhance the general ambiance.

ROAST GOOSE STUFFED WITH FRUIT *(gęś nadziana owocami)*: Wash a 6–7 lb goose and rub all over with salt, pepper, several cloves crushed garlic (or garlic powder) and dillseed. Smother inside and out with thickly sliced onions and let stand, covered, at room temp 3–4 hr or refrigerate overnight. When ready to cook, discard onions, place goose on rack in roaster and stuff using peeled, cored and quartered tart cooking apples mixed with 1 c diced, plumped prunes and/or mixed dried fruit and ½ c plumped raisins. The cavity may be tightly packed because apples decrease in volume during cooking. Sew up neck and tail opening, tie legs together with string and bake, uncovered, in preheated 350° oven 20–25 min per lb or until fork-tender. Baste with 1 c mead or Tokay wine and pan drippings. During roasting, prick goose with fork to release excess fat. Sprinkle sliced goose with a little ground cloves and ginger just before serving. Serve with buckwheat, barley or millet on the side. For a gravy combine 1 part pan drippings with 1 part boiling water and thicken with flour. Season to taste with salt, pepper, ground cloves and ginger. NOTE: In addition to winter entertaining, goose in one form or another has traditionally been served on St. Martin's Day (November 11).

TRIPE AND SAUERKRAUT *(flaczki w kapuście)*: Drain 2 qt sauerkraut and rinse lightly. Cut 1 lb precooked tripe into ½″ squares and mix into sauerkraut. Add 2 c reduced (gelatinous) veal stock (or 2 envelopes gelatin and 1 beef-bouillon cube dissolved in 2 c boiling water), 2 c German wheat beer (*Weizenbier* or *Weißbier*—wheat beer is no longer produced in Poland!), 1 c chopped onions, 1 T freshly grated horseradish root, 1 T dillseed, a 1″ stick of cinnamon, 2 t dry mustard, 2 T chopped fresh dill and 2 T honey. Stir, bring to boil, reduce heat and simmer 1 hr, uncovered, stirring frequently with wooden spoon to prevent scorching. Cover and simmer on low heat about 2 hr longer, stirring occasionally. When cooled to room temp, refrigerate. Simmer 1 hr before serving. This dish can be served in soup bowls and eaten with spoons. Bread torn into coarse pieces was often added to bowls by diners.

BAKED CHICKEN AND PRUNES *(kura pieczona ze śliwkami)*: Cover bottom of glass baking pan with onion slices, over it sprinkle 1 c shredded cabbage, add 1 lb prunes (with pits for authenticity—pitted prunes were unknown back then!), ¼ c chopped parsley and 20 juniper berries—all evenly distributed. Rub a 5-lb roasting chicken inside and out with butter and place several onion slices, prunes and juniper berries inside the cavity. Place chicken on bed of prunes and tuck pieces of 5 halved bay leaves into the chicken's indentations. Top the chicken with several bacon rashers. Mix ½ t ginger and ¼ t cinnamon with 1 c dry red wine and pour over chicken. Sprinkle with another ¼ c chopped parsley and 1 t dillseed. Cover and bake in preheated 375° oven 1½–2 hr. NOTE: Since this recipe was prepared without salt, be sure to have a saltcellar on the table. Serve with millet groats and peas and pork nuggets (below).

PEAS AND PORK NUGGETS *(groch ze skwarkami)*: Rinse 1 lb whole, yellow dried field peas in cold water, swishing them around to remove impurities. Drain. Place in pot cover with plenty of cold (preferably preboiled) water and soak overnight. Next day, cook in same water. Bring to boil and cook on high, uncovered, 10 min. Then add a bay leaf, reduce heat, cover and cook on low until tender (1–2 hr or more). Salt towards the end of cooking process. Drain, sieve (or process) and season with pepper and summer savory or marjoram. Garnish with ⅓–¼ lb pork fatback nuggets, fried to a deep golden brown. Some chopped onions may be fried up with the nuggets. NOTE: At present, this side dish has survived mainly as an accompaniment to boiled pork hocks *(golonka)*. At one time, it was as common as bread and potatoes are today.

LENTILS STEWED WITH PARSNIPS *(soczewica duszona z pasternakiem)*: Wash and drain 2 c lentils and simmer, covered, in 5 c water until tender (35–40 min). Peel 2 med parsnips, slice into ½″ rounds and cook, covered, in boiling salted water until tender (about 20 min). Drain. Combine cooked lentils and parsnips and garnish with ¼ lb diced slab bacon fried up with a chopped onion. Season mixture with ½ t ginger and garnish generously with chopped dill, parsley and scallion tops, chopped fine. Mix and serve as an accompaniment to roasts.

MIKOŁAJ REJ'S BEETS AND HORSERADISH *(ćwikła Mikołaja Reja)*: Although *ćwikła*, Poland's oldest, still-surviving relish or salad, goes back to the dawn of history, its first known recipe was penned in the 15th century by Mikołaj Rej, known as the "father of Polish literature." The proportions given below are this author's, since back then recipes simply said: "Take a little of this, add a little of that, etc." Scrub 4 large beets well but do not peel. Bake in preheated 375° oven about 1 hr or until fork-tender. Peel under cold running water. When cool enough to handle, cut each beet into 4 piece and slice the pieces thin. Toss with several T freshly grated horseradish root. Sprinkle with salt, 1 t–1 T bruised or crushed fennel and sprinkle with several T wine- or cider vinegar. Transfer to earthenware, crockery or glass bowl, cover with an inverted plate and cover container. Refrigerate or store in cool place several days to a week before serving.

CHERRY SAUCE, OLD POLISH, FOR GAME DISHES *(sos wiśniowy do dziczyzny)*: You can cook cherries from scratch if you like, but an easy way to achieve similar results is to use canned cherry-pie filling.

Place 2 c filling in saucepan, add 3 T wine vinegar or cider vinegar, ½ t ground cloves and ¼ t ground juniper and bring to boil. Stir in ½ c dry red wine. Heat briefly but do not boil. Switch off heat. Season with freshly ground pepper, stir, cover and let stand 5 min or so before serving. Serve hot over cooked game (venison, boar, pheasant and other game birds, hare, etc.). This sauce can create a wild-game-like atmosphere if served with domestic meat such as beef, dark-meat turkey, duck or goose. HINT: This easy-to-prepare sauce can help to Old-Polonize the run-of-the-mill chicken, turkey and roast beef often pushed by Anglo-mainstream caterers.

WILD GAME DISHES *(dziczyzna)*: Any of the game dishes listed in the Polish Holiday Banquet/Dinner-Party Entrées section lend themselves nicely to feasts with an Old Polish theme. NOTE: You may be able to get wild boar as well as American buffalo meat (which can double for Polish bison [*żubr*]) from specialty suppliers. NOTE: For an Old Polish ambiance, do not serve with potatoes (which were unknown in the Old Polish era), but groats (millet, barley, buckwheat, saffron rice), cooked (dried, yellow) peas and pork nuggets and bread. Stewed pears, cucumbers and figs (see below) might make a nice combination.

ROASTS *(pieczenie)*: In the Old Polish era, meat was mainly spit-roasted. You can approximate that method with a modern electric rotisserie. Baste roast frequently with butter and cook until fork-tender.

SAFFRON BABA, OLD POLISH *(baba staropolska z szafranem)*: Add a pinch of saffron to a ½ jg grain alcohol or vodka and let stand 1 hr. Mash 1¼ cakes yeast with 1 T sugar and drench with ⅔ c warm milk, stir in ⅔ c flour, mix, cover and leave in warm place until doubled in bulk. Beat 12 egg yolks with ¾ c sugar until light and creamy and add to risen yeast mixture along with 2⅓ c flour, 2 t vanilla sugar (or 1 t vanilla extract) and a pinch of salt. Work into a dough and knead at least 20 min (by hand or in mixer equipped with bread-kneading hook). Melt just over ¾ c butter and gradually work into dough until fully absorbed. Add ⅓–½ c raisins, 2 oz chopped candied orange rind and the saffron-alcohol mixture and work to blend ingredients thoroughly. Transfer to buttered, bread-crumb–sprinkled babka pans, filling them to only ⅓ of their height. Let them rise in warm place until they reach ¾ of the way to the top of the pan. Bake in preheated oven at 350° for 50–60 min, or until a pick comes out clean. When cool, glaze or dust with confectioners' sugar. Great at Easter or any time!

STEWED PEARS, CUCUMBERS AND FIGS *(gruszki z ogórkami i figami)*: In pot combine 4 c diced cucumbers (peeled and seeded), 1 c chopped dried figs, ⅔ c honey, 1¼ c water, ½ t cinnamon and ⅛ t ground cloves. Cover pot and simmer gently about 15 min. Add 4 c firm, underripe pears (peeled, cored and diced), cover and simmer another 5 min or until pears are cooked. Cool to room temp. Flavor with 1 T rosewater. This early compote was a side dish on the dinner table of the well-to-do or a dessert when drenched with sweet cream.

HONEY DRINK *(napój miodowy)*: This simple drink was once served cellar-cool in Old Polish manorhouses and even at the royal court alongside wine and mead as a refreshing summer beverage. Bring 3 c water to boil and pour over 2 T fennel seeds and ½ t ground cassia (Chinese cinnamon [*Cinnamonum cassia*]) in stoneware, crockery or heat proof glass container. Cover and let stand until cooled to room temp. Strain (discarding spices) and stir in ½–¾ c honey. Will keep up to a week refrigerated in a stoneware jug or glass bottle. For authenticity, take out of fridge at least 2 hr before serving so your honey drink is cool but not ice-cold.

HOT SAUCES AND CULINARY POLONIZERS

The hot sauces presented here are usually used to embellish main dishes (meat, fowl, fish), and some of them (esp. the mushroom sauces) can be a meal in themselves when ladled over grains, noodles or potatoes. They can also serve as culinary Polonizers—additions that impart a genuine Polish flavor to plain, Anglo-mainstream or otherwise ethnically nondescript foods. For instance, when the banquet-hall manager insists that only roast beef, chicken, turkey and the like are available for your affair, perhaps you can supply their chef with one of the recipes below or even provide the prepared sauce itself to be spooned over the portions or provided in gravy boats. Or, when you have to whip up a guest-quality meal in no time, these sauces can be ladled over the ready-to-eat meats available at your supermarket's hot-food counter. Plain-roasted meats are preferable to highly seasoned ones such as curry chicken or barbecue beef. The sauces (gray, black, cherry) in the preceding Old Polish Cookery section can also be used in this way. This section also shows how widely available American-style processed foods can provide shortcuts to traditional Polish delights.

MUSHROOM SAUCE, FRESH *(sos ze świeżych grzybów)*: Clean (preferably by wiping with damp cloth) and trim 8 oz fresh wild or domestic mushrooms and cook in 1½ c stock or water containing 1 grated onion. When done (20–25 min), strain stock and set aside. When mushrooms are cool enough to handle, slice or dice. In saucepan melt 2 T butter, add 2 T flour, stirring into a paste and gradually dilute with the mushroom stock, stir in ½ sour cream or sweet heavy cream and whisk till smooth. Add 1 crushed mushroom bouillon cube (optional) and 1 T chopped dill and salt and pepper to taste. Simmer briefly. Spoon over steak, roasts, chicken, turkey, poached meatballs, buckwheat groats, potatoes, noodles, etc. Portobello mushrooms are best!

MUSHROOM SAUCE, DRIED *(sos z suszonych grzybów)*: Soak 1½ oz well-scrubbed dried mushrooms (preferably king bolete) in 2 c warm water several hr, then cook in same water until tender (50–60 min). Cut mushrooms into thin strips or dice. Fry 1 chopped onion in 2 T butter until golden-tender. Add the strained stock, ½ c sour cream or heavy cream fork-blended with 1–2 T flour, 1 crushed mushroom bouillon cube (optional) and heat several min, whisking until smooth. Add the mushrooms, 1 T chopped parsley and salt and pepper to taste. Serve as above, except chicken and white-meat turkey for which the fresh mushroom sauce (above) is better suited.

MUSHROOM SAUCE, MIXED *(sos z grzybów mieszanych)*: For a larger quantity of sauce combine the fresh and dried mushroom sauces above. As a mushroom-sauce stretcher for an even greater quantity, dissolve 2 T flour in 2 c water, add 1 mushroom bouillon cube and heat to boiling. Add to the combined two mushroom sauces above. Simmer briefly. Excellent with roast beef and meatballs.

PRUNE SAUCE *(sos z suszonych śliwek)*: Cook 8 oz pitted prunes in water to cover. When they disintegrate, sieve or process. Melt 2 T butter in saucepan, stir in 2 T flour and 1½ c meat stock. Add the prunes and season to taste with salt and pepper, 1–2 T vinegar, ½ t ground ginger, ½ t marjoram and a pinch or 2 ground juniper. Bring to boil, stirring constantly. Pour over roast pork, beef, duck, goose and dark-meat turkey.

MIXED FRUIT SAUCE *(sos z suszu)*: Proceed as with prune sauce (above), but use 8 oz mixed dried fruit including raisins instead of prunes. Good with roast pork and roast fowl.

HUNTER'S SAUCE *(sos myśliwski)*: Fry 1 large finely minced onion, 1 grated carrot and 1 slice of grated celeriac in 2–3 T butter or oil on med-low until tender. Add ½ c puréed tomatoes and 1½ c cold meat stock in which 2 T flour has been dissolved, bring to boil and whisk until smooth. Add 2 cloves crushed garlic, 1 T chopped parsley, 1 jg red dry wine, 1 T wine vinegar, ½ t ground juniper and salt and pepper to taste. Simmer on low under cover 10 min. Let stand another 10 min for flavors to blend. Serve over game or domestic meats to which you want to impart a wild-game accent.

BASIC WHITE SAUCE *(sos biały podstawowy)*: This sauce can serve as the basis for numerous variations depending on what flavorings are added. Melt 2 T butter in saucepan, stir in 2 T flour and mix into blend but do not brown. Stir in 1 c cold milk, half & half, or ½ sour cream or plain yogurt fork-blended with ½ c milk. Heat to boiling, whisking the whole time until sauce thickens. Season with salt and pepper and (optional) a pinch of ground nutmeg. VARIATION: Replace half the milk, cream or yogurt with meat or vegetable stock. NOTE: Either version can be used as is or developed into the following sauces.

Dill Sauce *(sos koperkowy)*: Add 2 T fresh chopped dill to basic white sauce. (OPTIONAL: stir in 1–2 raw, beaten egg yolks and heat to boiling, whisking the whole time.) Good with poached or broiled fish, poached meatballs, chicken and veal.

Sorrel Sauce *(sos szczawiowy)*: Trim a handful (about 3 oz) sorrel leaves of stems, wash well, chop fine and cook in 1–2 T butter until fully wilted. Add to basic white sauce. Season with a little sugar and salt. Good with bland-tasting foods like boiled meat, poached meatballs, poached fish and hot hard-cooked eggs.

Horseradish Sauce, Hot *(sos chrzanowy na gorąco)*: Depending on sharpness desired, stir in 1–2 heaping T prepared horseradish and season to taste with a little lemon juice and sugar. Simmer briefly. Good over boiled beef, tongue, fish and hot hard-cooked eggs.

Mustard Sauce, Hot *(sos musztaradowy na gorąco)*: Proceed as with horseradish sauce (above), substituting brown Polish-style prepared mustard for the horseradish. Good over boiled beef, tongue, hot hard-cooked eggs and frankfurters.

Caper Sauce *(sos kaparowy)*: To basic sauce add 1–2 T capers and 1–2 t of their marinade, stir and simmer until bubbly. Cover and let stand 10 min for flavors to blend. A gourmet sauce for fish (esp. poached), boiled meat, poached meatballs and hot hard-cooked eggs.

POLONAISE TOPPING *(tarta bułka zrumieniona na maśle)*: Although Poles have no special name for this topping and simply describe it as "bread crumbs browned in butter," this simple but elegant embellishment has come to be known worldwide by the French adjective *polonaise* (short for *à la mode polonaise*, "in the Polish manner"). Even the most inexperienced chef is able to prepared plain boiled vegetables: cauliflower, string beans, carrots, brussels sprouts, etc. A spoonful of polonaise topping is all that is needed to turn a plain boiled vegetable into a gourmet delight. This topping is also good on boiled potatoes, *pierogi* and *kopytka*. See Cauliflower Polonaise for the recipe, page 151.

CREAM OF SORREL, SOUP, MOCK *(zupa szczawiowa fałszywa)*: This is an example of using convenience items in a way the manufacturer never considered. Cook ½ a 10-oz package frozen chopped spinach according to directions on package. When cool, chop. Prepare 2 cans of cream of potato soup according to directions on can. Add the spinach and bring to boil. Remove from heat and sour to taste with citric acid crystals. (Real sorrel is naturally sour, while spinach is not!) Serve in soup bowls containing sliced hard-cooked eggs.

SAUERKRAUT AND BEANS: *(kapusta z fasolą)*: To stewed sauerkraut (see Cooked Vegetables and Main-Dish Accompaniments, page 152), add a 12 oz can of American-style baked beans or pork and beans (including their tomato sauce) and a 12 oz can plain navy beans, drained. VARIATION: Fry up ½–¾ lb skinned or skinless sliced or diced *kiełbasa* with 2 chopped onions and add to pot of sauerkraut with sausage and beans *(kapusta z kiełbasą i fasolą).*

SAUSAGE AND BEANS *(fasola z kiełbasą)*: Dice ½ lb skinned, smoked *kiełbasa*, and brown with 1 chopped onion in 2 T oil. Drain and reserve liquid from a 12–16 oz can American-style baked beans or pork and beans. To liquid add 1 T mustard, 2 T vinegar, 1–2 cloves garlic, crushed, ¼ t pepper and 1 T marjoram. In pot mix the desauced pork and beans with 3–5 c plain white canned beans. Add the *kiełbasa* and onions and the sauce and simmer, covered, 15 min on low heat. (OPTIONAL: Add 3–5 soaked and cooked diced pitted prunes.) VARIATION: For a heartier meal, double the amt of *kiełbasa*. For a purely vegetarian dish, omit the sausage altogether and add only fried onions (make sure the baked beans are meatless as well!).

BREADED PORK CUTLETS *(kotlety schabowe)*: Instead of bone-in American-style pork chops, cut away the bones (which make an excellent soup stock) and pound meat to a thickness of ¼″–⅓″. Season, bread and fry to a nice golden brown the way you would with bone-in pork chops. (For detailed recipe see Banquet/Dinner-Party entrées, page 86).

DOUGH BAKING, EASY *(łatwe wypieki)*: Refrigerator crescent-roll dough that comes in a tube can be used as a shortcut for various Polish-style baked goods the manufacturer never dreamed of. It is ideal for *paszteciki* (little handheld pastries usually served with clear soups) and *pierożki* (small baked dumplings). It can also encase *kulebiak* (a savory, loaf-shaped pie often containing sauerkraut or cabbage) and *pieróg* (a savory loaf containing buckwheat filling). To use, start by pressing down with flour-dipped finger on the manufacturer's perforations (on dough-sheet) to obliterate them. Use to make the following:

- *Paszteciki*: cut each dough-sheet into 6–8 squares, place a spoonful of filling on each, roll up, tucking ends under or fold into a triangle and bake according to pkg directions
- *Pierożki*: cut circles in dough-sheet with biscuit-cutter or glass, place a dollop of filling at center of each, fold dough over filling, pinching edges together, and bake as above
- *Kulebiak* or *pieróg*: arrange filling on dough, fold 1 flap over filling to overlap the other flap, place seam-side down on baking sheet, tuck ends under and bake as directed on pkg.

NOTE: Refrigerator biscuit dough other than crescent rolls as well as frozen puff-pastry dough may also be used in the above recipes.

COMPOTE/FRUIT DRINK, EASY *(kompot najłatwiejszy)*: Following a hearty meal, rather than a rich dessert many Poles would prefer a refreshing homemade fruit drink known as *kompot.* By Polish standards, every canned fruit in syrup is a compote. Combine the syrup from 1 or more kinds of canned fruit and dilute with preboiled water until you get the taste you want. The amt of water will depend on whether the fruit is in heavy, med or light syrup (i.e. contains more or less sugar). If still too sweet, a little lemon juice should fix the problem.

POLISH BANQUET/DINNER/SUPPER MENUS

Before presenting several sample menus, a few remarks about banquets and dinner-parties are in order.

FORMAL BANQUET *(bankiet tradycyjny)*: These are increasingly rare in today's more casual and cost-conscious era, but at times an occasion warranting a truly elegant, gourmet reception may arise, possibly connected with a commemorative event, ball or other gala. When that occurs, let it not be said that Polish-Americans are at a loss how to go about it. Here are some things to consider.

1. Banquet site: The setting should be commensurate with the intended rank of the planned event, hence an elegant gourmet banquet would be more at home in an upscale hotel dining room or banquet hall than an upstairs hall over a corner grocery in the old Polonian neighborhood. The premises should be appropriately decorated with garlands, flowers, candelabras, possibly a decorative scroll or banner over the head table indicating the banquet's guest of honor or purpose.

2. Announcing of guests: At a truly formal affair, guests are announced on the basis of the printed invitations they present as they enter the banquet hall or ballroom. They are then greeted by the hosts who have strategically positioned themselves near the entrance.

3. Hors d'oeuvres and apéritifs: This is usually a stand-up course, sometimes called a cocktail hour, allowing guests to circulate and socialize. At the most elegant affairs, dinner-jacketed waiters bring apéritifs and hors d'oeuvres round to the guests wherever they may be standing or sitting. Other waiters follow close behind collecting empty glasses, cocktail picks, used napkins, etc. The varied snacks (canapés, finger foods, relishes) are not meant to fill up on, but rather are the light accompaniments for alcoholic drinks. According to Polish tradition, vodka and flavored cordials and brandies (usually around 80 proof) are the preferred tipple, although beer and wine can be provided for those who prefer them. For recipe suggestions see Apéritifs, Hors d'oeuvres, page 64.

4. Starter/appetizer course: This is a sit-down course. After guests have mingled, socialized, imbibed, snacked and broken the ice, the call goes out: *„Prosimy miłych Państwa do stołu."* ("Ladies and Gentlemen, dinner is served.") The table, at which placecards are often used to indicate who sits where, may be laden with platters containing cold starters: meat, fish, eggs, salads, relishes, bread and butter and decanters of spirits. VARIATION: Rather than self-serve platters, each guest may find an identical predished portion on his/her salad plate. NOTE: This course is not meant to fill up on but to dull the edge of one's hunger. After this course is a good time for a speech or presentation.

5. Soup course: At a multi-course banquet full of rich foods a light, clear, refreshing soup is preferable to a thick, hearty stick-to-the-ribs potage. Hence the popularity of *czysty barszcz czerwony*, often served with filled pasties or savory pastry fingers. Also popular are broths, bouillons and other clear soups, usually served in twin-handled barszcz cups or (in their absence) teacups. In a formal banquet setting, predished portions are brought to guests by waiters.

6. Hot starter or fish course: By today's American standards, when a symbolic appetizer and main course often constitute an entire banquet, wedding or dinner-party, this course may seem unduly extravagant. But I have included it for the benefit of those who may occasionally wish to re-create the atmosphere of the kind of socials held in the Polish manorhouses, mansions and townhouses of the 19th and pre-World War II 20th century. Other than a light fish course, it might include fried mushrooms or *bigos*. Any of the entrées listed among the main courses may be a hot starter when served in smaller portions and without all the trappings (cooked vegetables, starchy supplement, salad, etc.) that traditionally accompany the main course. The hot starter course may be dished out by very experienced waiters to each guest individually or predished portions may be brought to each guest. The least formal way is to serve hot starters on self-serve platters. This course is usually accompanied by red or rosé wine for red meats and white wine with fish and light-meat poultry.

7. Main course or roast: The main course of a festive dinner or banquet was known as *pieczyste* (roast course) and nearly always comprised roast veal, beef, pork or game as well as roast poultry with all the trimmings. The meat or fowl may be dished out to each guest individually by experienced waiters or brought in predished portions. Such accompaniments as cooked vegetables, grain/pasta/potatoes, etc. may be served the same way or set out on platters. Dry red, rosé or white wine is provided, depending on the meat it is to accompany.

8. Salad: The French practice of serving green salads as a separate course following the main meat course is occasionally encountered on the Polish banquet scene, but in general Poles prefer salads that accompany the main course.

9. Cheese and fruit: At formal banquets patterned on the traditional French model a variety of cheese plus breadstuffs and butter are often served as a kind of pre-dessert course.

10. Dessert, after-dinner drinks, coffee: Various cakes, pastries, ices, puddings, cooked-fruit desserts, etc. are traditionally served at the end of the meal, often accompanied by liqueurs, sweet dessert wines, brandy and strong coffee.

SEMI-FORMAL BANQUET *(uroczyste przyjęcie)*: This kind of less formal banquet is far more widespread nowadays. Although a bit more streamlined and less involved, it need not and should not be unelegant. Some things to consider:

1. Banquet site: An elegant, although possibly slightly less posh and pricey banquet site might be chosen for what I have termed a "semi-formal banquet." The premises should be appropriately decorated (see point 1 for Formal Banquet, page 193).

2. Hors d'oeuvres and apéritifs: Arriving guests may be greeted by the hosts but usually they are not formally announced the way indicated for a Formal Banquet (page 194). Rather than waiter service, a refreshment buffet (table, bar, etc.) can be provided, at which guests can serve themselves. These would include prepoured drinks and various fingerfoods, snacks and hors d'oeuvres. A linen tablecloth, cut flowers and candelabras will enhance the presentation. Even here waiters or servers should keep the buffet tidy, replenish platters, pour drinks and clear away any dirty plates, napkins and silverware.

3. Starter/appetizer course: At a less formal banquet, guests would probably find self-serve platters waiting for them at the table, although pre-dished portions are not uncommon. Placecards would be less likely than at more formal affairs.

4. Soup course: This course would not differ from that at the Formal Banquet (page 194). Or it might be skipped altogether.

5. Main course: The hot starter or fish course (see Formal Banquet) would be less likely at a semi-formal banquet, hence the main meat course would directly follow the soup or, if soup is not served, the starter course. It may be served in pre-dished portions or family-style with platters of food placed on the table for guests to help themselves.

6. Dessert, after-dinner drinks, coffee: This course is the same as in the Formal Banquet (page 195).

BUFFET-STYLE DINNER *(przyjęcie bufetowe)*: Buffet-style service may be economical (by virtue of not requiring much hired help), but it is the antithesis of gracious dining and does not lend itself to elegant multi-course receptions. Guests unfamiliar with Polish cuisine often end up putting a hotch-potch of incongruous foods on their plates. The program may be delayed and it often takes quite some doing to get the proceedings back on track. NOTE: Buffet service may be satisfactory at smaller gatherings such as house parties. At larger receptions, serving only a single course (e.g., appetizers, desserts) buffet-style may not be too disruptive.

DINNER-PARTY *(proszony obiad)*: This is usually held in the home and attended by invited guests, hence its Polish name *proszony obiad* (invited dinner). This is usually more casual than either the formal or semi-formal banquets described above, but that is not to suggest that it cannot be gracious and elegant. Ordinarily the hosts greet arriving guests who present the lady of the house with cut flowers (an odd number). If it is a name-day party, then the one celebrating his/her feast day gets the flowers. Truly elegant guests bring one bouquet of flowers for the lady of the house and another for her husband or other family member in whose honor the party is being given. Usually, snacks and drinks are provided at a self-serve buffet and the man of the house may serve as bartender. The sit-down portion of the meal follows the typical Polish entertaining style: cold starters, soup, main course and dessert. See sample menus, page 197.

SUPPER-PARTY *(proszona kolacja)*: This is probably the simplest and least formal type of house party. Thanks to its simplicity, ease of preparation and serving, and resultant lower costs, it could have numerous applications on Polonia's community scene in situations where a full-course banquet or dinner-party is not required. Unlike other forms of entertainment, it has a number of variations.

I.

- **Cold starter course**: herring, fish in aspic, hard-cooked eggs (deviled or in sauces), cold roast and smoked meats, pâté, vegetable salads, relishes, spirits, mineral water, juices, soft drinks
- **Cakes**, other desserts, tea or coffee

II.

- **Hors d'oeuvres**, apéritifs
- **Full hot main course**: meat, fowl or fish, cooked vegetable, starchy supplement, salad
- **Cakes**, other desserts, tea or coffee

III.

- **Snacks**, finger-foods, and drinks
- **A single "short" hot dish**: *bigos*, pierogi, tripe, steak roll-ups, creamed mushrooms, *gołąbki*, beef stroganoff, etc., plus bread, butter, relishes
- **Cakes**, tea or coffee

IV.

- **Assorted canapés**, beverages
- **Cakes**, other desserts, tea or coffee

SAMPLE BALL/BANQUET/RECEPTION MENUS

NEW YEAR'S EVE/MARDI GRAS* BALL: Here is the actual menu and presentation style of the New Year's Eve ball at which my wife and I rang in the 21st century, accompanied by a group of friends in Warsaw's Old Town:

- **Cold dishes**: assorted cold smoked meats, assorted cold roast meats, roast pork loin à la Varsovienne in aspic, salmon in aspic, deviled eggs (stuffed with mushrooms), walnut and pineapple salad, smoked-chicken salad, herring in fruit and vegetable salad, additions: tomatoes, cucumbers, pickled mushrooms, olives, horseradish, bread and butter
- **Beverages**: mineral water, fruit juice, carbonated soft drinks, wine, beer, vodka (500 ml [about 1 pt] per couple)

*The main difference between the New Year's Eve spread and a Mardi Gras party would be the abundance of *pączki* and *faworki* at the latter.

- **First hot course**: pork tenderloin stuffed with prunes, potato puffs, salad bouquet (served at about 10 P.M.)
- **Dessert**: Viennese-style cheesecake, assorted sweet biscuits and teacakes, fresh fruit; coffee or tea
- **Champagne toast** at midnight (750 ml bottle per couple)
- **Second hot course**: chicken in sweet and sour sauce with rice (served at 2 A.M.)
- **Clear beet *barszcz*** (served in teacups at 4 A.M.)

SEMI-FORMAL BANQUET: This is the type of affair better Polish hotels prepare for conferences, conventions, reunions and other gatherings; Polonian groups have numerous occasions to hold such events, which are more popular nowadays than formal banquets.

- **Hors d'oeuvres and apéritifs**: many of the hors d'oeuvres and beverages described in Polish Holiday/Banquet/Dinner-Party Favorites (e.g., rolled and skewered hors d'oeuvres, wines, spirits, etc.) would be appropriate for this initial stand-up course that allows banquet-goers to socialize
- **Starter course**: turkey in Malaga aspic, smoked salmon with lemon, assorted salads, relishes, bread and rolls, butter
- **Soup**: consommé with puff-pastry pellets *(groszek ptysiowy)*
- **Hot fish course**: walleye polonaise (with chopped egg and dill toppings)
- **Main course**: roast pork loin stuffed with prunes, dilled potatoes, bouquet of Polish salads
- **Cheeses**: this course is optional and is chosen by those who like this French custom of serving different cheeses and biscuits after the main course
- **Dessert**: assorted Polish cakes—cheesecake, poppy-seed roll, walnut torte, fruit cake
- **Tea or Coffee**
- **After-dinner drinks**: cognac, liqueurs, dessert wines

FORMAL BANQUET: The following is the menu served at Kraków's Pod Różą Hotel at a 10-year class reunion banquet held on July 2, 1892. (NOTE: There's no typographical error in the date—the reunion actually took place towards the end of the 19th century!)

- **Hors d'oeuvres and apéritifs**: vodkas and Warsaw-style hors d'oeuvres
- **Soups**: crayfish soup, *barszcz* à la Radziwiłł with *paszteciki*
- **Cold starter**: smoked salmon with tartar sauce
- **Hot entrée**: tenderloin steak with vegetable garnish, asparagus, cauliflower, green peas
- **Second hot entrée**: young rotisseried pullets (chickens)

- **Follow-up**: compote and lettuce
- **Dessert**: ice cream, fruit, cheeses
- **Beverages**: Black coffee, Hungarian white wine, Austrian red wine

TRADITIONAL PATRIOTIC-THEME BANQUET: By and large, the Polish-American banquets held to commemorate Polish Constitution Day (May 3), Pułaski Day, and Kościuszko anniversaries have followed the following menu patterns:

- **Upscale Anglo-mainstream banquet food**: scotch, martinis, shrimp cocktail, roast beef, lobster, etc.
- **Polish-American peasant/blue-collar fare**: *kapusta, kiełbasa, gołąbki,* meatballs, etc.
- **Mainstream community-supper food**: baked chicken, pork chops, etc. with *kiełbasa* or *pierogi* added as an afterthought

Perhaps the time has come to kick things up a notch and expose Polonian banquet-goers to some of the dishes enjoyed by people like Pułaski, Kościuszko and their compatriots living in the late 18th and early 19th centuries. That was a time when Sarmatian (Old Polish) culinary tradition was vying for the hearts and stomachs of the Polish gentry with what they perceived as the new-fangled French gourmet/powdered-wig culture, of which Poland's last king, Stanisław August Poniatowski, was an ardent advocate.

- **Soup**: creamed beet soup with meat-filled pierogi *(kołduny)* or beef broth with barley or grated noodles *(zacierka)*
- **Cold starters**: pike in aspic with horseradish sauce; sliced, cold larded roast beef *(sztufada)*; veal tongues in aspic; gherkins, capers, sour-cured apples, spiced/honeyed apricots, spiced pears, *ćwikła*, pickled mushrooms, brined dill pickles
- **Hot starter**: ginger-flavored tripe with marrow dumplings (prepare tripe as indicated in this book but increase the amt of ginger to make it the main flavor accent!)
- **Hot entrées**: roast beef, Hussar-style, roast leg of venison in mushroom sauce, ox tongue* in gray sauce, roast duck with capers, roast pullet (young chicken) in dill sauce
- **Accompaniments**: buckwheat groats, pearl barley, garnished with fatback nuggets (potatoes were still not common at the turn of the 19th century), creamed sorrel, stewed sauerkraut with capers, honeyed turnips with

*In English, the term "ox tongue" sounds a bit more quaint and archaic than beef tongue and is better suited to an historic theme meal; in Polish only one term (*ozór wołowy*) exists.

nutmeg, buttered carrots garnished with chopped parsley

- ✦ **Dessert**: fruit preserves (thick, cooked down), honeyed pears, marzipan (almond) confections
- ✦ **Wines**: mead, Hungarian Tokay, Burgundy (red), Rhine (white)

KING STAŚ'S THURSDAY DINNERS: King Stanisław August Poniatowski (affectionately referred to Król Staś), a patron of the arts and learning, was known for his famous Thursday dinners, to which he would invite prominent politicians, thinkers and community leaders. In the 1990s, Warsaw Mayor Paweł Piskorski picked up on the tradition by holding Tuesday breakfasts to talk over current issues with leading businessmen and activists. Perhaps somewhere in Polonia someone will eventually come up with Saturday suppers or a Friday *podwieczorek* (tea) at which matters of Polish-American interest could be discussed over tasty Polish-style treats. King Stanisław August's Thursday dinners were mainly a pretext to get together and discuss various topics of the day. Their culinary aspect was therefore secondary and only a few of the foods served have been pieced together by historians. The rest is a matter of speculation.

- ✦ **Starter**: oysters
- ✦ **Soup**: *barszcz* or broth
- ✦ **Meat**: roast lamb and roast grouse
- ✦ **Dessert**: rose preserves
- ✦ **Beverages**: water, old Tokay, Spanish wine

WARSAW DINNER-PARTY: The following are two favorite dinner-party spreads that have been served over the years at nameday parties and other festive occasions:*

I.

- ✦ **Cold starter**: creamed herring, deviled eggs (stuffed with *kiełbasa*), pork pâté with horseradish sauce, assorted bread and rolls, butter
- ✦ **Spirits**: chilled clear and flavored vodkas, wine
- ✦ **Soup**: clear red *barszcz* with salty pastry fingers
- ✦ **Hot entrée**: roast pork loin with prunes
- ✦ **Accompaniments**: lettuce with vinaigrette, dilled new potatoes, braised red cabbage
- ✦ **Compote**: apple-cherry
- ✦ **Dessert**: *szarlota* (apple cake), *sernik z owocami* (fruited cheesecake)
- ✦ **Follow-up**: coffee, tea, cognac

---

*See *Polish Heritage Cookery* for any recipes not found in this book.

II.

- ✦ **Cold starters**: mock lobster polonaise (smoked-halibut salad); carp in aspic à la juive (with raisins), horseradish sauce; assorted cold roast and smoked meats, relishes, bread and rolls, butter
- ✦ **Spirits**: chilled clear and flavored vodkas, Burgundy wine
- ✦ **Soup**: onion soup with croutons
- ✦ **Hot entrée**: beef tenderloin à la varsovienne
- ✦ **Accompaniments**: saffron rice, asparagus or cauliflower polonaise, tomato salad (sliced tomatoes garnished with chopped chives) or *mizeria* (cucumbers in sour cream)
- ✦ **Dessert**: ice cup, *karpatka* (Carpathian mountain cake)
- ✦ **Follow-up**: coffee, tea, cognac, liqueurs

FESTIVE FAMILY DINNER: Here are two Polish family-style dinners that could be served at a First Holy Communion party*, graduation, small home wedding reception, nameday party or other festive occasion in a reassuringly familiar, down-home setting.

I.

- ✦ **Cold starters**: boiled ham, smoked pork loin, *baleron* (smoked picnic ham), mayonnaise-laced mixed vegetable salad, relishes, bread, butter, vodka*
- ✦ **Soup**: chicken soup with egg noodles or sorrel soup with hard-cooked eggs
- ✦ **Main course**: roast chicken polonaise (with dill-flavored bread and liver stuffing)
- ✦ **Accompaniments**: dilled new potatoes, peas and carrots, *mizeria* (sliced cucumbers in sour cream)
- ✦ **Compote**: strawberry
- ✦ **Dessert**: walnut torte, rhubarb cake, coffee, tea

II.

- ✦ **Cold starters**: tomatoes stuffed with fish salad, eggs in mustard sauce, sliced veal in aspic, leek salad, spiced plums, pickled mushrooms, pickled pumpkin, homemade fruit cordial*
- ✦ **Soup**: creamed mushroom soup (made with dried bolete mushrooms)
- ✦ **Main course**: breaded pork cutlets
- ✦ **Accompaniments**: mashed potatoes, stewed sauerkraut, lettuce with sour cream or (in the colder months) grated carrot/apple/horseradish salad
- ✦ **Compote**: wild plum or mixed
- ✦ **Dessert**: plum cake, Wedel chocolate wafer torte, coffee, tea

---

*Alcohol should not be served at First Holy Communion parties if the First Holy Communicant is to feel that this is his/her very special spiritual experience and not just another excuse for the grown-ups to eat, drink and be merry.

POLISH FEST/PICNIC/COMMUNITY-SUPPER FOODS

Summer Polish fests, club picnics, parish suppers and other such community events held throughout the year are times many people have come to associate with Polish foods. Any of the dishes found in this book can be served on such occasions, but the type of event and general circumstances should be taken into account. Serving fancy hors d'oeuvres or gourmet banquet fare to be eaten on paper plates and with plastic forks might be somewhat out of place. Another thing to consider is the available facilities. Some organizers may have a fully equipped school cafeteria or other kitchen facility at their disposal, where foods can be prepared from scratch and refrigerated until needed. At other times, simply using the facilities to warm up home-produced or store-bought foods may be more convenient. At some outdoor events (fests, fairs, picnics), an electrical outlet may be the only convenience available to event-organizers, enabling them to bring in their own electric roasters, microwave ovens, steamers, electric kettles and other appliances. This section will therefore focus on the most convenient methods of preparing, warming and serving typical festival foods. Crowd quantity recipes have been provided for the *bigos* and pea soup. NOTE: In a departure from the rest of the recipe chapter, the Polish names below are listed first to indicate the way they should be displayed on signs or menus.

BIGOS (Polish hunter's stew—crowd quantity): In Polish tradition, *bigos* is a cool- and cold-weather dish, served from the start of the hunting season (autumn) on through Mardi Gras. Historically, it was less common at Easter, esp. in years when the holiday came late: mid to late April. That was because by Easter the family's supply of barrel-cured sauerkraut had often run out and also because by then people were craving the lighter dishes of spring. In a Polish-American setting, *bigos* is enjoyed year-round. Here are some hints about how to prepare it in larger quantities:

- ✦ An economical way to prepare *bigos* for a community event is to have club or committee members donate frozen, cooked, leftover meat from their home freezers. Advance notice should be given so enough meat can accumulate. Since the more varieties the better, this can be cooked pork, beef, veal, turkey, chicken, duck, goose, game, *kiełbasa* (fresh or smoked), ham, bacon, even a few meatballs and frankfurters. To prepare meat for *bigos*, cube cooked meat, freeze and keep frozen till needed.
- ✦ Feel free to use less expensive *zwyczajna* (utility grade) *kiełbasa* if available at your Polish butcher's or some of the economical American brands of "Polish sausage" on the market. In a dish of many long-simmering

ingredients, the inclusion of top-of-the-line *kiełbasa* will not really improve the taste of your *bigos* but may adversely affect your group's fund-raising effort.

- ✦ In summer and autumn, when cabbage is plentiful and inexpensive, it may be more cost-effective to use more fresh shredded cabbage in your *bigos* and less sauerkraut at those times of year. For instance: Add 1 qt sauerkraut to 2–3 large heads of shredded cabbage, using the reserved sauerkraut juice to sour the *bigos* to taste.
- ✦ Unless you have a fully equipped kitchen at your event venue, it is probably best to prepare the *bigos* at home and keep it hot at the activity site in an electric roaster or stovetop soup pot.

To prepare bigos in quantity, you will need 7–9 quarts combined of sauerkraut and firmly packed shredded cabbage in any proportion you want. For this recipe use 3–4 qt sauerkraut. Drain well, reserving liquid. Rinse very lightly. Scald with boiling water to cover and cook 1 hr from the time boiling resumes. Separately, scald 3 shredded heads of cabbage (totalling 9 lb) with boiling water and cook, uncovered, 20–30 min. Drain sauerkraut and cabbage, combine the two, add an equal or slightly smaller volume of combined cooked cubed meat and sliced smoked *kiełbasa* (a good proportion is 3 parts meat to 1 part *kiełbasa*). In gauze or linen bag, place 5 bay leaves, 20 peppercorns, 5 grains allspice and 10 juniper berries), tie securely and fasten to pot handle by string for easy removal. Add 3 lb pitted prunes and 10 large cooking apples, peeled, cored and cut into large cubes. Simmer at med-low temp (325°) in field kitchen, large stovetop pot or several roasters in oven at least 3 hr, stirring occasionally to prevent scorching. When *bigos* cools to room temp, refrigerate until ready to use. Add 3–4 mushroom bouillon cubes and simmer it at least another 2 hr. Season to taste with salt, pepper and caraway or dillseed. Marjoram can also be added. HINT: If there is too much liquid (and the *bigos* is soupy), pour some of it off and stir a little flour into the *bigos*. (OPTIONAL: 2–3 c dry red wine or dark beer [stout, porter, bock] may be added at the start of the second day's simmering session.) Serve with rye bread or potatoes and cold beer, clear vodka or Żubrówka. PORTIONS: about 50.

GROCHÓWKA ŻOŁNIERSKA (Polish army-style pea soup—crowd quantity): This hearty pea soup is one of the things Poles fondly recall from their army days and it is often served on patriotic occasions, especially Polish Soldier's Day (August 15), and at Polish veterans' affairs. Essentially it does not differ from the pea soup people cook at home except that it is made in large quantities and is cooked for hours in a field kitchen (a huge, tire-mounted kettle). In large soup pot combine: 3 gal water; 5½ lb split yellow peas (or hulled whole yellow dried peas, presoaked several hr or overnight and drained); about 3 lb mixed diced meats: slab bacon, smoked *kiełbasa*, smoked hocks or ribs (deboned), fatty ham, scraps or end-pieces of lunch meat, cut-up wieners, etc.; 8 of each: carrots, parsley roots, onions and leeks, diced; 2 small celeriacs, peeled and diced; 3–4 bay leaves and ¼ c salt. Bring to boil, stirring frequently, reduce heat as low as possible, cover tightly and simmer the living daylights out of it (!) 4–5 hr. IMPORTANT: Stir frequently! Towards the end add 3 lb peeled, diced potatoes and cook until they are very soft. Several (2–3) mushroom bouillon cubes may be added (optional). Season *grochówka* with a handful of marjoram and at least 2 T ground pepper to taste. If soup is too thick, dilute with some boiling water. Provide salt, pepper and marjoram for guests to custom-season their portions. Serve with rye bread. PORTIONS: about 50.

ZUPA OWOCOWA Z GRZANKAMI (cold fruit soup with croutons): This refreshing hot-weather treat may be enjoyed by those who do not care for such stick-to-the-ribs selections as pea soup, *kapusta*, and tripe. It can be made from one fruit such as sour cherries, strawberries or blueberries or a combination of these and other fruit, including apples, pears, plums, etc. (See page 130.) It may be served ice-cold, cool, at room temp, warm or piping hot. The cooler versions are better suited to summer activities.

MIELONE KOTLETY (fried meatballs/Polish "burgers"): Break up 3 slices stale French bread or bread rolls into bowl and drench with milk to cover. When soggy, combine with 1¼ lb ground pork, pork and beef or pork/veal/beef mixture. Add 1 egg and work well by hand to blend ingredients. Salt and pepper. Form large meatballs or thick oval patties, roll in flour and brown on both sides in hot lard or oil. Reduce heat, cover and simmer another 10 min or so until fully cooked. Drain on absorbent paper. This can be a main course served with buckwheat groats, potatoes, braised beets, sauerkraut, salad. Or, serve in a bun as a kind of Polish "burger" *(kotlet mielony w bułce)* with Old Polish plum sauce or Polish-style mustard and a dill pickle on the side.

KLOPSIKI/KOTLECIKI/SZNYCELKI W SOSIE (meatballs in gravy): Soak ½ c bread crumbs in ⅔ c milk until soggy and combine with ¾ lb ground pork and ½ ground beef. Add 1 egg and 1 finely chopped onion simmered in 1 T butter. Work by hand until consistency is uniform. Salt and pepper to taste, form golfball-sized meatballs or slightly larger, roll in flour or flour/crumb mixture and brown in hot fat on all sides. Either cover and continue simmering on low until fully cooked or transfer to pot, add 1 c stock, cover and simmer on low 10–15 min. Dissolve 1 T flour in 1 c milk and add to pot. Bring to boil and simmer briefly. Salt and pepper to taste. Serve over buckwheat with braised beets or sauerkraut on the side.

FLACZKI (zesty Polish-style tripe soup): This is another Polish favorite at fests and suppers. (See page 79.) Serve with rye bread and provide pepper, cayenne (or Tabasco), marjoram, paprika and ginger to allow guests to custom-season their portions. For Warsaw-style tripe, provide grated yellow cheese as a topping. Vodka is a frequent accompaniment to this hearty dish, which definitely has more adherents among the male half of the population.

KAPUSTA (stewed sauerkraut): Most Polish-American visitors to Polish fests, picnics and other such club and parish doings come expecting to get *kapusta* as the traditional accompaniment for *kiełbasa*, pork cutlets, meatballs, boiled pork hocks and other meats. For the recipe, see Cooked Vegetables and Main-Dish Accompaniments, page 152. Your *kapusta* is easily kept hot and ready to serve at the festival site in an electric roaster. All sauerkraut and cabbage dishes improve when heated or reheated. By rights, the sign should read *"kapusta kiszona duszona"* (stewed sauerkraut), but the familiar "K" word alone should strike a respondent chord in most Polish-American fest-goers.

KIEŁBASA Z KAPUSTĄ (Polish sausage and sauerkraut): This is a Polish fest-goer's all-time favorite. See Easter section for preparation method, page 117. Keep hot and ready to serve at the festival site in an electric roaster.

KIEŁBASKI Z RUSZTU (grilled *kiełbasa*): Cut smoked *kiełbasa* into 3–4″ serving-sized pieces or use the smaller grillers. Cook on charcoal or electric grill well away from flame, turning frequently, until evenly browned on all sides. These can also be cooked on a rotisserie. HINT: To ensure even cooking, score each piece of *kiełbasa* by cutting halfway through at an angle on one side at ¼″ intervals. Serve with rye bread or boiled potatoes with sauerkraut on the side.

KIEŁBASKI W BUŁECZCE (grillers in a bun, Polish hot dogs): These are wiener-sized Polish sausages that are a handy festival food since they are served in a bun. Grill or steam and serve in hard rolls (rye or crusty French bread type) with Polish-style mustard. The soft hot-dog rolls do not stand up to these sausages very well.

SZASZŁYK PO POLSKU ("shish-kiełbasa"): This is a Polish take-off on the Middle Eastern shish kebab. On a skewer alternate ½″–¾″ pieces of smoked *kiełbasa* with ½″ onion slices, fresh mushroom caps and bell pepper pieces of roughly equally size. Brush with oil, sprinkle with salt, pepper, garlic powder and paprika and cook on rotisserie or grill, making sure that all sides are evenly cooked. They are ready when the onion is tender.

KASZANKA/KISZKA (buckwheat sausage, black pudding): There are basically 3 different ways of reheating and serving this tasty black sausage: 1) reheat serving-size (4″–5″) lengths of *kiszka* on a grill or in lightly oiled or vegetable-sprayed skillet until lightly browned on the outside and heated through; 2) cut *kiszka* into 1″-thick rounds and fry on both sides until hot and crusty, allowing 3–4 such rounds per serving; 3) Remove from casing, break up and fry like hash. Serve plain or topped with fried onions. Provide rye bread, mustard and/or horseradish and dill pickles (see page 176).

KASZANKA DIETETYCZNA ("diet" *kiszka*): For those who love *kiszka* but don't need the extra fat and cholesterol, do the following: Remove whatever amount of *kiszka* you want from casing, place in lightly greased skillet and break up with spatula. Add anywhere from ½ to the same amount of plain, cooked buckwheat groats (*kasza gryczana*) and mix well until fully blended. Fry until hot and crusty. Season with salt, pepper and marjoram. Serve topped with fried onions or plain with brined dill pickles and fresh sliced tomatoes on the side. Mustard and horseradish should also be provided. NOTE: *Kiszka* already contains buckwheat groats. By adding more, you are simply increasing the fiber and carbohydrate content of this dish.

OGÓRKI KISZONE/KONSERWOWE (dill pickles, brined and vinegar-type): Brined dill pickles (made without vinegar) are a great combination with many picnic meats. American-born festivalgoers may prefer the vinegar type (the kind sold in supermarkets labeled "Polish-style dill pickles"), so be sure to also have some of those on hand as well.

PARÓWKI (wieners, frankfurters): You can give this popular festival food a Polish touch by getting veal frankfurters from a Polish deli. If only American-style franks are available, then at least serve them in a crusty wheat (French-bread–type), rye or whole-wheat hard roll and provide Polish-style mustard on the side.

PLACKI KARTOFLANE (potato pancakes): These are the favorites of many, but for best results they should be fried shortly before serving. Prepare the grated-potato batter (see page 141) at home and use it to fry the pancakes at the festival site as orders come in. Provide salt, sugar and sour cream for customers to choose from. NOTE: These can also be served with mushroom gravy as a main course.

KOTLET SCHABOWY (breaded pork cutlet): Most every fest-goer, regardless of ethnic background, will enjoy these delicious cutlets (see page

86). Pound slices of fresh pork loin (pork chops with the bone removed) very thin before breading and frying to a deep golden brown. They may be served as a main course with potatoes and salad, or as a "fast food" (see next entry).

KOTLET SCHABOWY W BUŁCE (pork-cutlet sandwich): If you pound the cutlets very thin, after frying, 1 cutlet may be big enough to make 2 sandwiches. Serve in split crusty rye, whole-wheat, French or kaiser roll with a splotch of Polish-style mustard.

MŁODE KARTOFELKI (new potatoes): To people used to getting instant mashed potatoes at every turn of the way, these will be a real treat. Truly new, walnut-sized potatoes need not be peeled since the thin skin comes off under running water with a nylon kitchen scrubber. After boiling and draining, keep hot in electric roaster. Drizzle each portion with melted unsalted butter and fresh chopped dill just before serving.

MIZERIA (sliced cucumbers and sour cream): This is a classic Polish salad but the trick about serving this at a festival site is not to add the sour cream until ready to serve. Keep the sliced, salted, peppered, lightly vinegar-sprinkled cucumbers in a bowl (see page 157) and use a slotted spoon to dish out each portion. Top each portion with a dollop of sour cream just before handing it to the customer. (OPTIONAL: Each portion may be garnished with a little fresh chopped dill.)

KOMPOT (compote, homemade fruit drink): This traditional Polish "chaser" to wash down a meal is a nice change-of-pace from those syrupy colas and other carbonated soft drinks. It can be made with one or more in-season fruits. The rough proportions are 1 lb cleaned (hulled, pitted or peeled) fruit, ½–1 c sugar and 4–6 c water. Cook briefly (until fruit is tender), cool and serve. NOTE: A pinch of cinnamon, ground cloves or nutmeg with a sprinkle of lemon juice will sharpen the flavor of this after-dinner beverage. VARIATION: For a poached-fruit-type dessert eaten with a spoon, use only 2–3 c water.

PĄCZKI (Polish dougnuts): Everyone loves these luscious, jam-filled doughnuts at any time of year. (See page 97.) In hot weather the sugar glaze will become sticky, so perhaps unglazed *pączki* would be preferable at summer events. NOTE: *Chruściki/faworki* are less suitable for outdoor summer fests because they don't stand up well to jostling and tend to wilt in hot weather.

RÓŻNE POLSKIE WYPIEKI (assorted Polish baked goods): Good sellers at Polish food concessions include *babka*, *placek*, *chałka*, *szarlotka*, *makowiec, sernik, jagodzianki*, etc. NOTE: Cakes glazed with icing or containing soft, creamy or runny fruit fillings are best avoided in hot weather.

TRUSKAWKI ZE ŚMIETANĄ (strawberries and sour cream): This is a nice, light refreshing finale to a summertime meal. Dish out portions of sugared halved strawberries as needed and top each serving with a dollop of sour cream.

MLECZNY COCKTAIL TRUSKAWKOWY (Polish strawberry milk shake): Rather than using today's widespread imitation strawberry syrup, prepare this creamy, refreshing shake from only natural ingredients. For each portion combine ⅓–½ c sugared strawberries, and 1 c chilled sour milk, *kefir* or buttermilk. Whirl briefly in blender or milkshake mixer until frothy/creamy and serve.

OGÓRKI Z MIODEM (honeyed cucumbers): To many, this treat will be "something different," but most Americans who have sampled it really go for it. See page 170.

SIMPLE PICNIC/OUTING/CAMPFIRE TREATS

This final recipe section deals with simple snacks and picnic lunches that can be enjoyed during hikes and bike trips, at campsites and other places where ingenuity and the ability to make do, not fancy appliances, are what counts. In fact, this back-to-basics approach may be a refreshing change of pace from all the high-tech gadgetry that now seems to be closing in on us all at every turn of the way.

OLD-FASHIONED POLISH PICNIC *(starodawna majówka)*: Whether you hike, ride a bike or drive to some wooded out-of-the-way place, stop to rest on a riverbank or row a boat to a secluded little island you can relive the simple pleasures of a more relaxed, slower-paced era with an old-style picnic lunch. It might include some hard-cooked eggs (don't forget the salt and pepper!), *kabanosy* (thin, dry *kiełbasa* that requires no refrigeration), whole small firm tomatoes, dill pickles, radishes and bread. Cold roast chicken and/or breaded pork cutlets are also good. Include some in-season fruits—cherries are esp. good and stand up to handling and jostling much better than strawberries and raspberries do. Firm plums are also OK. If you lack a portable cooler (or simply do not want to get loaded down with too much equipment), wrapping cold bottled beverages (beer, soft drink, juice) in newspaper will keep them pleasantly cool for hours.

OLD-FASHIONED POLONIAN PICNIC *(starodawny piknik polonijny)*: Some readers may still remember the Polish-American picnics that predated the era of beverage coolers and charcoal grills. I recall the picnics my family used to hold at places like Belle Island (an island park in the Detroit River) or Dodge Park north of the city. A big metal *balia* (washtub) containing a block of ice was used to keep the beer and soft drinks cold. No cooking was done on the spot, and all the food was prepared at home and brought to the picnic site. There was baked *kiełbasa*, breaded pork chops and roast chicken, potato salad, tomatoes, radishes, dill pickles, etc. Naturally there was plenty of Polish rye bread and unsalted butter. Apple cake, cheesecake and other home-baked goods were also in good supply. The Detroit Polonia also had private picnic groves such as Warsaw Park, Szwajcarska Dolina (Swiss Valley), Zielony Gaj (Green Glen) and Wanda Park which featured live music, dance pavilions, and food and beverage concessions. (Wanda Park, the home of the Detroit area's Polish war veterans, is still going strong!)

CAMPFIRE POTATO BAKE *(kartofle pieczone w ognisku)*: When in a field picking potatoes, the best you can do is to shake and wipe excess soil off your potatoes with your hand. After a wood fire has turned to ashes and glowing embers, throw small potatoes into it. Cover them with hot ashes and allow them to cook. When tender (test them with a sharpened stick!), pull out of campfire. When still hot but cool enough to handle break open and enjoy with a pinch of salt (if available) for flavoring. Only the white pulp is eaten and the charred skin can be thrown back into what's left of the fire.

KIEŁBASA ROAST *(kiełbaski pieczone w ognisku)*: Glowing embers are better to roast sausages than a roaring bonfire. Find a long forked stick and with penknife strip bark from the tines and sharpen them. Impale a 3″–4″ piece of smoked *kiełbasa* on each forked stick and roast high enough above heat source so *kiełbasa* browns evenly on the outside and is heated through. Too hot a fire will burn the skin to a crisp before the inside gets cooked. VARIATION: Instead of the forked-stick method, a sharpened single-point stick can be run down through the center of the sausage which is cooked by constantly turning the stick over the campfire. Either way, provide rye bread and mustard.

POLISH HOT POT *(prażonka biwakowa)*: Line bottom and sides of heavy, preferably iron pot with tight-fitting lid with cabbage leaves. On top of cabbage arrange in layers: thick-sliced bacon slices, sliced onions, 2 layers sliced potatoes and salt and pepper generously. Continue layering until ingredients are used up (top layer should be bacon). Cover with cabbage leaves, place lid on pot and wrap entire pot with 2 layers of heavy-duty aluminium foil. Place pot into hot ash- and ember-filled pit large enough to accommodate it. Shovel more embers round the sides and on top of pot, cover with soil and pat down. It should be ready in several hr. (OPTIONAL: Sliced smoked *kiełbasa* may be included in addition to or instead of the bacon.)

CAMPFIRE BIGOS *(bigos biwakowy)*: *Bigos* never tastes better than in the great outdoors at any time of year. But preparing it from scratch under primitive camp conditions would be a daunting task. The solution is to prepare it at home (see page 79) or wherever conditions permit, bring it along and heat it over a campfire. A cast-iron pot with a tight-fitting lid is best but any cookpot with handles allowing it to be suspended over the flame will do.

BEANS AND BACON *(fasola z boczkiem)*: This simple dish will satiate hearty appetites in the great outdoors. Fry up ¼ lb diced slab bacon with 2 large chopped onions until nicely browned. Add 5–6 c well-drained canned white beans (navy, Great Northern, etc.) and simmer until beans are heated through. Season with 2 T vinegar and salt, pepper and (optional) marjoram and/or savory to taste. Provide plenty of bread. VARIATION: For a meatier version, fry up some sliced or diced smoked *kiełbasa* with bacon and onions. Most any diced meat (leftover chops, roast, wieners) may be added.

CAMPFIRE CHICKEN *(kurczak biwakowy)*: Since this is a fairly time-consuming operation, this recipe is recommended more as a demonstration of how cooking was done under primitive conditions rather than a practical tip for your camping trip (unless you're the adventurous type). After building an open fire, create a primitive spit by planting two forked sticks opposite each other beyond the reach of the flames. Split a fryer chicken in half down the back, rub all over with oil and salt and pepper. Impale the two halves horizontally about 2–3″ apart on a green stick stripped of its bark and position over campfire, resting ends in the forked sticks. Cook slowly at a height ensuring even cooking without burning, turning chicken every few min. Depending on the size of the chicken and intensity of the heat source, this may take an hr or more. Baste occasionally with 1 heaping T butter dissolved in 1 c boiling water.

CAMPFIRE GROATS or RICE *(kasza lub ryż biwakowy)*: Bring 4 c water, containing 2 T oil and ½ t salt to boil. Add buckwheat groats or rice gradually. Bring to boil, stir, reduce heat, cover and simmer until water is absorbed. Wrap pot in several layers of heavy-duty aluminium foil and place in pit dug to snugly accommodate it. There should be at least 8″ between top of pot and ground surface. Cover pot with soil and pat down. It'll be ready when you get back from a morning at the lake.

<u>FISH STORED IN HORSERADISH LEAVES</u> *(ryba w liściach chrzanowych)*: This is not a recipe but a way of storing freshly caught fish at out-of-the-way campsites where refrigeration or even ice are unavailable. Behead, gut and scale fish, rinse, dry, salt generously and wrap snugly in horseradish leaves. Dig a hole at least 1′ deep in a cool, shady places, place at the bottom of the hole and cover with soil. The ethereal oils in the horseradish leaves act as a preservative and should keep fish from spoiling for 8–10 hr. <u>NOTE</u>: This may not work in very hot weather, so smell the fish after unwrapping it before rinsing and cooking.

<u>FISH COOKED IN CABBAGE LEAVES</u> *(ryba pieczona w liściach kapusty)*: For this dish you will need a burned-down campfire with plenty of glowing embers and hot ash as for campfire potatoes (see page 209). Rub cleaned fish all over with oil and salt and pepper. Wrap in cabbage leaves (horseradish leaves may also be used) and encase in damp, freshly dug clay. Fill a little pit with hot ash and embers, add the clay-encased fish and top with some more ash and embers. Cover with soil, pat down with shovel and go for a several-hour hike or swim. It should be ready to enjoy when you get back to camp.

POLISH FAST FOOD

While Polish treats have yet to make it on America's fast-food circuit, Polock Johnny's of Baltimore (with 17 outlets at its height) was set up by Polish-born Jan Kafka in 1921, decades before McDonald's made the scene. The tradition is being carried on by granddaughter, Margie Kafka. The house speciality remains the Polock Johnny, a plump, savory link of smoked *kiełbasa* served on a bun with brown mustard and other garnishes of preference. A developing, upscale restaurant chain in Poland is Chłopskie Jadło.

Not all Polish dishes lend themselves to the fast-food format. That is especially true of those in gravies and sauces as well as foods that have to be eaten with a knife and fork. But that is true of the foods of other nationalities as well. Even a cursory glance at the fast-food scene reveals the popularity of simple, handheld foods such as hamburgers, hotdogs, fries, pizza, tacos and Kentucky-style chicken.

Here are some dishes that could easily become fast foods:

Polish pasties (*Paszteciki*)—hot, filled, savory, handheld pasties are an immediate hit with Americans who have tried them and seem ideally suited to the fast-food scene. Pasties filled with meat, meat and mushrooms, just mushrooms, sauerkraut and mushrooms and the especially delicious, dill-flavored rice/egg/onion vegetarian filling are sure to go over.

Hot apple-beety (drink)—Hot clear red *barszcz* is the perfect match for *paszteciki,* but beets are not a favorite food of most American young people, to whom fast food is largely addressed. Perhaps a bit of marketing is required to reorient their habits. A strongly apple-flavored beet drink like Hortex Barszczyk might be the answer if offered under some catchy name like the above (alluding to the popular American dessert known as Apple Betty or apple crumble).

***Kiełbasa* in a bun**—Grilled, hot-dog-sized, smoked Polish sausage served in a crusty, split rye or wheat roll, mustard or horseradish accompaniment

Battered *kiełbasa* on a stick—Hot-dog-sized smoked Polish sausage, impaled on a wooden skewer, dipped in crêpe batter and fried to a nice golden brown

Pork cutlet in a bun—Poland's popular boneless, breaded pork cutlet, fried to a golden brown and served with an equal-sized tomato slice in a crusty bun slathered with mustard-flavored mayonnaise sauce

Polish "burger"—Thick Polish-style *kotlet mielony* (ground-meat patty/meatball) served in a crusty bun with mustard or possibly, sour-cream-laced sliced cucumbers.

Polish mushroom burger—A fried, breaded patty made of ground fried, fresh mushrooms and onions (bound together with egg and bread crumbs and seasoned with salt, pepper and dill) might be an interesting alternative for vegetarians in the crowd.

Battered-fried Polish mushrooms—Rehydrated, cooked dried mushroom caps, battered and deep-fried, might become an interesting alternative to French-fried onion rings. Fresh mushroom caps (esp. portobello) can also be breaded and deep-fried to a nice golden brown.

Mini-pierogi—Since cutting normal-sized pierogi with the side of a plastic fork is not very convenient, perhaps tiny bite-sized *pierogi* would be better suited to a fast-food format.

Deep-fried mini-pierogi—Rather than being boiled, or boiled and fried, the tiny *pierogi* mentioned above can also be deep-fried to a nice golden brown. Drain on absorbent paper before serving.

***Bigos* in a bowl**—Perhaps one dish served in a bowl (just as chili is) would not be a bad idea, and *bigos* is the likely choice. Even if today's younger Americans are not generally crazy about sauerkraut, more than just teenagers frequent fast-food places.

Pączki—Polish doughnuts are a natural on the fast-food circuit, especially if their surface is unglazed and unsugared, since those can be messy to handle.

FRUIT AND VEGETABLE GARDENING, POLISH-STYLE

Not all the ingredients used in Polish cuisine are readily available in every American supermarket, and that is particularly true of certain garden produce. Besides, it is often more convenient to pop into the garden than to drive to a supermarket even for those varieties commonly found in its produce department. And, there is a certain satisfaction in growing your own in your backyard vegetable patch. Here are some suggestions:

BEETS *(buraki)*: To make a delicious baby-beet soup called *botwinka*, you need the greens and immature roots of baby beets that are rarely available commercially. Growing your own will enable you to enjoy this treat early in the season and prepare all kinds of other beet dishes (*buraczki, barszcz, ćwikła,* etc.) when your beets mature.

CELERIAC *(seler)*: Stalk celery has never been widely used in Polish cuisine. When Poles say *seler*, they mean celeriac (root-celery), but that is not always easy to find in America. That's why growing your own is a good idea for all Polish food fanciers who have their own vegetable patch. This root vegetable (which grows underground with green leaves protruding) is one of the classic ingredients of *włoszczyzna* (Polish soup greens). It is also prepared as a cooked vegetable in its own right, is great in mixed-vegetable salads and can even be precooked and then fried like a breaded cutlet.

CHIVES *(szczypiorek)*: These fine, subtly onion-flavored greens add flavor and color to a wide variety of dishes including white cheese, scrambled eggs, soups, salads, sauces, fish and gravy-type dishes. It's available in supermarkets, but it's more convenient to have it handy, ready to be snipped when needed.

CURRANTS *(porzeczki)*: Currants are another berry-type fruit far better known in Poland than America. Blackcurrants have much more vitamin C than citrus fruits and are great in syrups, juices, jams and alcoholic cordials. Redcurrants are also enjoyed by many, and there are even whitecurrants.

DILL *(koper)*: This is one of Poland's favorite herbs. Finely chopped, the fragrant feathery leaves impart an unforgettable flavor to boiled new potatoes and other vegetables, poultry stuffing, soups, sauces and fish dishes. The mature dill stalks are used to make dill pickles. Even if you don't have a vegetable garden, dill will grow along a fence, behind the garage or in other such out-of-the-way places. Some apartment-dwellers even grow it in a window or balcony flower-box. Be aware—it grows 4–6′ tall!

GOOSEBERRIES *(agrest)*: One of Poland's favorite garden berries is nowhere nearly as well known in America. They are excellent in preserves, syrups and compotes and can be used in an interesting sauce for meats. Gooseberry bushes have extremely sharp thorns and a row of them can be planted to successfully keep out unwanted stray animals.

GREEN/SPRING ONIONS *(dymka, szczypior)*: Chopped scallions are a nice garnish for most salads, white cheese, and cooked vegetable dishes. And scrambled eggs are superb when fried in chopped greens onions simmered in butter.

GREENGAGE PLUMS *(renklody)*: Large, yellowish, pinkish or red plums usually meant for eating. They are also used in jams and other preserves.

HORSERADISH *(chrzan)*: Prepared horseradish is easy enough to find in the market, but some recipes call for grated horseradish roots. This root vegetable spreads underground enabling you to dig up a root whenever you need it.

ITALIAN PLUMS *(węgierki)*: Known in Polish as Hungarian plums, they are widely used in Polish cookery to make *powidła* (plum butter), jams, syrups and cakes.

LEEKS *(pory)*: This is another ingredient of standard Polish soup greens which comprise carrots, leeks, parsley roots or parsnips, onions and celeriac. Leeks also make a delicious soup and cooked vegetable and are great in salads.

MARJORAM *(majeranek)*: Whereas dill is Poland's favorite fresh herb, marjoram is the most widely used dried herb. The stalks of mature marjoram are cut, tied together in bunches and suspended upside down in a warm place. When fully dried, the leaves are stripped off and sieved to get homemade rubbed marjoram. It beautifully brings out the flavor of pork dishes, meatballs, *gołąbki,* soups, *bigos,* roast duck and goose as well as bean dishes. Marjoram is the main flavor accent in *kiszka* and West Poland *kiełbasa.*

PARSLEY *(pietruszka)*: Although this green is more widely available in America than dill, having your own fresh-picked parsley whenever you need it is certainly more convenient than dashing down to the store or doing without. The finely chopped greens are used in poultry stuffing (together with dill) and to garnish potatoes, vegetables, soups and salads. The parsley root is one of the traditional soup greens.

PEARMAINS (*papierówki*): Pearmains are one of the earliest variety of apple to ripen (in most years, ready to eat in June). The Polish name refers to its paper-thin skin which is always a greenish yellow and never turns red.

POTATOES (*kartofle/ziemniaki*): Although potatoes are certainly available in even the smallest grocery, finding real Polish-style walnut-sized *młode kartofelki*—the kind you don't have to peel since their thin skin easily comes often under running water with a nylon scrubber—is not always easy. Naturally, you have to have a fair-sized garden to make growing potatoes worth your while.

RADISHES (*rzodkiewka*): Although easy to find in supermarkets, there is nothing like crunchy garden-fresh radishes to liven up salads and lend color to platters. They are cooked whole until fork-tender in boiling salted water and garnished with Polonaise topping (butter-browned bread crumbs). The young greens can be chopped and used to garnish salads and white cheese like chives.

RUSSET APPLES (*szara reneta*): These tart apples are regarded by Polish homemakers as the best variety for cakes, duck and goose stuffing, compotes and other cooking needs.

NOTE: If your interest in gardening runs to flowers, don't look to this book for guidance. All I know about Polish flowers is that red geraniums are often found in the flowerboxes of peasant cottages and tall hollyhocks frequently grow along its walls. Mums are meant for the dead and used to decorate graves and it is now common to bring the hostess of a dinner-party or the name-day celebrant an odd number of cut flowers: 3, 5, 7, 9 or more, but never a dozen! If you need more information than that, consult the books written by Polonia's No. 1 expert on Polish flowers and herbs—the Buffalo area's Sophie Hodorowicz-Knab (see Bibliography, page 217).

Bibliography

NOTE: The titles are given in italics. The author's translation of all titles in languages other than English is given in brackets following the original title.

Abodaher, David J. *No Greater Love–Kazimierz Pulaski.* Philadelphia: Copernicus Society of America.

Anders-Silverman, Deborah. *Polish-American Folklore.* Urbana/Chicago: University of Illinois Press, 2000.

Benet, Sula. *Song, Dance and Customs of Peasant Poland.* CT: Polish Heritage Publications, Cornwall Bridge, 1996.

Budrewicz, Olgierd. *Polska dla początkujących* (Poland for Beginners). Warsaw: Interpress Publishers, 1976.

Chłapowski, Marcin. *Polish Przewodnik Handlowy* (Polish Business Directory). Toronto: Master Printing Inc., 1998.

(Collective Work.) *Feasting with Tradition.* McKeesport, PA: Holy Family Polish National Catholic Church, 1977.

(Collective Work.) *Kitchen Secrets.* Detroit: Altar Society of St. Bartholomew RC Church.

(Collective Work, Marie Sokołowski and Irene Jasiński, ed.) *Treasured Polish Recipes for Americans.* Minneapolis: Polanie Publishing Co., 1972.

(Collective Work, Maria Grymska and Janina Nicewicz-Kosińska, ed.) *Wigilia i święta* (Christmas Eve and the Holidays). Warsaw: Prószyński i Spółka, 1999.

Culinary Arts Institute Staff. *Polish Cookbook.* Melrose Park, IL: Culinary Arts Institute, 1978.

Czachowski, Hubert and Święch, Iwona. *Wigilia—czas oczekiwania, czas magii* (Christmas Eve—A Time of Anticipation and Magic). Toruń: Top Kurier, 2000.

Czerniewicz-Umer, Teresa. *Poland—Architecture, Parks, Museums, Maps, Manors, Sanctuaries.* Warsaw: Wiedza i Życie, 2002.

Czerny, Zofia. *Polish Cookbook.* Warsaw: Państwowe Wydawnictwo Ekonomiczne, 1975.

de Gorgey, Maria. *A Treasury of Polish Cuisine.* New York: Hippocrene Books, 1999.

Dembińska, Maria (adapted by William Woys Weaver). *Food and Drink in Medieval Poland.* Philadelphia: University of Pennsylvania Press, 1999.

Fedak, Alina. *Polish Cooking.* Warsaw: Galeria Polskiej Książki Exlibris, 2001.

Ferenc, Ewa. *Polskie tradycje świąteczne* (Polish Holiday Traditions). Poznań: Księgarnia Św. Wojciecha, 2000.

Gałązka, Jacek and Juszczak, Albert. *Polish Heritage Travel Guide to USA and Canada.* Cornwall Bridge: CT Polish Heritage Publications, 1992.

Gil, Leszek Jozef. *Informator Polonijny* (Polish Phonebook). Chicago: Lewomax Publishing Co., 1998.

Hodorowicz-Knab, Sophie. *Polish Country Kitchen Cookbook.* New York: Hippocrene Books, 2002.

———. *Polish Customs, Traditions & Folklore.* New York: Hippocrene Books, 1993.

———. *Polish Herbs, Flowers & Folk Medicine.* New York: Hippocrene Books, 1995.

———. *Polish Wedding Customs & Traditions.* New York: Hippocrene Books, 1997.

Hoskins, Janina W. *Polish Genealogy and Heraldry.* New York: Hippocrene Books, 1990.

Klikowicz, Olga. *Goście przy rodzinnym stole* (Guests at the Family Table). Warsaw: Oficyna Wydawnicza, Watra.

Krysa, Rev. Czesław Michał. *A Polish Christmas Eve.* Lewiston, NY: CWB Press, 1998.

———. *The Signature of Spring.* The Orchard Lake Schools, 1991.

Krzyżanowski, Julian (ed.). *Słownik Folkloru Polskiego* (Dictionary of Polish Folklore). Warsaw: Wiedza Powszechna, 1965.

Kulikowski, Andrzej. *Heraldyka szlachecka* (Noble Heraldry). Warsaw Wydawnictwo "Château," 1990.

Leonilla, Siostra. *Ciasta Siostry Leonilli* (Sister Leonilla's Cakes). Warsaw: Wydawnictwo Sióstr Loretanek, 1997.

Łebkowski, Marek. *Kuchnia Polska* (Polish Cuisine). Warsaw: Reader's Digest Przegląd, 1997.

Martin, James Conroyd, *Push Not the River*: Elibris Corp., 2000.

Mielniczuk, Marcin and Staniszewski, Tadeusz. *Stare i nowe gry drużynowe* (Old and New Team Games). Warsaw: Wydawnictwo Telbit, 1999.

Nowakowski, Jacek and Perrin, Marlene. *Polish Touches.* Iowa City: Penfield Press, 1996.

Ogrodowka, Barbara. *Święta polskie* (Polish Holidays). Warsaw: Wydawnictwo Alfa, 2000.

Paul, Allen. *Katyń—Stalin's Massacre and the Seeds of Polish Resurrection.* Annapolis: Naval Institute Press, 1996.

Peszkowski, Rev. Zdzisław. *Wieniec modlitw* (Wreath of Prayers). Orchard Lake, MI: Polonian Liturgical Center.

Peterson, Joan and David. *Eat Smart in Poland.* Madison, WI: Ginkgo Press, 2000.

Pienkos, Donald E. *For Your Freedom Through Ours.* Boulder, Colorado: East European Monographs, 1991.

Samull, Donald. *Polish America—Guide to Polish Landmarks Across America.* Dearborn, MI: published by the author, 2001.

Sart, Marek. *Polish Heritage Songbook.* Cornwall Bridge, CT: Polish Heritage Publications, 1995.

Skrzypczak, Bolesław. *Alcoholic Drinks from Poland.* Warsaw: Agpol.

Strybel, Robert. *Christmas the Polish Way.* Scranton: Polish National Union of America, 1987.

Strybel, Robert and Maria. *Polish Heritage Cookery.* New York: Hippocrene Books, 1993, 1997.

Szczypka, Józef. *Kalendarz Polski* (Polish Calendar). Warsaw: Instytut Wydawniczy PAX, 1984.

Śliwa, Zuzanna. *Dom polski* (The Polish Home). Poznań: Podsielki-Raniewski i Spółka.

Śliwerski, Wojciech. *Harcerskie gry i zabawy* (Scout Games and Amusements). Warsaw: Horyzonty, 1998.

Wojnowski, Tadeusz. *A Polish American's Guide to Poland.*

Wróbel, Paul. *Our Way.* Notre Dame, IN: University of Notre Dame Press, 1979.

Wysocki, Rev. Józef. *Rytuał rodzinny* (Book of Family Rituals). Olsztyn: Warmińskie Wydawnictwo Diecezjalne, 1986.

Wytrwał, Joseph A. *The Poles in America.* Minneapolis: Lerner Publications Co., 1969.

Index

Printed in the USA
CPSIA information can be obtained
at www.ICGtesting.com
JSHW011702060824
67674JS00003B/201